TOM
CLARKE

THE TRUE LEADER OF
THE EASTER RISING

MICHAEL T. FOY

The
History
Press
Ireland

First published 2014

The History Press Ireland
50 City Quay
Dublin 2
Ireland
www.thehistorypress.ie

British Library Cataloguing in Publication Data.
A catalogue record for this book is available from the British Library.

ISBN 978 1 84588 776 6

Typesetting and origination by The History Press

Contents

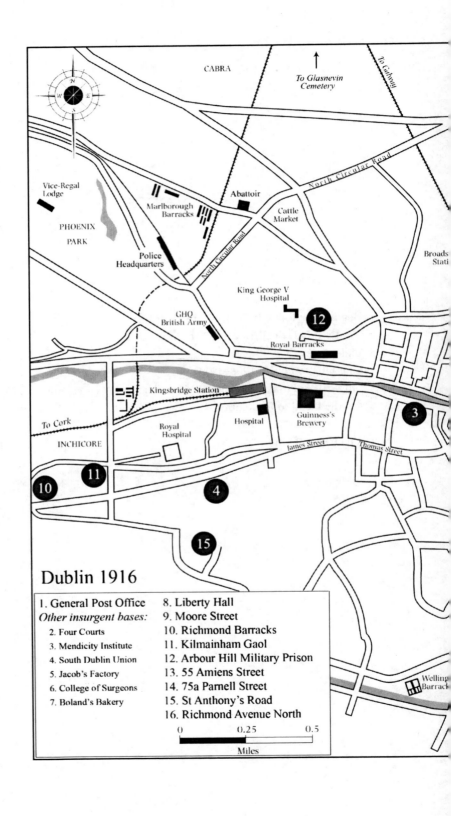

Dublin 1916

1. General Post Office
Other insurgent bases:
  2. Four Courts
  3. Mendicity Institute
  4. South Dublin Union
  5. Jacob's Factory
  6. College of Surgeons
  7. Boland's Bakery

8. Liberty Hall
9. Moore Street
10. Richmond Barracks
11. Kilmainham Gaol
12. Arbour Hill Military Prison
13. 55 Amiens Street
14. 75a Parnell Street
15. St Anthony's Road
16. Richmond Avenue North

0   0.25   0.5

Miles

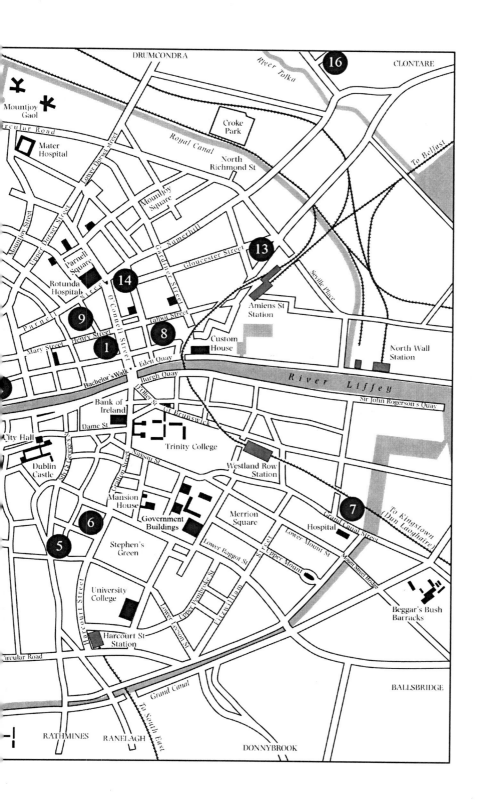

Acknowledgements

Once again I have to acknowledge the invaluable contribution of my friend and former colleague, Walter Grey. Besides our many enjoyable discussions about Tom Clarke, Walter read various drafts of the book and made many constructive suggestions for improvement. I am forever in Walter's debt. I also want to thank my oldest friend, Dr Brian Barton who suggested that I write a life of Tom Clarke. Dr Timothy Bowman, Dr Michelle Brown and Stewart Roulston read and commented on the book's final draft. I also received important help from Liam Andrews, Ken Boden, Lisa Dolan, Rev. Barbara Fryday, Gerry Kavanagh, Colette O'Daly and John Tohill. Once again I am indebted to Helen Litton who indexed the book. I would also like to express my gratitude to three members of The History Press Ireland: Beth Amphlett who commissioned the book, Ronan Colgan, and Gay O'Casey who edited the text.

Michael T. Foy

1

Beginnings:
Tom Clarke, 1857–1883

In the year 1847 when much of rural Ireland was in the throes of the Famine, a 17-year-old farmer's son from Co. Leitrim joined the British Army. For James Clarke that was not an unusual choice as a member of the small, scattered Protestant minority near the western fringe of Ulster and loyal to the British connection. Seven years later as a soldier in the Royal Artillery he was fighting in the Crimean War at the battles of Alma and Inkerman and taking part in the siege of Sevastopol. After the conflict ended in February 1856, his regiment transferred to Clonmel, Co. Tipperary where James was promoted to bombardier.

In Clonmel James met Mary Palmer, a Roman Catholic servant girl. On 21 May 1857 they married in Clogheen at Shanrahan Anglican parish church. Like many of her social class at the time, Mary could not read or write and made her mark in the register. Since in that period the Church of Ireland – to which James belonged – alone issued marriage licences, Roman Catholics like Mary often married under its auspices, though she insisted that any children the couple had would be raised in her religion.

Thomas James Clarke, the subject of this book, was their firstborn. Hitherto it has been accepted that Thomas was born in 1858 at Hurst Park Barracks on the Isle of Wight where James's Royal Artillery regiment was stationed at the time. One historian, though, has asserted that Thomas was born at Hurst Castle – an abandoned fort on the Hampshire coast that had not had a military garrison for over 150 years and which during the eighteenth century had become a favourite haunt of smugglers. But the records show no Thomas James Clarke born on the Isle of Wight or in the nearby county of Hampshire during the entire 1850s, nor is anyone of that name listed in the British Army's births and baptisms for England and Ireland during 1857 and 1858. Furthermore, Clarke's widow Kathleen asserted that her husband had been born on 11 March 1857 and celebrated his fifty-ninth birthday just before the Easter Rising in 1916. The inference is that Thomas James Clarke must have been born out of wedlock in Co. Tipperary.[1] Over the next twelve years, James and Mary had three more children – two girls, Maria and Hannah, and a younger son, Alfred. In April 1859, James, Mary and their then only child Thomas accompanied the regiment to South Africa, almost drowning on the way when their ship was involved in a serious collision.

After five and a half years the Clarke family returned to Ireland and, after being honourably discharged from the Royal Artillery in January 1869, James joined the staff of the Ulster Militia Artillery. With no married quarters available in the militia barracks, James and his family lived in Dungannon, a rather drab provincial town in Co. Tyrone whose arid social life came to a dead stop on Sundays. Evenly balanced between Protestants and Catholics, the town was dominated by its centuries-old sectarian struggle between Unionism and Nationalism. Tyrone had been a cockpit of religious and political antagonism since the Ulster Plantation and the county was also a heartland of the great O'Neill clan that in Tudor and Stuart times had provided two notable rebels against English power – Hugh O'Neill, Earl of Tyrone and his nephew, Owen Roe. This bitter county was the centre of Thomas Clarke's small world. Only the newspapers connected him to outside events and he travelled little, apparently never even visiting Belfast, 50 miles away.

Now known universally as Tom, Clarke attended St Patrick's National School in Dungannon. Under the monitor system he became an assistant teacher but was eventually let go because of falling rolls. Clearly intelligent and well read, Tom became an enthusiastic amateur actor in Dungannon's Dramatic Club. But politics was his all-consuming passion and he came to espouse the cause of Irish independence. This commitment divided the Clarke family because his father had for decades served proudly as a British soldier and his brother Alfred had also enlisted in the Royal Artillery. Any early influence that his mother, who came from a very different background, might have had on Tom's ultimate political beliefs remains a matter for conjecture. When James Clarke warned his son that defying the British Empire meant banging his head against a wall, Tom retorted that he would just keep going until the wall fell down. His rebelliousness was certainly not rooted in a miserable childhood. The Clarkes were a happy family and Tom respected and admired his father, rejecting only his army uniform; the bonds with his mother and siblings stayed strong and harmonious. Much more influential in shaping his political consciousness was Tom's time in South Africa. Increasingly hostile to the British Army, he came to regard it as an imperial garrison that oppressed not the black population – then politically invisible – but the Boers, Dutch settlers for whom Tom developed a lifelong sympathy. But it was on his return to Ireland that Tom's political ideas really crystallised. Only a few years after the Fenian Rising of 1867 the British Army and Royal Irish Constabulary were still highly vigilant – and visible – in Co. Tyrone. And in bitterly divided Dungannon memories of the Irish Famine remained vivid, while an agricultural depression during the late 1870s exacerbated a traditionally turbulent relationship between landlords and tenants. The town also experienced frequent sectarian rioting between Protestants and Catholics.

In 1878 Tom attended an open-air meeting outside Dungannon addressed by John Daly, a national organiser of the Irish Republican Brotherhood (IRB). A superb public speaker with a powerful physique, imposing presence and magnetic personality, the 33-year-old Daly's oratory mesmerised audiences and his vision of an independent Ireland left Clarke deeply impressed. Suddenly Tom realised that his mission in life was to destroy every vestige of British authority in Ireland – Crown, Viceroy, Army and the Dublin Castle administration, the entire colonial system. He espoused the same goal as Wolfe Tone, his greatest historical inspiration. Almost a century earlier, Wolfe Tone, the father of Irish republicanism and instigator of the 1798 Rebellion, had set out 'to subvert the tyranny of our execrable government, to break the connection with England, the never-failing source of all our political evils, and to assert the independence of my country'. And from this goal Tom himself was never to deviate. Later in 1878, after the Dungannon meeting, Clarke and his best friend Billy Kelly joined a Dramatic Club excursion to Dublin where Daly swore them into the IRB.[2] But after becoming the organisation's Dungannon secretary, a disillusioned Clarke discovered that his idealised vision of the IRB as a sword for smiting England was very different to the drab reality of a society that had seriously lost its way. He was to spend the rest of his life remedying that situation.

Founded in both Ireland and America in 1858, the IRB was a secular, secret, oath-bound revolutionary movement dedicated to achieving Irish independence. Organised in circles, IRB members underwent clandestine military training, preparing to rise in Ireland when England became involved in a major war. Through conventional battle the IRB hoped to defeat British forces, establish a revolutionary government and win international recognition for an independent, democratic Irish republic. The IRB's American counterpart – which became known as the Fenian Brotherhood – channelled men, weapons and funds to Ireland and after the American Civil War ended in April 1865, thousands of former Union and Confederate soldiers crossed the Atlantic hoping to fight in an Irish rebellion. But the British government struck first in September 1865 by arresting and imprisoning most IRB leaders and detaining hundreds more. This pre-emptive strike ensured that when the insurrection finally occurred in 1867, it was a complete anticlimax. The only significant action was at Tallaght outside Dublin, where police fired on and routed columns of rebels. After the abortive rising everything fell apart. With most IRB leaders in prison and the organisation itself bereft of energy and purpose, the Fenian Brotherhood collapsed into squabbling factions. By 1871 Prime Minister Gladstone believed it was safe enough to give an amnesty to the imprisoned IRB leaders, especially as constitutional nationalism was gathering strength in Ireland where a Protestant lawyer, Isaac Butt, had established a Home Rule movement.

One IRB leader, John Devoy, believed 'it was a wonder that the men of the organisation, after such a series of defeats, had the recuperative power to reorganise the movement'.[3] But somehow it did survive. However, to prevent another hopeless rebellion, the Supreme Council changed its constitution and stipulated that henceforth the support of a majority of the Irish people was required for the IRB to inaugurate war with England. In the 1874 Westminster general election, the Supreme Council even supported Home Rule candidates. But within three years this co-operation ceased as most IRB members became disillusioned with constitutional politics, though even then four Supreme Council members dissented and were forced out. So by the time Clarke joined the IRB in 1878, it was more like a talking shop than a revolutionary conspiracy. And when he finally got some action it proved sterile and self-defeating. In August 1880 a nationalist Lady Day parade through Dungannon led to clashes between Catholic and Protestant mobs in the so-called 'Buckshot Riots'. A newspaper reported that after police in Irish Street fired buckshot into crowds, 'the firing was returned with interest from revolvers and by repeated showers of stones from the crowds of desperate men, many of them inflamed by drink, almost rushing on the points of the bayonet in the eagerness of their attack'.[4] Clarke and Kelly were among the shooters and despite eluding a subsequent round-up, the heat was on. Since Tom was already unemployed, they decided to leave for America, departing from Dungannon on 29 August 1880 and sailing a fortnight later from Londonderry. For Clarke this was a leap in the dark. But though it meant abandoning everything and everyone he knew, Tom was always a fearless gambler and no doubt hoped that in America his revolutionary career might finally take off.

After a fortnight's voyage Clarke's steamer arrived at Castle Garden on the island of Manhattan, then New York's reception centre for European immigrants. Later many of them recalled the excitement of sailing up one of the largest natural harbours on earth and realising – even before its first skyscraper was built – that New York's high-rise buildings promised them a new life in which the sky was indeed the limit. Pressing through a huge hall thronged with people conversing in many languages, Clarke was now a world away from Dungannon. Finally, immigration officials processed him and Kelly into a vibrant and astonishingly diverse metropolis of industry, finance, commerce and entertainment. This was the city that never slept. Here social life was exciting and liberating and iconic landmarks were everywhere from the Statue of Liberty and Broadway to Times Square and the world's longest suspension bridge in Brooklyn.

By 1880 over a third of New York's 1.5 million inhabitants were Irish or of Irish descent, concentrated mainly in the cheap housing of Brooklyn and Manhattan's 'Little Dublin'.[5] Urban Protestant America regarded the Catholicism of the Irish as alien and subversive and many Irish slid into lives of crime, alcoholism and violence. Even though by the 1880s Irish immigrants like Clarke were much better educated than previous generations of illiterate peasants, many still worked at dirty, dangerous semi-skilled and manual jobs. With no waiting relatives or friends and lacking a house and job, Clarke and Kelly faced an uncertain future. But the New York Irish had stuck together, building a vast support network of social, military and athletic clubs, and it was through these that the pair came to board with another Dungannon man, Pat O'Connor. He also gave them jobs in his shoe shop, although after a couple of months they shifted to Brooklyn's Mansion House hotel where Clarke worked as a storeman and Kelly as a boilerman.

However, politics was never far away and Tom and Kelly joined the Napper Tandy Club, a branch of Clan na Gael, then the leading republican organisation in Irish America. Founded in June 1867, the Clan was a revolutionary society committed to Ireland's liberation by force of arms. It had only really taken off after January 1871 when Gladstone released IRB leaders like John Devoy, Jeremiah O'Donovan Rossa and Thomas Clarke Luby and immediately exiled them to America. Joining the Clan, Devoy and O'Donovan Rossa quickly emerged as the dominant figures in Irish-American nationalism and in time both men would also dramatically change Tom Clarke's life. Devoy's forceful, single-minded personality and organising talent quickly attracted 15,000 members to the Clan from across America and in 1875 his fund-raising ability had persuaded the cash-strapped IRB to reunite

with the American wing. A year later Devoy pulled off a sensational coup
by dispatching a sailing vessel, the *Catalpa*, to rescue a group of transported
Irish soldiers from a prison in western Australia. He then established a joint
Revolutionary Directorate linking Clan na Gael and the IRB (with America
the dominant partner). Devoy now stood at the zenith of his political power
but ironically by the time Tom reached America in late 1880, Devoy had
split the Clan and precipitated his own downfall. This was because Devoy's
triumphant Australian rescue had raised his followers' expectations to
completely unrealistic levels. Many outlandish ideas for attacking England
now circulated, including a Clan submarine fleet that would destroy the
Royal Navy and starve the enemy into submission. Devoy rejected all such
schemes and dismissed as fantasy predictions of an imminent Irish revolution.
Instead he favoured joining with Ireland's landless peasantry and Isaac Butt's
Home Rule party in a broad national front that would campaign for gradual
political and economic progress in Ireland. By 1880 this so-called New
Departure policy had established an alliance between the Clan, Home Rulers
now led by Charles Stewart Parnell, and Michael Davitt's Land League.

However, this semi-constitutionalism went against Irish republicanism's
entire *raison d'être* of violent struggle against British rule. An authoritarian,
Devoy had suddenly sprung his gradualist policy on a bemused membership,
many of whom regarded it as heresy. Devoy's leading critic and the champion
of militarism was Jeremiah O'Donovan Rossa, a charismatic former IRB
leader from Co. Cork. Once he and Devoy had been best friends until incom-
patible personalities and policies drove them apart. Studious, reserved and
teetotal, Devoy was very different from the gregarious, chaotic O'Donovan
Rossa, an alcoholic famous for his spectacular benders in Broadway bars.
When O'Donovan Rossa's atavistic hatred of England led him in early 1880
to advocate assassinating Queen Victoria and wiping out the entire House of
Commons with chemical poison, Devoy expelled him from the Clan. But
O'Donovan Rossa regarded Devoy's policy as treasonous to the Clan and he
didn't go quietly, taking a minority of radicals with him. Even many members
who stayed in the Clan harboured serious doubts about Devoy's leadership.
While his New Departure appealed to the head, O'Donovan Rossa's demand
for immediate, violent action to humiliate England appealed to the heart.
In any struggle for the republican soul, Devoy was ultimately bound to lose.

After establishing his own radical organisation, the Skirmishers,
O'Donovan Rossa set out to literally blow Devoy's 'heresy' to pieces.[6]
He recruited volunteers and solicited funds for a bombing campaign in
England that would embrace an openly terrorist strategy of 'indiscriminately,

deliberately, recklessly and uncaringly destroying civilian life, property and security in the pursuit of military and political ends. Randomness and ruthlessness are intended to sap confidence in the state, to create irresistible pressure on the government to reach an accommodation with the terrorists'.[7] Contemptuously dismissing civilised warfare as 'trash', O'Donovan Rossa planned no-warning attacks on British government buildings, transport systems and even places of entertainment. By consciously targeting civilians, he intended creating a general panic that would destroy the British public's faith in the authorities and catapult Ireland's cause on to a worldwide stage.

O'Donovan Rossa's operatives commenced their bombing offensive in January 1881 with an explosion at Salford army barracks in Lancashire that killed a young boy. Despite a shoestring budget that necessitated them using cheap gunpowder, they gradually fomented a reign of terror, making the civilian population fearful of 'an invisible adversary who could strike at any moment unsuspected and unknown by those around him, hidden and protected by anonymity'.[8] Many Clan members became uneasy at O'Donovan Rossa forcing the pace and grabbing all the headlines and glory, at their organisation being outdone by a 'revolutionary showman'[9] who was emerging as the first bogeyman of a new terrorist age. Most of O'Donovan Rossa's operatives were Clan defectors and there was a fear of more members leaving to join him. Clarke – himself a natural Skirmisher – was probably torn between his own warlike instincts and his loyalties as a Clan official. But he regarded unity as an overriding principle, especially after the internal strife that had destroyed the Fenian Brotherhood and disabled the IRB. Furthermore, Tom's political antennae must have detected that increasing rank-and-file discontent in the Clan would soon change either the organisation's policy or its leadership and probably both. And since the Clan's membership and financial resources were far superior to O'Donovan Rossa's Skirmishers, any bombing campaign by it was bound to be far more destructive. Clarke would have wanted to be part of that.

Clan members' dissatisfaction at a lack of action finally erupted in August 1881 during an annual conference (the 'Dynamite Convention') at Chicago. One observer, Henri Le Caron, recalled that:

Nothing was talked of but the utter lack of practical effort which had characterised the past two years. The whole question of active operations came up and was debated at great length. Many of the delegates present attacked both the Revolutionary Directorate and the Executive Body for having practically done nothing.[10]

Devoy was unable to hold the line and resigned his presidency, leaving delegates 'determined that some outward and visible sign should be given England of its power of doing mischief'.[11] His successor was Alexander Sullivan, an archetypal city boss whose political machine dominated Chicago. Ambitious and unscrupulous, Sullivan was a lawyer with a well-deserved reputation for his iron nerve, ruthlessness and a coldly ferocious temper. He always carried a pistol and had once been acquitted by a packed jury after killing a school principal for allegedly insulting his wife; later he shot and wounded a political rival. Clearly Sullivan was not someone for whom violence was a distasteful last resort.

Anxious to make up for lost time, Sullivan intended outdoing O'Donovan Rossa with a Clan bombing campaign in England that would use powerful dynamite instead of gunpowder. Irish Republicans regarded dynamite as the nineteenth century's weapon of mass destruction and a radical alternative to their traditional but unsuccessful strategy of mass rebellion and open warfare. Vastly exaggerating its destructive power, they had dreams of airships bombing English cities and explosives teams crossing the Atlantic to incinerate London, inflicting on it the same devastation that Rome had once visited upon Carthage. Such visions had transfixed Clan delegates to the Chicago convention and one recalled that although 'the word dynamite finds no single place in the official records of the assembly it was in the air and in the speeches from start to finish'.[12] Sullivan told his confidante, Henri Le Caron, that America alone would control, fund and staff the bombing campaign in England, hermetically insulating it from the IRB in Ireland and Great Britain. Although employing Irish and British members with local knowledge might have been preferable, Sullivan distrusted an IRB Supreme Council that opposed bombing and feared it might sabotage his strategy. He also believed the Royal Irish Constabulary had penetrated the IRB and told Le Caron – almost certainly wrongly – that the Royal Irish Constabulary had forty agents in America trying to infiltrate the Clan.

Sullivan delegated the selection and training of Clan members for bombing missions in England to Thomas Gallagher, a 32-year-old doctor. Born in Glasgow to Irish parents from Donegal, Gallagher had emigrated early to America where he joined Clan na Gael and graduated from a New York medical school. With a lucrative practice in Brooklyn he became a dapper man about town, sporting a gold-tipped walking cane, but Gallagher's strident hatred of England and his knowledge of chemicals took him into much darker territory. Le Caron recalled him going on and on about 'making experiments in the manufacture of explosives and advocating their use.

He was quite enthusiastic in their praise and so carried away by his subject that he expressed his willingness to undertake the carriage of dynamite to England and to superintend its use there'.[13] After Sullivan granted his wish, Gallagher established a training school to instruct Clan recruits in the manufacture and use of dynamite.

John Kenny, the president of the Clan's Napper Tandy Club who had sworn in Clarke and Kelly, recalled a meeting at which:

> A secret call was issued for volunteers to do something more than talking for Ireland. The nature of the work was not stated but it was intimated. One of the first to volunteer for that job was young Clarke. It was no boyish adventure with him. He was a sensible and thoughtful young fellow who fully realised the risks to be undertaken. Tom Clarke came to me that night and quietly asked to have his name sent to the proper quarters for service in any capacity.[14]

Clarke certainly met Sullivan's criteria about recruits being loyal and intelligent young bachelors with no close personal ties: Tom had no wife, children or even a girlfriend to worry about if things went wrong and he had also deliberately severed contact with his family in Ireland. A Tyrone accent would also enable him to melt into London's large Irish population. After being vetted Tom was chosen. Billy Kelly had volunteered at the same time as Clarke but was turned down. At Gallagher's training school in Brooklyn, Tom learned about handling and detonating dynamite, clearly impressing the doctor who brought him to a deserted part of Long Island where he gained experience by blasting rocks with nitroglycerine. After graduating with honours, he made it on to Gallagher's bombing team. His time had finally come.

An audacious bombing campaign in England undoubtedly appealed to Tom's dramatic imagination, offering him a starring role in a lethal form of street theatre that would soon usher in a new world of global terrorism. Not long before, Clarke had been teaching in a rural Ulster backwater, but now, along with other fanatical young men – 'dynamite evangelists' – he stood poised to travel vast distances and strike at the very heart of the British Empire. Secretive, single-minded and ruthless, with no moral qualms about killing civilians, Tom was well suited for such a dangerous venture. In his mind the rules of war apply did not apply to England and its people; they were liable to be attacked anywhere – in government offices and crowded shops or on the streets, buses, trains and underground system. Tom was not squeamish about causing deaths and casualties and it could have been him, not O'Donovan

Rossa, who declared that 'I believe in all things for the liberation of Ireland. If dynamite is necessary for the redemption of Ireland then dynamite is a blessed agent of the people of Ireland in their holy war. I do not know how dynamite could be put to better use than in blowing up the British Empire'.[15] Drinking from the same well of rage and visceral hatred as O'Donovan Rossa, Tom would let nothing stand in his way, not even an IRB Supreme Council opposed to bombing. Nor was he bothered about operating in an English capital teeming with soldiers, policemen and the newly formed Special Branch of Scotland Yard. Dangers such as premature explosions, imprisonment and even execution concerned him not at all.

In October 1882, Sullivan sent Gallagher on a reconnaissance mission to England.[16] Posing as an American tourist, he spent a couple of months gathering intelligence on security measures and potential targets like the House of Commons, Scotland Yard and government offices in Whitehall. Returning to America, Gallagher submitted to the Revolutionary Directorate a favourable report on the prospects for a bombing campaign in England. Impressed, Sullivan approved one commencing in early April 1883, appointed Gallagher as its leader and allocated him funds. Gallagher could not wait to get started and wearied Le Caron by talking about 'nothing but dynamite, its production, its effectiveness and the great weapon it was soon to prove against the British government'.[17] But it is surprising that in Sullivan's small circle nobody queried Gallagher's obvious vested interest: a bombing campaign's most enthusiastic supporter had been chosen to assess its chances of success. Having done so much to get the bandwagon rolling in the first place, Gallagher would have had great difficulty halting it even had he wanted to.

The Clan's bombing campaign was lamentably flawed from start to finish. Sullivan and the Revolutionary Directorate had seriously overestimated Gallagher's ability, swayed perhaps by his professional standing and confident manner. In reality Gallagher was just as inexperienced a conspirator as the men he led. Tom's fate now rested in the hands of an amateur who was about to give a master class in ineptitude. And in another way Gallagher was not quite what he seemed, because he was secretly working both sides of the street. While nominally a Clan member following Sullivan's instructions, Gallagher had surreptitiously allied himself with O'Donovan Rossa, the politician he most admired, in a dual allegiance that made Gallagher effectively a Skirmisher, piggybacking a free ride on the Clan's superior resources. Furthermore, despite Sullivan's boasts about a blanket of absolute secrecy, a British intelligence agent had infiltrated his operation. Ironically this was none other than Henri Le Caron, the very person Sullivan had cautioned about the necessity of preventing enemy penetration. For fifteen years this 'Prince of Spies' had been reporting on the Clan's activities and leaders. But despite warning the British government in general terms about what was coming, Le Caron could not provide Special Branch with the bombers' identities, hiding places and intended targets. Initially at least, the authorities had to rely on catching a lucky break.

Gallagher organised his mission in two separate phases. First, he decided that tight security at ports made smuggling commercially manufactured dynamite into England too risky and planned instead to produce explosives in the country itself. Only when a stockpile was ready would he and the other team members cross the Atlantic to commence attacking strategic targets in London. But Gallagher had only assembled a small group and his operation was under-resourced from the start. In late January 1883 he sent just one person, Alfred George Whitehead, in advance to the English midlands city of Birmingham. In this unfamiliar location, Whitehead was expected by himself to rent and convert premises into a shop that he alone would run as a front for a bomb-making factory in which he would manufacture gelignite. And although secreting Whitehead far away from London certainly increased operational security, it meant that highly unstable nitroglycerine would have to be transported by train over a hundred miles south to the English capital.

After giving Whitehead a couple of months to set himself up in Birmingham, Gallagher and the others sailed separately to England during March 1883. The first conspirator out was John Curtin, an iron moulder who arrived in Liverpool after visiting his parents in Co. Cork. Alfred Lynch, a 22-year-old coach painter using the pseudonym 'Norman', followed on 13 March with orders to stay in London and await Gallagher's further orders. Lacking a strong personality and completely untrained in explosives, Norman was probably selected because of his pliability, someone whom Gallagher could use as a glorified errand boy. Gallagher himself embarked on 14 March, travelling on the same ship – but in a different class – as his alcoholic brother Bernard and another passenger, William Ansburgh. Whether Bernard Gallagher and Ansburgh were actually connected to the plot is still unclear. Clarke was last out, leaving from Boston in the guise of Henry Hammond Wilson, supposedly an Englishman returning home. Sworn to secrecy, Tom confessed many years later that it had been one of the hardest things in his life not telling even his best friend Billy Kelly that he was going thousands of miles away on a mission.[18] Now working in another Long Island hotel, Kelly first learned about Tom's disappearance when a suitcase of his belongings arrived for safekeeping along with a note warning him to stonewall any inquiries from Tom's family.[19] On the voyage to England and for the second time in Clarke's life, he nearly drowned when his ship hit an iceberg, but a passing vessel rescued the passengers and brought them to Newfoundland. Tom then completed his journey to Liverpool.

Whitehead, meanwhile, had been building up his cover in Birmingham. On 6 February 1883, he bought premises 2 miles south of the city centre that he eventually opened as a paint and wallpaper shop, an ideal front for purchasing the chemicals needed to make nitroglycerine. Whitehead dispersed the fumes through a back kitchen funnel connected to the chimney. To keep watch over his arsenal, Whitehead took lodgings in rented rooms next door to his shop. Unsurprisingly, he was soon unable to cope with serving customers while secretly manufacturing dynamite, so he hired a 13-year-old boy to work the counter. The youth proved remarkably incurious, even after an explosion at the rear of the shop that Whitehead dismissed as an accidental pistol discharge. If Whitehead had been further along in manufacturing explosives, he, the boy and many residents nearby would have perished. But employing a very young assistant and packing an inordinately large number of boxes into such small premises was always likely to create suspicions about Whitehead's business. Near the end of March 1883, a supplier tipped off police who secretly entered the shop and discovered its true purpose. It was the intelligence breakthrough that Special Branch so desperately needed and Birmingham detectives immediately began covert surveillance of Whitehead's customers and visitors. On 28 March they got lucky when Thomas Gallagher travelled from London to inspect Whitehead's progress. Shortly after Gallagher's arrival they were unexpectedly joined by Clarke who had just travelled from Liverpool — evidence of Gallagher's inability to co-ordinate the conspirators' movements and organise effective counter-surveillance. In quick order the police had identified three prime suspects.

The next day Gallagher and Clarke travelled together by train to London, where Tom took lodgings in a private house situated among an Irish community near Blackfriars Bridge. Inexperienced and inadequately trained, Tom then sent Whitehead an uncoded letter containing his new address; he also revealed his intention of returning to Birmingham to collect explosives that would be used to start bombing the capital. On 5 April 1883, Clarke helped Whitehead pour 80lbs of nitroglycerine into rubber fishing stockings and pack them into a case. He then took it by cab to Birmingham's main railway station and caught the return train to London. A detective had tailed Clarke's cab but lost it in the heavy traffic. Just after Tom had left, Norman turned up at Whitehead's shop. Norman had been holed up at a Euston

Square hotel in London until Gallagher dispatched him to Birmingham to bring nitroglycerine back to the capital. After collecting a wooden trunk packed with 200lbs of explosives, Norman went by taxi to Birmingham railway station, where he sent Gallagher a telegram arranging for them to meet at Euston Station in London. Norman then travelled south on the 6 p.m. train, but in the next compartment were Birmingham detectives who had sent a telegram warning Special Branch in Scotland Yard about Norman's imminent arrival. At 9 p.m. Gallagher met Norman at Euston Station and they went by taxi towards a hotel in the Strand where Norman was to store the explosives. But Special Branch detectives shadowing the pair lost track of Gallagher when he slipped out of the cab just before it reached the hotel. After a few hours waiting in vain for him to reappear, they gave up, went inside and arrested Norman.

British authorities then began rounding up the remaining suspects. Early on 5 April 1883, Birmingham police raided Whitehead's accommodation and arrested him. They also discovered Clarke's uncoded letter to Whitehead containing his Blackfriars address which, incredibly, Whitehead had not destroyed. The Birmingham police next advised Scotland Yard detectives to discreetly watch Clarke's lodgings. Just after lunchtime Tom returned there accompanied by Gallagher and Chief Inspector Littlechild of Special Branch arrested them both. By then police were searching Norman's room in Euston Square where they discovered a telegram from Gallagher's Charing Cross hotel. They then searched Gallagher's room and found a letter from Curtin's London address. Soon afterwards detectives apprehended Curtin. Like a circular firing squad, the conspirators had destroyed each other through messages they should neither have sent nor retained. William Ansburgh's London address was also found in Gallagher's hotel room, although the two men had apparently never met again after crossing the Atlantic. An inebriated Bernard Gallagher was detained in the family home town of Glasgow where he had been on a never-ending pub crawl since arriving from America.

It had been a close call for Special Branch. Although they arrested Gallagher's entire team and seized 500lbs of nitroglycerine, things could have turned out very differently but for civilian alertness and the conspirators' own folly. On separate occasions, detectives trailing Clarke and Thomas Gallagher had lost them and only luck facilitated their eventual capture – still in possession of enough explosives to inflict carnage on London. It must have galled Tom and Gallagher to have come so close to success only to fall into enemy hands at the last moment, and to be rounded up so quickly, Gallagher after only ten days in England and Clarke a day less. Literally overnight Tom's situation had changed dramatically, from potentially holding the power of life and death to a state of utter helplessness. He and the other Irish prisoners were remanded to Millbank Prison, an immense yellow-brown fortress on the north bank of the Thames close to the Houses of Parliament and the Old Bailey, where they would soon stand trial for treason-felony. A mightily relieved public craved to know what these 'monsters' looked like, but at that time newspapers lacked any photographs to satisfy its curiosity. Even the Prince of Wales was intrigued and had his private secretary approach the governor about the possibility of Edward inspecting the prisoners 'quite privately'.[20] But ultimately the royal tour of Millbank never materialised.

However, police photographs of the bombers did exist, taken very shortly after their arrest, still in civilian clothes.[21] Millbank's governor presented them to the head of the prison service, Sir Edmund du Cane, jocularly apologising for the poor image of an agitated Whitehead, 'taken by the instantaneous process whilst the gentleman was objecting and great was his vexation when he realised that we had secured his likeness!!'[22] But Clarke's photograph was very different. Not despairing or blankly uncomprehending, he was sitting in an armchair dressed like a middle-class businessman or academic. Captured and on remand, he knew that his life had just changed forever – and not in a good way – yet he remained composed and dignified, his eyes locked unflinchingly on the camera. Silently, Tom seemed to be marshalling his resources for battles soon to be fought.

Although presumed legally innocent, Tom was treated as a convict from the time of his arrest. Apart from a daily hour of exercise and attendance at chapel, he was held in solitary confinement, a regime that Michael Davitt, a former Fenian prisoner in Millbank, regarded as 'a very terrible ordeal'.[23] Davitt especially remembered hearing:

> The voice of Big Ben telling the listening inmates of the penitentiary that another fifteen minutes have gone by. What horrible punishment has not that clock added to many an unfortunate wretch's fate by counting for him the minutes during which stone walls and iron bars will a prison make.[24]

And there were other reminders of a noisy, joyful world just beyond reach such as the strains of a band in St James's Park and railway engine whistles 'with the suggestiveness of a journey home'.[25] Things hadn't changed much by Clarke's time. Although he conceded that the Irish prisoners 'were not treated with exceptional severity',[26] the surveillance was close and continuous. They were not allowed to converse and Tom was caught out twice when he tried. Written messages were also forbidden, but despite having no pens or pencils they succeeded in communicating with each other: 'A fellow has no business in prison unless he is resourceful and observant'.[27] But the mental desolation was a different matter:

> Looking back now to my imprisonment in Millbank I get a picture of a dreary time of solitary confinement in the cold white-washed cell with a short daily exercise varying the monotony. Day after day all alike, no change, maddening silence, sitting there in that cell, hopeless, friend-less and alone with nothing in this world to look forward to but that one note occasionally coming to me from one or another of my poor comrades, Gallagher, Whitehead and Curtin who were in the same plight as myself.[28]

The authorities spent almost three months strengthening their case against Gallagher's team. They had Whitehead on manufacturing and possession, Clarke and Norman on possession, and could prove Thomas Gallagher's association with all three men. The police had also seized incriminating documents. But evidence against the rest was weaker and largely circum-stantial; charging them all initially with treason-felony was problematic. There were no captured maps or notes detailing targets, vital in persuading a jury that the defendants had really intended using the dynamite in a deadly fashion. So the prosecution caught a lucky break when a chastened Norman, his mind concentrated wonderfully by five days in prison and the prospect of thousands more, contacted Scotland Yard and offered to become a prosecu-tion witness. And what a story he had to tell. In his version he, a young man, trusting and naive, opposed to violence and with no real interest in Irish politics, had been dropped right in it by a manipulative Thomas Gallagher. Norman claimed that the doctor had accompanied him around London pointing out bombing targets like the Houses of Parliament ('This will make a great crash when it comes down') and Scotland Yard ('That will come down too').[29] The prosecution knew that if Norman could sell himself convinc-ingly to the jury as a victim of Gallagher's manipulation, it would clinch their case. And to secure his testimony, it gave Norman a sweet deal: no jail time, a new identity in a foreign country and possibly – republicans believed undoubtedly – piles of money for a fresh start in life.

The trial of Clarke and the others began on Tuesday 22 June 1883 at London's Central Criminal Court, the Old Bailey, and because of the great demand for seats at the 'Dynamite Conspiracy' trial, admission was by ticket only.[30] The Lord Mayor welcomed its three presiding judges, Lord Chief Justice Coleridge, Master of the Rolls, Lord Justice Brett and Mr Justice Grove. For their protection, barricades had been erected at various court entrances, while policemen flooded the nearby streets to deter a rescue attempt, an explosion or hostile crowds: 'The prisoners were brought to and taken away from court under a strong guard of mounted police, the appearance of the van and its armed escort causing much excitement as it passed through the streets'.[31] The six accused men knew nothing about Norman's pre-trial negotiations with the prosecution and on the first day a journalist reported that 'when Norman appeared, instead of going into the dock, he proceeded with chief inspector Littlechild to the witness box. I shall never forget the look of consternation on the faces of the prisoners as he was being sworn by the court'.[32] All the defendants pleaded 'Not Guilty'. Five were legally represented – two by QCs – but Clarke acted as his own defence counsel. Whether handling explosives or appearing before the three most senior judges in the land, Tom demonstrated his great self-control, confidence and a willingness to stand alone. But he was also determined to keep the conspiracy's secrets to himself and knowing that the less he said in court the better, Clarke declined to testify on his own behalf. Most of what he did say in court was a lie, including his continued insistence that he really was 22-year-old Henry Wilson and a punning claim that he worked as a clerk. Resisting grandstanding, Tom limited himself to interventions designed to create reasonable doubt. Trying to undermine the credibility of eyewitness identification, he successfully extracted admissions from his Birmingham cab driver and Whitehead's young shop assistant that they did not conclusively recognise him. But a detective insisted Clarke was the man he had tried following to Birmingham's central railway station. And while Norman admitted never having met Clarke and could not connect him directly to the plot, he had already sunk Gallagher, with whom Tom had been arrested – and at Tom's accommodation where a significant amount of explosives was present. If jury members connected the dots, then Clarke was in serious trouble.

Since no defendant testified, the trial lasted only four days. Clarke declined to make any closing arguments and after the Lord Chief Justice's summing up, the jury needed just an hour and a quarter to convict him, Thomas Gallagher, Whitehead and Curtin, though it acquitted Ansburgh and Bernard Gallagher. Thomas Gallagher buckled on hearing the verdict, swearing on his mother's grave that he was the victim of a tragic miscarriage of justice and had never even met O'Donovan Rossa, the plot's supposed mastermind. Gallagher's denials failed to sway the Lord Chief Justice who sentenced all four convicted men to penal servitude for life. Spectators cheered, as did the crowds gathered outside when they heard the news. Clarke shouted at the judge, 'Good-bye we shall meet in Heaven'.[33] He remembered being 'hustled into the prison van, surrounded by a troop of mounted police and driven at a furious pace through the howling mob that thronged the streets from the Courthouse to Millbank Prison. London was panic-stricken at the time'.[34]

NOTES

1 The question of Tom Clarke's place and date and place of birth has been complicated by anonymous and erroneous notes deposited in his private papers at the National Library of Ireland. Accepting these at face value, Gerard MacAtasney in his book *Tom Clarke: Life, Liberty, Revolution* stated that Clarke was born in 1858 at Hurst Castle on the Hampshire coast. Later in the nineteenth century, Hurst Castle was re-fortified with a military garrison but only after a government report of 1859 by which time the Clarke family was in South Africa. Writing almost eighty years before MacAtasney, Louis Le Roux in his book *Tom Clarke and the Irish Freedom Movement* had apparently realised this error and assumed that the anonymous writer of the notes must have meant Hurst Park Barracks on the Isle of Wight where Clarke's father's regiment was then stationed. Kathleen Clarke also reinforced her claims about Tom's age by asserting that he was 26 years old when he went to prison in June 1883 and 41 years old when he was released in September 1883 ('A Character Sketch of Tom Clarke', NLI MS 49,355/12). I am grateful to the General Register Office for Births, Marriages and Deaths, Southport, England for the information concerning births in Hampshire and the Isle of Wight in 1857 and 1858. Both MacAtasney and Le Roux also accepted the incorrect dating by the writer of the anonymous notes of 31 March 1857 as the occasion of Clarke's parents' marriage. I am grateful to the present rector of Shanrahan Church, Rev. Barbara Fryday, for providing me with a copy of the marriage certificate. There is also a marriage certificate with the same details at the General Register Office, Dublin.

2 In his life of Clarke, Louis Le Roux asserted that Daly had sworn in Clarke and Kelly in 1882 – a time when both men were living in America. However in a letter to the *Irish Press* on 4 March 1937, he corrected himself by writing that he had a statement from Kelly saying that he, Clarke and a few other friends had been sworn into the IRB in 1878. For Clarke and Kelly's friendship, see William (Billy) Kelly, BMH WS 226 and also Kelly's manuscript notes on the early life of Tom Clarke in Ireland and America, NLI MS 44,684/1.

3 John Devoy, *Recollections of an Irish Rebel*, p. 254.

4 *Belfast Telegraph*, 18 August 1880.

5 For the New York Irish, see Jay P. Dolan, *The Irish Americans: A History*. Also Ronald H. Bayor and Timothy Meagher, *The New York Irish*.

6 For the Clan split and the onset of the dynamite campaign, see Terry Golway, *Irish Rebel: John Devoy and America's Fight for Ireland's Freedom*, pp. 139–45.

7 Seán McConville, *Irish Political Prisoners, 1848–1922*, p. 328.

8 Shane Kenna, 'The Politics of the Bomb' in Fearghal McGarry, *The Black Hand of Republicanism: Fenianism in Modern Ireland*.

9 Seán McConville, *Irish Political Prisoners, 1848–1922*, p. 336.

10 Henri Le Caron, *Twenty-Five Years in the Secret Service*, pp. 187–8.

11 Ibid., p. 187.

12 Ibid., p. 188.

13 Ibid., p. 192.

14 Lecture on Clarke by John Kenny, *Gaelic American*, 12 January 1924.

15 O'Donovan Rossa quoted in Jonathan Gannt, *Irish Terrorism in the Atlantic Community 1865–1922*, pp. 132–3.

16 For the dynamite campaign in England, see Shane Kenna, *War in the Shadows: Irish American Bombers in Victorian Britain*. See also K.R.M. Short, *The Dynamite War: Irish American Bombers in Victorian Britain*.

17 Henri Le Caron, *Twenty-Five Years in the Secret Service*, p. 192. See also pp. 200–1.

18 Kathleen Clarke in a letter to the *Donegal Democrat*, 9 October 1964. There is a copy in the Seán O'Mahony Papers, NLI MS 44,101/4.

19 Billy Kelly, William (Billy) Kelly, BMH WS 226 and NLI MS 44,684/1.

20 Letter from the Governor of Milbank to Sir Edmund Du Cane, 23 April 1883. Papers of Sir Edmund F. Du Cane, MSS. Eng. Misc. d. 956-8. 961 Bodleian Library, Oxford University.

21 The original photographs are deposited in the Du Cane Papers, Bodleian Library, Oxford.

22 Letter from the Governor of Milbank Prison to Sir Edmund du Cane, 23 April 1883, Du Cane Papers, Bodleian Library, Oxford.

23 Michael Davitt, *Leaves from a Prison Diary*, p. 171.

24 Ibid., p. 172.

25 Ibid.

26 Clarke in a lecture he gave in 1899 to Dublin's '98 Club, a year after his release from prison. Clarke's copy, sadly incomplete, is in the Clarke Papers, NLI MS 49,354/6.

27 Clarke, *Glimpses of an Irish Felon's Prison Life*, p. 12.

28 Ibid., pp. 12–13.

29 K.R.M. Short, *The Dynamite War*, p. 132.

30 *The Times*, 12 June 1883. This newspaper carried extensive reports on the trial on 12, 13, 14 and 15 June 1883.

31 *The Times*, 12 June 1883.

32 *Reynolds Weekly Newspaper*, 22 April 1883. Cited in Shane Kenna, *War in the Shadows*, p. 143.

33 *The Times*, 15 June 1883.

34 Tom Clarke, *Glimpses of an Irish Felon's Prison Life*, p. 11.

2

'An Earthly Hell': Prison 1883–1898

After returning to Millbank, Clarke was immediately initiated into the English convict system. First fitted out in a khaki uniform, he then had his hair cropped and became literally just a number as prisoner J464. Finally a senior officer read out to him the rules and regulations that he was to obey absolutely:

> Nothing in them startled me like the one that stated, 'Strict silence must at all times be observed; under no circumstances must one prisoner speak to another'. When I thought of what that meant in conjunction with another paragraph, 'No hope of release for life prisoners till they have completed twenty years, and then each case will be decided on its own merits', and remembered with what relentless savagery the English government has always dealt with the Irishmen it gets into its clutches, the future appeared as black and appalling as imagination could picture it.

Another Irish prisoner declared that 'the announcement never failed to stagger even the most hardened and reckless criminal'.[1]

Convicts normally spent the first nine months of their sentence in solitary confinement, but since Millbank usually held only remand prisoners, Clarke, Gallagher, Whitehead and Curtin were soon transferred out. Awakened suddenly on 25 August 1883 and ordered to dress quickly, they were hand-cuffed in a chain gang, surrounded by a posse of armed officers and escorted to a nearby railway station. Their destination was Chatham Prison, about 30 miles east on the southern shore of the Medway estuary and situated just outside the town itself.[2] At this time Chatham exuded British military and industrial power, with forts and army barracks protecting its great naval dockyard while ships plied one of Europe's busiest waterways, constantly replenishing the wharves, workshops and warehouses. For decades inmates from England's largest public works prison had been extending the dockyard, building new basins and dry docks; now Clarke too was destined to toil here for many years, helping to raise more great monuments for his captors. Alighting from their train at Chatham, Clarke's party was put in a horse-drawn Black Maria and driven to the prison's reception hall, where an officer recorded Tom's name, religion, occupation, place and date of birth. Clarke still insisted that he was Henry Hammond Wilson, born in Great Yarmouth in Norfolk and three and a half years younger than his real age of 26.[3] Warders measured Clarke's height and weight, gave him a medical examination, took his photograph and recorded details of his complexion, hair and eye colour. After bathing he was escorted along corridors and walkways to a cell.

Stretching almost half a mile, Chatham Prison held 1,700 convicts and housed another 2,000 people. The governor, Captain Vernon Harris, and his two deputies had their own living quarters, while accommodation was provided for senior officers, over a hundred warders and their families, four chaplains, two doctors, nurses, scripture readers, civil guards and schoolmasters. The grounds contained a chapel and infirmary, an administrative block with offices for Harris and his deputies, a reception office and a search room for visitors. There was also a library, a warders' mess room and a staff reading room as well as a cookhouse and a bathhouse. An edifice in the middle contained the convict cells. Chatham Prison resembled a small factory town with workshops that employed inmates as tailors, shoemakers, printers, blacksmiths, carpenters, wheelwrights and fitters. Other prisoners laboured in an iron foundry, cultivated gardens and vegetable plots or dressed stone brought from quarries at Portland in Dorset.

As a high security prison, Chatham had a permanent military presence, a guardroom stocked with weapons, armed sentries at the main gate, an army barracks nearby and a police unit that investigated criminal offences committed inside the gaol. A former army officer, Harris ran his prison with 'clock-like precision'.[4] He had personally recruited many former soldiers and sailors as warders and they shared his belief that 'discipline was a first duty and to exact it from others a second of at least equal importance'.[5] Their attitude chimed with Gladstone's Home Secretary, Sir Edward Harcourt, who rejected the dynamitards' claim to be prisoners of war and implacably denied them political status. Harcourt encouraged Harris to treat Clarke and his comrades as felons. So did the Director of Prisons, Sir Edmund du Cane, an austere and intellectually brilliant civil servant who for decades had seen off successive Home Secretaries while outlasting every prison reformer. Enjoying such high-level protection, Harris's hard-line approach meant that 'everyone must conform and either fall out or be crushed'.[6]

The Governor's stringent controls were partly intended to prevent the Irish convicts hatching escape plots or enlisting outsiders to spring them from prison. There were precedents. In 1867 Fenians had freed two republican leaders from a horse-drawn police van in Manchester and three months later they also exploded a bomb outside Clerkenwell Prison in London, killing a dozen civilian bystanders. Harris's anxieties about security swelled as Special Branch hunted down the remaining dynamitards in London, Liverpool and Glasgow and imprisoned them at Chatham, twenty-one in all. To prevent any breakouts on his watch, he kept the prison permanently on high alert, ordering that every vehicle entering and leaving be searched, right down to the baker's and butcher's vans. Designating the Irish convicts as Special Men, he concentrated them in a separate penal block that was located a considerable distance from the ordinary prisoners. Hidden away from an unsympathetic English public and abandoned even by many Irish nationalists, Clarke did not anticipate getting his freedom for a very long time – if ever. Such oppressive isolation left the Special Men feeling like the Forgotten; one wrote that 'we, the Irish convicts, were virtually in a living tomb, cut off from everything and hearing no human sounds but hard words and harsh orders from the warders'.[7]

Chatham's regime enforced discipline among prisoners right from the start by driving out rebelliousness and making them malleable. Except for short exercise periods and attendance at chapel, Clarke was initially confined to his cell all day, spending many dreary hours picking oakum. This involved separating lengths of old ship's rope into coils by sliding them back and forth on his knee and removing tar and salt from the strands which would later be used to caulk the seams of wooden ships. Such repetitive and intellectually deadening work was 'a dreadful and cruel occupation. It annoys the fingers and was monotonous to madness'.[8] When Clarke finally entered the main prison population in early 1884, vigilant warders mounted close surveillance upon him virtually every waking minute and frequently throughout the night as well. They also searched him and his cell regularly for weapons and contraband. Ordinary rub-downs occurred routinely at least four times a day, but it was the prison officers' twice monthly 'disgusting' body examinations, conducted with 'the most repugnant minuteness', that left Clarke feeling utterly violated. After stripping him naked on a bench, they probed every orifice with a lamp and he never forget their mocking running commentary or 'the indecent and hurtful way some of the officers mauled me'.[9] However, Tom hated even more the systematic sleep deprivation inflicted only on the Special Men; Clarke's nightmares occurred during his waking hours. After every working day he would return wearily to his cell and throw himself down on the floor longing only for oblivion, but even when a bell rang and he retired to bed, it was difficult to nod off. And sleep, when it finally came, was constantly interrupted by a loud noise that resembled cannon fire, made by inspecting officers banging cell doors behind them. Once every hour a warder peered through a 'Judas hole' in cell doors: any prisoner who pulled a blanket over his head received a bread-and-water punishment and if he turned away the warder would shine a flashlight on a wall before slamming the peephole shut:

> This went on night after night, week after week, month after month for years. Think of the effects of this upon a man's system and no one will wonder that so many were driven insane by such tactics. The horror of those nights and days will never leave my memory. One by one I saw my fellow prisoners break down and go mad under the terrible strain.[10]

Harris's most effective weapon in preventing the dynamitards from conspiring was a rule of perpetual silence that banned prisoners from conversing. Clarke even had to raise a hand first before being allowed to address a warder. Deputy Governor Griffiths conceded that:

> A very vicious system for reports and punishments was in force at Chatham. All intercommunication was forbidden and the rule was strictly enforced by a stringent and meticulous discipline. It was easy to go wrong, very difficult to do right. Misconduct was scrupulously inter-preted, the shadow of a 'report' would hang heavily over the whole body of convicts and might result in punishment for very trifling offences.[11]

Harris's warders punished inmates for moving their lips, turning a head, keeping an untidy cell, hesitating to obey an order and not closing up in the ranks. To Clarke this was a cruel system of 'perpetual and persistent harassing which gave the officers in charge of us a free hand to persecute us just as they pleased. It was made part of their duty to worry and harass us all the time. Harassing morning noon and night and on through the night'.[12] But Chatham's warders saw it very differently. Believing Clarke and his comrades capable of mass murder, these ex-servicemen felt that they were in a sense still at war against a cunning and dangerous enemy and so they never let their guard down when around them, brooking neither argument nor delay. Furthermore, even a hint of them fraternising with prisoners risked official censure and accusations of trafficking contraband. Griffiths acknowledged that 'almost invariably they were brusque and abrupt in manner, seemingly unsympathetic and little given to weakness as they would have deemed it, to gentle and conciliatory treatment of their charges'.[13] Clarke often felt like a verbal punchbag when warders bellowed orders at him like a parade ground sergeant-major 'with as much fuss and noise as if I were a whole regiment of soldiers'.[14] Another Irish prisoner compared his incarceration to being 'enveloped by a shroud' and that 'the nagging, the ordering about, the mental kicking and hammering crushed him to a pulp'.[15] Clarke hated almost every officer, but apart from Governor Harris he most despised 'Bully' Parker whom he once witnessed hooting with laughter while punching and kicking a simple-minded prisoner unconscious. Only two of the staff at Chatham ever showed him any kindness – an Irish infirmary nurse who threw bread into his cell and whispered news items, and a Cockney who warned him to avoid a prison informer.[16]

Besides stringent control mechanisms, Harris laid on hard labour, hard fare and a hard bed. However, while ordinary prisoners at least had stools and mattresses, Clarke's 12ft by 7ft whitewashed cell contained only a wooden stump – fastened to the cold stone floor and situated too close to the wall – and an uncomfortable plank bed. There was also a chamber pot, a bowl of water and a broom for sweeping the cell clean – but no table – and walls were bare apart from a copy of the prison rules. With no sunlight and an iron grating covering a gaslight, reading at night was difficult and sometimes impossible, weakening Clarke's eyes and necessitating glasses in later life. The heavy door had a spyhole, a flap through which meals were passed and a gap at the bottom through which he slid out his broom. Tom took meals alone in his cell using a tin knife and a wooden spoon to consume food and water that many prisoners considered part of their punishment. Unappetising, stodgy, lacking in variety and frequently cold, Clarke's diet consisted of small quantities of cocoa, bread, frequently rotten potatoes, molasses, tough stringy meat, oatmeal that tasted like gum, plum duff and gruel. After going hungry for years on end, his appetite was finally worn away, though sometimes even the meagre helpings shrank when he was put on a punishment diet of bread and water – something Clarke regarded as 'systematic starvation'.[17] Deputy Governor Griffiths believed that eventually the same food with the same flavour, prepared in the same way and served in the same order, 'became almost nauseous and the palate of even the hungriest man craves with almost maddening desire for a change'.[18] Famished inmates on worksites wolfed down railway grease and ate handfuls of earth-worms sprinkled with salt; so many reported sick to get a taste of medicine that nurses concocted jars of unpleasant liquids to deter these 'malingerers'. Cod liver oil became a much sought-after luxury. But at least Clarke's wiry frame didn't soften into middle-aged flab. Entering prison at only 9½ stone, he actually shed another 7lbs over the next fifteen years.[19]

Once a week warders marched Clarke in his underclothes to a bathhouse that lacked stools and pegs on which to hang garments. As two club-wielding officers stood guard, he plunged into water that was always deliberately kept very cold but after only a minute or so they ordered Clarke out again, whacking him 'to help me dry' if he dressed too slowly. Predictably such poor hygiene meant a pungent smell suffused the prison and though Clarke said he was well acquainted with the unpleasant odours of asylums and workhouses, Chatham's seemed uniquely repugnant – 'a strange blend of metallic aromas, natural fibre matting, carbolic soap or disinfectant and a hint of boiled meat and the sickly smell of the unwashed (the latter two sometimes indistinguish-able from each other)'.[20] Adding to his nausea, the whiff of warders' tobacco, beer and hair oil also drifted around corridors and wafted into prisoners' cells.

There were few creature comforts at Chatham; no hairdresser, for instance, and no reclining chair. Before Clarke's time a warder slid a razor under a cell door and collected it when the convict had finished shaving and cutting his own hair – a system hurriedly abandoned after an inmate rolled out four fingers instead.[21] The Governor then allocated prisoners two dozen scissors with which to trim each other in the corridors once a week. Blunted through constant use and with their screws loose, these implements were potentially lethal in clumsy hands and it was just Clarke's luck to receive his short back and sides from Chatham's very own demon barber – 'A crazy character who imagined himself at times to be an astronomer, I knew my mad matey very well with his head away up in the air and his tense drawn face with the fixed, lack-lustre eyes that told its own tale of insanity'. Until hair croppers were introduced a few years later, Clarke sat on a stool in 'terrible torture' as this trainee Sweeney Todd snipped away furiously, leaving a trail of cut ears and flowing blood:

> It was a sight when sitting in the body of the church on Sunday morning
> to look along the lines of cropped heads and see the havoc that had
> been wrought upon most of the unfortunate lags' skulls – regular ridges
> of cuts in many cases where the skin had been clipped away.[22]

Exercise facilities for long-term prisoners were similarly poor. They were allowed a daily one-hour stroll around a small yard that was surrounded on three sides by high buildings that blocked out sunlight. Even the smaller of the ordinary convicts' two yards was four times as big. Clarke complained that he was harassed by vindictive warders who made him walk fast in summer heat but slowly during the cold of winter.

Clarke's day began early. Awakened at 6.30 a.m. by a ringing bell, he washed himself, tidied the cell and slid his broom out under the door to a warder who then passed him breakfast. An hour later he was in chapel for a short service during which, as Deputy Governor Griffiths recalled, sparrows frequently twittered a lovely accompaniment 'to the gruesome chorus of so many hundreds of unfortunates expiating their offences against the law'.[23] Even more incongruously, the lusty singing of hymns such as 'Oh, Be Joyful' and 'Now, Let Us Lift Our Cheerful Voices' muffled the ribald lyrics belted out by old lags. Afterwards in the prison yard, Clarke joined one of many labour gangs being searched for any tools, disguises or food that prisoners could use in an escape. Some gangs then marched to workshops in the artisans' yard, while warders, armed guards and a deputy governor on horseback escorted a long column out through the main gate. According to Griffiths, 'each officer was strictly responsible for his quota and was required to bring them back dead or alive'.[24] Parties wound their way down to the banks of the Medway or crossed a small bridge and fanned out over nearby St Mary's Island. Often battling severe weather and icy winds, they filled in dams and built stone retaining walls or else dropped down into the great basins to excavate mud that was then pulled along railway lines to landfills. In the fields prisoners wheeled clay to kilns that made bricks for the construction projects around Chatham: 'It was a busy scene on every side, a scene of incessant often arduous and painfully harassing toil'.[25] Prisoners could only watch achingly as ships disappeared over the horizon. Almost certainly, security considerations prevented Clarke and the other Special Men ever working outside and certainly the jobs listed in his Chatham labour record were done in the artisans' yard. Until February 1886 he was a cleaner, then an iron moulder until March 1889, followed by a month as a darner in the tailor's workshop and finally a stereotyper.[26]

When a recall bell rang at noon, all activity ceased immediately, and tools were collected, counted and locked up. Outside parties then marched back to the prison 'with a listless air of great fatigue'. Counted and meticulously searched, prisoners then consumed a midday meal before resuming work. It was, Griffiths said, 'a harsh and unlovely regime' of 'rigorous and relent-less' treatment,[27] one that verged on cruelty as competing 'taskmasters' and

'slave drivers' demanded that their work party achieve the highest quota.
Labouring outside and inside the prison was exhausting and dangerous.
On the Medway, prisoners drowned, broke their limbs and lost body parts.
Clarke spent three years as an iron moulder producing 3 tons a week of
heavy castings from molten metal, working in fierce heat that saturated his
clothing and thick leather boots. Other Irish prisoners broke stone with
mallets, pulling muscles, jarring bones and blistering their hands. Even in
high summer, labour never ceased later than 5 p.m. and though some men
would visit the bathhouse, most went to their cells. There, Clarke often lay
motionless on the floor until suppertime, after which he was locked inside
for another twelve hours.

Spending years in both Millbank and Dartmoor Prisons convinced one
prominent Fenian, Michael Davitt, that:

> The first two years of penal servitude are the hardest to bear and
> test mental endurance more than the whole of the remainder of an
> ordinary sentence. Liberty has only just been parted with. The picture
> of the outside world is still imprinted upon the memory and home and
> friends haunt the memory.[28]

Clarke initially drew comfort from his memories of good times but constantly
recycling them brought him diminishing enjoyment until eventually 'they
have been trod over so much that they are too stale to arouse any further
interest'.[29] Another prisoner despaired that 'not a ray of hope could endure,
not even the consolation of their memories of the past, for those memories
also waned, growing more dim by the end of each succeeding day'.[30] Clarke's
adjustment was made even more difficult by his intense feelings of isolation
because, while Gallagher, Whitehead and Curtin were fellow conspirators,
they were not close friends. He never established deep trusting relation-
ships easily and one associate thought Clarke 'very selective in his choice of
friends'.[31] From the start Clarke believed he was really fighting a lone battle.

Deprived of liberty, Tom's sense of loss was all-consuming. Short of escape
or death, he would almost certainly serve decades before even being considered for release. He also missed his family, although it had been on Clarke's
insistence that they were not told about his arrest, conviction and imprisonment. Now there would be no revolutionary conspiracy, social intercourse,
fresh air and the freedom to wander in town and countryside. And he was no
longer master of his own destiny now that the enemy made every decision
that affected his life:

There I was in the first flush of manhood cut off from friends and from all the joys and pleasures of life and doomed to life by torture in an earthly hell … The prison gates closed out from us a great many things that we had been familiar with … During these years we heard practically nothing from the outside world.[32]

Once a voracious reader, Clarke no longer saw even a newspaper, heard about wars, the fall of governments or momentous events such as Gladstone's First Home Rule Bill of 1886 and the downfall of Parnell in 1891. At Chatham 'only three elements had any meaning for the convict: work, diet and sleep'.[33] Although intellectually curious, Clarke now existed in an intellectual wasteland with no access to stimulating literature when he had already realised that someone whose mind was 'well stocked with healthy ideas will take longer to break down'.[34] The prison library was really only a storeroom from which a chaplain distributed loans – probably charitable donations – that Clarke called trashy books of fiction, 'stories of servant girls in love, stories of adventure for the boys, stories for babies of the "Ba, Ba, Black Sheep, Have You Any Wool?" kind, and so on, were the class of book they generally threw into our cells'. But most spectacularly inappropriate was one stamped 'Protestants only', 'an extraordinary book, one of the fiercest anti-Popery books I have ever read, although I had read through some hot stuff of that kind in Ulster, where I was raised'.[35] And as a dedicated smoker, Tom never adjusted to the absence of tobacco in prison. Decades later he remarked that 'I had the same craving on my last day in prison at the end of 15 years'.[36]

Metaphorically, Clarke had only just begun traversing a barren landscape, one that stretched to the horizon and far, far beyond. The passage of time and chronic boredom weighed heavily on him, with Chatham's repetitive, sterile labour offering little relief. During these 'dark and hopeless years',[37] he dreaded deteriorating into a mental vegetable, contentedly engaging in mindless activity, mixing up his days and confusing names, people and places. The greatest danger of this happening lay in Chatham's silent system, against which even the most educated, optimistic, physically fit and strong-willed prisoner fought a losing battle. Clarke believed it would ultimately drive him – and everyone else – insane. He had witnessed it devastating prisoners' personalities, eroding their memories and eventually leaving them barely able to enunciate words properly. Longing for human contact, many prisoners found that 'the temptation to speak in these dead-houses, to move one's tongue was more than irresistible',[38] yet even whispering 'good morning' to a fellow convict incurred punishment. Gradually the silent system ground a prisoner down, shattering his nervous system and mentally exhausting him until he could think of nothing but his own wretched misfortune: 'The end – insanity – for that poor mortal is then near at hand'.[39] According to Clarke, '"Who next" was the terrible question that haunted us day and night – the ever recurring thought that it might be myself added to the agony'.[40] One day he thought his own number was finally up when a loud buzzing suddenly started in Clarke's ears and persisted despite his repeated slapping: 'All night long it kept buzzing away and with a queer sickening feeling the thought came to me that I was nearing the insanity mark'.[41] Yet puzzlingly, the noise ceased whenever he left his cell. Clarke's anxiety mounted for a few days until he accidentally noticed a new telegraph wire running between the prison and an adjoining military barracks, fastened over his cell and insulated at the ventilator opening where it emitted the buzzing sound. Overjoyed that his sanity remained intact, Clarke wanted to shout to the heavens – but that was against the rules.

Clarke's prison memoirs repeatedly accused the British government, its prison service and Governor Harris of conspiring 'to drive us all mad or to kill us. Some of us realised the situation early in our imprisonment and saw that the mercilessly savage treatment was meant to smash us'.[42] But Professor Seán McConville's definitive study of Irish political prisoners rejects the contention that it was official policy to exact systematic revenge on the Special Men. Certainly tough measures were 'authorised at the highest level of the convict service but it is doubtful if the Home Office had exact knowledge of the regime and its draining effects – either at the official or the political level. The charge against them is indifference rather than vindictiveness'.[43] The Victorian prison system emphasised punishment rather than rehabilitation and 'penal servitude demanded and enforced unremitting, unreserved and manifest submission and this principle was especially expressed during Edmund du Cane's headship of the convict system'.[44] The silent regime, for instance, was not unique to Chatham but mandatory for every convict in every English prison. Deputy Governor Griffiths witnessed many ordinary prisoners go insane. Megalomania was especially prevalent; some men claimed to be great inventors, one insisted he was King of the Moon and another boasted about his sister being Queen of New York. Religious mania was also rampant. Prisoners rattled off prayers, texts and hymns or launched themselves into impassioned theological debates; some acted despondently while others walked around with heads held high, exalted and superior. Warders prevented many suicides through strict surveillance and the use of canvas jackets, belts and padded cells. Griffiths saw desperate prisoners mutilate themselves for a long spell of recuperation in hospital. Although regular nightly cell checks imposed an enormous strain on the Irish prisoners, Harris and his warders had every reason never to drop their guard around the Special Men. Furthermore, Clarke and his comrades were never subjected to corporal punishment – unlike ordinary prisoners who received as many as thirty-six lashes for punching and kicking warders, throwing bricks and stones and threatening them with shovels and hammers. Maintaining order at Chatham was a dangerous occupation. Yet Clarke became fixated on the idea that the prison was a battleground in a Manichean struggle between good and evil, one with Harris as its satanic face. Despite Griffiths, a perceptive and enlightened prison reformer, regarding his boss as 'a firm but equable and strictly impartial governor',[45] Clarke lacerated Harris as 'a regular devil', a 'Pontius Pilate'[46] who habitually washed his hands of all responsibility. No doubt regrettably, Clarke could only engage in character assassination by reciting mocking rhymes about 'That thundering thief, Our Chatham chief'. Harris was the first, but not last, of Clarke's great hate figures, a focus for all his antagonism. If he did not enter Chatham with a streak of paranoia, then he certainly left that way.

In August 1884 Clarke was suddenly and unexpectedly rescued from abject misery when to his 'grief and surprise' he recognised John Daly at morning chapel. Sitting beside him was James F. Egan, 'then a stranger to me'.[47] Clarke and Daly had last met in America just as Tom set out on his dynamiting mission. Intending to assist Clan bombers in England, Daly followed later in the summer of 1883. Until April 1884 Daly lived in Birmingham, lodging with Egan, an old Limerick friend until he was entrapped by a Special Branch agent and arrested when collecting four packets of explosives from Birkenhead railway station. He got penal servitude for life. Egan himself was framed, receiving twenty years after police discovered dynamite and supposedly incriminating documents in his garden. Incarcerated at Chatham, Daly's forceful personality and Egan's irrepressible good humour lifted Clarke and the three men established a mutual support system:

We soon came to know each other better, and before long were fast friends. The ordeal they went through under my eyes for years is a test of manhood as severe and searching as mortal man could be subject to, and I know with what spirit they met it and went through it. We three were so closely identified with each other in prison that to speak of my prison life without mentioning them would be impossible.[48]

Clarke, Daly and Egan set about devising ways of evading official surveillance and communicating with each other. Egan invented a code of signals,
while Daly ran a 'post office', passing on thousands of notes written with
tiny pieces of black lead pencil that he had supplied to the Special Men:
'Never a week passed but I received a voluminous note from John Daly –
and some weeks two or three notes – and he received the same from me.
This went on for about eleven years. As with Daly, so with Egan, for the
eight years he was with us'.[49] Clarke gleefully anticipated every missive,
perusing them with nervous delight and chuckling over Egan's comic
sketches. After warders discovered some of Clarke's notes during searches
of other prisoners, they hunted for Daly's clandestine system, ransacking
the three men's cells and collecting bucketfuls of paper remnants they had
dropped through the wall ventilators into horizontal air shafts. But Clarke,
Daly and Egan only expressed mock bewilderment when confronted with
the haul. They had covered their tracks with 'the utmost care and crafti-
ness'[50] by ensuring that 'not a single note was ever put into the ventilators
without first being put into the mouth and reduced to pulp by rolling it
between the hands'.[51] Clarke revelled in his ability to repeatedly outfox
Harris and his officers in a never-ending battle of wits, little victories that
kept him going.

Clarke's 'inventive genius'[52] enabled him to create a cell telegraph.
Remembering that Morse code relied on two different sounds represented
on paper by a dot and a dash, he devised an alphabet based on the dull knock
of knuckles on a wall and the sharp crack of a button. But Tom still needed to
pass it on to the other Special Men. Without at that time having any lead to
write a note, he used a stolen needle to laboriously perforate a sheet of brown
paper and form letters alongside corresponding dots and dashes:

> It was slow work, especially as the vigilant eye of the officer peeping
> every now and then into my cell obliged me to conceal the paper
> when I heard him approaching. It took me nearly two days to write
> that note, but when it was finished it was plain and readable. On the
> Saturday following I concealed it in my stocking when going into the
> net compartment to Gallagher and threw the note over the partition
> to him. He got it safely and within a week we were able to converse
> freely through the wall dividing our cells. On the following Saturday
> I had another note ready for another of my comrades and so on week
> by week till we were able to send telegrams along through six or
> seven cells.[53]

Clarke also spent many long winter nights telegraphing fellow prisoners. Putting their ears to a wall made airtight connections through which they could hear him tapping messages from four or five cells away. In turn, Clarke himself loved receiving Daly's stories about a spider that he had tamed and trained and for which Clarke supplied flies and moths. Daly drew great solace from his cell companion; perhaps like Robert the Bruce he considered it a harbinger of ultimate victory.

Deputy Governor Griffiths believed that prisoners were happiest when they 'allowed themselves to be carried along without protest or hesitation, adapting themselves to the monotonous movement'.[54] But Clarke regarded docile collaboration as tantamount to death, and even though he had foresworn open defiance in prison, his natural belligerence kept landing him in trouble. After he complained regularly to Harris about his letters being delayed and reported warders for assaulting inmates, prison officers marked Clarke down as an agitator. They weren't wrong. For his part, Tom alleged that they falsely accused him of non-existent offences and tried to entrap him into breaking prison rules. During one punishment session, the very warder who had denounced him allowed Clarke out of his cell to go to the toilet. On the corridor floor he noticed some pieces of broken bread and despite the officer seemingly looking the other way, Clarke sensed that the officer was setting him up for a charge of stealing food: 'I was absolutely starving and could have eaten it ravenously but like a flash a revulsion of feeling came and in my impotent rage and misery I uttered curses fierce and bitter against English villainy as ever Irishmen uttered'.[55] But Clarke also pushed, bent and circumvented the rules whenever he could. Starting early in December 1883 with 2 days of bread and water punishment for signalling to an inmate in an adjoining cell, he was punished fourteen times between 1883 and 1890, twice as many times as Gallagher and seven times more than Curtin.[56] The vast majority of his offences consisted of communicating with fellow prisoners either by signalling or talking, though once he was accused of fighting in the iron foundry. However, being caught never stopped Clarke: 'We were able to communicate with each other in spite of all their watchfulness and strictness. "Where there's a will there's a way". Pen or pencil had we none, what of that; a fellow has no business in prison, unless among other qualifications he is resourceful and observant'.[57] Tom exhibited these qualities after he noticed his cell door turned on pivots embedded in lead. When the warder turned his back, Clarke used scissors from the tailoring shop to dig out some lead and wrote on brown paper guidance for the Special Men on how to correspond with each other. Next day Clarke propelled the note by hand like a marble and started a chain of Special Men shooting it from cell to cell. During the warders' 'ever-lasting'[58] searches of the prisoners, they all hid notes in their mouths, while Clarke secreted the precious lead in his broom handle.

Influenced by Daly writing notes in the editorial style of a newspaper, Clarke brazenly launched his own single-page news-sheet. Outwitting five alert warders in the printers' shop, he surreptitiously set up the type for a front page, laid tissue paper on the bed of his stereotyper's oven, inked it over and then placed it on a letter typing press. After Clarke pulled down the top plate, the paper printed beautifully every time. He called his publication 'The Irish Felon, Published at Her Majesty's Convict Prison Chatham by Henry Hammond Wilson'. It mixed a leading article that 'was as treasonable as a leading article could be'[59] with spoof news articles, an essay denouncing the English prison system and a poem mocking Harris. Clarke basked in satisfaction at the literary vengeance that he had wreaked upon the governor, claiming Harris never 'suspected that while he and his assistants were striving with might and main to destroy us, body and mind, we were indulging in such amusements and having such jibes at him'.[60] Moreover Daly's 'coughing and choking in his cell that evening told me he was enjoying the perusal of it'.[61]

Tom brought courage and resilience to his battle for survival. He soaked up every punishment thrown at him, shrugging off three days' punishment on bread and water or an occasional punch from a warder. But even Clarke's powers of endurance were tested by forty days' solitary confinement in the Arctic cell – Chatham's coldest – during an exceptionally cold winter. Deprived of underwear and surviving on a starvation diet, he battled below-zero temperatures and a strong north-easterly wind, conditions so extreme that only his unbreakable willpower got him through. Clarke's physical and mental strength had vindicated his own motto, 'clench your teeth and never say die':

> Talk of hunger and cold! Many a day I was forced to chew the rags I got
> to clean my tinware in an effort to allay the hunger pangs. By the time
> I had finished that terrible forty days I was so weak that I was unable
> to straighten myself or to stand upright and I could not walk without
> staggering like a drunken man.[62]

Clarke also acquired a useful weapon to combat Chatham's all-pervasive surveillance that included a warder in fustian shoes creeping stealthily along corridors and peering through spy holes into the cells: 'No sound betrayed him to the prisoner inside. This made it very difficult to write or read notes with safety'.[63] Despite Clarke's vigilance, his eyes and ears were useless for advanced warning, so he developed a remarkable sense of smell, detecting, like a sniffer dog, 'the silent sleuth outside my door. Many a time it gave me timely warning. Never did it fail me'.[64]

Realising that in Chatham it was senseless to 'bang your head against the wall', Tom accepted that he would have to wear a humiliating convict uniform, undertake forced labour, apparently conform to prison rules and put up with official punishments. Nor would he attack warders or go on hunger strike to protest against his treatment. Forty years later a friend recalled Clarke laughing

> at the sensational reporting of hunger striking by Mrs Pankhurst and the English Suffragettes. There was no reason for him and his fellow prisoners to resort to hunger strikes, for hunger and cold were their daily portion during their imprisonment. Clarke did not want to die that way. He wanted to live and strike a blow at his foe and he did. He said England feared one live Irishman with an effective weapon more than she feared an army of hungry Suffragettes.[65]

But Tom would never, of course, actively co-operate with the British authorities or give up information about himself, his comrades and the Clan's leaders, organisation and plans: 'I was convicted under an assumed name and up to the time of my conviction and for long after, the authorities knew absolutely nothing about me'.[66] Even the age he volunteered was false. Special Branch's dossier on him consisted of the results of less than a fortnight's surveillance between Clarke's arrival in Birmingham and his arrest in London, and Clarke was determined not to give up any more details. He even left his family in Ireland, the IRB and close friends in New York in the dark about his arrest, conviction and imprisonment. When Millbank's governor requested the name of someone to whom his money could be sent for safekeeping, Clarke did not fall into the trap.

Throughout his imprisonment, Clarke was sustained by an unquestioning sense of moral superiority over the ordinary prisoners. They might once have been bankers, lawyers, doctors, policemen, artisans and labourers, but in his eyes they were now 'wastrels and scoundrels'.[67] Tom despised them as 'dregs raked in from the gutters', imprisoned for wicked and ignoble crimes:

Never for one moment did I forget I was an Irish Political Prisoner and in spite of it all, never felt any degradation. On the contrary, I wore that convict garb with a certain amount of pride and took satisfaction in the thought that all her laws and with all her power the great England could not force me — one of the mere units of the rank and file — to regard myself as one of the criminal class any more than I could ever be forced to regard myself as English.[68]

Clarke's proud self-image was strengthened by a conviction that his own trail of tears had already been travelled by previous generations of Irish revolutionaries, some of them right to the gallows. Faltering now or giving in would only betray their suffering and sacrifices: 'Many of our revered dead have trod that path and it was these memories that inspired me with sufficient courage to walk part of the way along that path with an upright head'.[69] Nor could Clarke abandon his fellow dynamitards, a band of brothers, 'plucky and self-reliant comrades fighting the same fight in the same spirit of "no surrender". Throughout the whole time we stood loyally by each other'.[70] Bound together by nationality, politics, religion, revolutionary commitment, identical sentences and now place of abode, their group loyalty proved unshakeable. United in defiance of their captors and resolved never to surrender, none broke ranks, turned informer or sought a pardon.

To avoid slipping into irreversible depression, Clarke worked incessantly to occupy his mind:

It was ever present before me that if I were to 'let go' of myself madness was inevitable … It required, at times, all the effort I was capable of making to enable me to choke off despondency and wrench the mind away from dwelling upon the miseries of such a life.[71]

For many hours he would count every bolt in his cell door, perforation in the ventilators, brick in the walls and then the entire prison, before rearranging them into pyramids, squares and end-to-end, calculating the dimensions. Next he counted the buttons on the prison population's clothes as well as arrows stamped on prisoners' uniforms. Clarke also kept hair samples from his weekly cuttings and used a micrometer to establish that during thirteen years, over 6ft of hair had been snipped off his head. Helped by a manual, he also learned shorthand and eventually worked his way through the entire Bible twice, constantly getting faster. Curious to discover his speed but lacking a watch, he ingeniously estimated it by measuring strikes from the prison church's clock against his pulse rate of seventy beats a minute. Clarke's motto throughout was 'Keep your thoughts off yourself all you can', but other survival rules included 'Where's the use of pulling a long face over it', 'Guard your self-respect — If you lost that you'd lose the backbone of your manhood' and 'Keep your eyes wide open and don't bang your head against the wall'.[72]

Inevitably in some ways prison changed Clarke as a man, but his politics remained unalterable, a fanatical, all-consuming republicanism that never dimmed. Nevertheless, any hopes of one day returning to the political battle-field depended on Tom forging a new persona to sustain him through the long years that lay ahead. Naturally impulsive and quick-tempered, he had quickly grasped the pointlessness of raging against his captors and indulging in futile gestures of resistance. Instead he re-invented himself, acquiring self-discipline and steely determination. Eventually Clarke acted, talked and even looked very differently — laconic, inscrutable and grave with wary eyes that gave nothing away. Carefully weighing up both his own words and the people to whom he spoke, Clarke cultivated an impassive exterior and by turning a face of stone to the world, he robbed his captors of the satisfaction of seeing him suffer or indeed any other emotion: 'Don't grin. Don't let them see you grin'.[73] Undefeated, he seemed living proof of the dictum that anything that does not kill you makes you stronger. Although still Daly's junior partner, he had won the older man's respect and at Chatham an air of authority, even charisma, began enveloping Tom Clarke. But it was a costly transformation. Clarke's icy controlled exterior masked emotions he had driven deep inside his soul, where they remained permanently bottled up, a damage his wife saw for herself; how 'years of prison torture with the silent system enforced rigorously made him a very silent man. Those terrible years developed the habit of repressing every sign of emotion and made him suspicious of every stranger'.[74] And Clarke's intolerance and inability to compromise crystallised into something even more formidable, a world of black and white in which Clarke would never again trust anyone not standing unequivocally on his side.

Even after Daly and Egan's arrival, Clarke still felt himself in 'a fight against frightful odds'.[75] As Deputy Governor Griffiths acknowledged, there was at Chatham

a rigid, almost barbarous rule from which all solace and alleviation was scrupulously eliminated. There was no light in the lot of the Chatham convicts, no horizon to which they could look for coming relief, all around was flat, stale and unprofitable, a dull monotonous round of iron, unchangeable routine with little or no sympathy for them.[76]

Between 1883 and 1890, this regime gradually drove seven Special Men insane: Gallagher, Whitehead, Duff, McCabe, Devaney, Flanagan and Casey. It overwhelmed a few of them very suddenly, but sometimes Clarke could see it coming: 'Being thus closely in touch with Gallagher and Whitehead as time went on I noticed them change and get queer, and I knew that step by step their reason was giving way'.[77] He first realised Whitehead was losing it when he saw him kneeling on the floor of the carpenter's shop stuffing crushed glass into his mouth:

> I picked up some of the fragments that he had dropped, and asked him 'What do you mean by eating this glass; don't you know it will kill you?' He replied in a dull listless way to all my questions 'A pinch of it will do you no harm' and then left.[78]

Clarke implored the Catholic chaplain, Father Matthews, to intervene with the Governor on Whitehead's behalf but the priest refused, fearful that Harris might accuse him of 'hobnobbing' with prisoners. Soon afterwards it dawned on Whitehead himself that he was losing his battle with insanity:

> Can I ever forget the night that poor Whitehead realised he was going mad. There in the stillness, between two of the hourly inspections, I heard the poor fellow fight against insanity cursing England and English brutality from the bottom of his heart and beseeching God to strike him dead sooner than allow him to lose his reason. Such episodes are ineffable on the memory, they burn their impress into a man's soul.[79]

Clarke, Daly and Egan wrote letters publicising the seven men's misery, but prison authorities suppressed them. Clarke then appealed in vain to the Governor: 'Oh I fancy I hear the laugh of triumph brutal Harris used to give on these occasions'.[80] All Tom thought he could see was a pitiless desire by the British authorities to inflict retribution on the Special Men:

> Everyone inside the prison walls – officers and prisoners – priest, parson and doctor knew right along that they were insane. The English Home Office knew it, but their vengeance had to be sated whether the victims went mad under the torture or not. For seven or eight years knowing well that they were insane, the authorities continued to punish them in the most cruel manner for their irrational acts for which they were in no sense accountable.[81]

But Clarke was never very good at – indeed he rarely tried – empathising with his enemy or seeing that they might have reasonable motives for their behaviour. His tunnel vision reduced every issue and situation to one of right and wrong, blinding him to every explanation except an official conspiracy to destroy the Special Men. Perhaps as a born conspirator Clarke could not imagine the British authorities behaving any differently from himself. By 1890 Whitehead's sanity had disintegrated and he was blaming imaginary 'mischievous beings' for influencing important people on the outside to have his sentence prolonged. Other Special Men claimed that they had an ability to shut down their body organs or that prison doctors were injecting them with drugs in order to burn away half their stomachs.

A former soldier, Harris quickly discovered that in prison as in war the first casualty was truth. Chatham abounded with confidence tricksters, counterfeiters and scam artists whose criminal careers had thrived on exploiting other people's credulity. The governor did not trust any prisoner and least of all the Irish Special Men. He knew some inmates specialised in bogus displays of insanity that Chatham's physicians had difficulty distinguishing from genuine cases of madness and that Doctor Gallagher was ideally qualified to feign mania and coach others to mimic it. But by dismissing Clarke's claims, Harris created a vicious circle in which Gallagher, Whitehead and others erupted in violent tempers or refused to obey orders, so incurring punishments that only deepened their melancholy. Despite his failure, Clarke had shown considerable moral courage in challenging the prison authorities. He could do no other because, while Gallagher, Whitehead and the others were not friends like Daly and Egan, they were comrades he was honour-bound to defend. Loyalty and unity meant everything to Clarke, one facet of a steely character that would not bend. And in accepting responsibility for protecting Gallagher, Clarke had changed the balance of their relationship. He was no longer a subordinate but a potential leader.

Chatham's medical staff had less trouble detecting physical ailments such as diarrhoea, enteritis, dyspepsia, vomiting, colds, influenza and 'gaol fever'. The prison food also caused flatulence, indigestion and piles. When Clarke himself arrived at Chatham, the prison doctor had pronounced him healthy and he remained in generally good shape. Usually suffering only an occasional cold, his first stay in the infirmary was not until June 1888, when he received three weeks of treatment to a right foot burnt accidentally in the iron foundry. On 5 April 1889, Tom was back complaining of palpitations, but after three days the doctor diagnosed a heart murmur as pulmonary and not due to any organic disease. Discharged 'much relieved', Clarke returned soon afterwards for another nineteen days with the same problem. Finally, in early January 1890 he was in for five days with influenza. One month later during a medical examination, Clarke reported a slight pain over his left ribs but not the heart and though the heart murmur persisted, it never proved life threatening.[82]

When convicted, Clarke had severed contact with his family and friends, until on 2 October 1885 he was suddenly brought to a reception room where a 'relative' was waiting to see him. In fact, it was his old Dungannon friend, Billy Kelly, who in New York had recognised Clarke from newspaper drawings of the Old Bailey defendants. After travelling to Ireland, he waited nine months before receiving permission to visit Henry Hammond Wilson. At their meeting Kelly arranged to exchange letters with Clarke, though he also returned to Chatham in February 1887.[83] Then Tom received a visit from a genuine relative, his sister Maria. When she emigrated to America, Kelly persuaded Clan leaders to let her travel to England and meet Tom, posing as Maria J. Wilson. On 5 February 1889, brother and sister were reunited after eight years apart. Nine months later they met again.[84] Clarke's happiness at seeing Kelly and Maria can only have been equalled by his astonishment a fortnight later when he was ushered into a room to see his old nemesis, Chief Inspector Littlechild, the Scotland Yard detective who had arrested him almost six years earlier. Sitting at a table in front of the fire, Littlechild radiated a bogus amiability, greeting Tom as Mr Wilson ('that was the first time I had ever been addressed as "Mr" in prison') and apparently with no hard feelings on his part. Clarke was unconvinced: 'I knew Scotland Yard methods. And that he was there to do a stroke of business'.[85] He was right.

The Chief Inspector was a bit player in the political drama then gripping England and Ireland. Its origins lay in the election in 1886 of Lord Salisbury's hard-line Conservative government, strongly supported by *The Times* newspaper. In March 1887, it published facsimile letters purporting to prove that Parnell supported murder in Ireland. Salisbury responded by establishing a Special Commission which began investigating the accusation in September 1888, with Littlechild trawling for evidence of collusion between Parnell and the American Clan. Ingratiatingly he invited Clarke to dictate a preliminary statement and testify later before the Commission. Undeterred by Clarke's flat refusal, he persisted for another three-quarters of an hour, alternating flattery and intimidation, good cop, bad cop all rolled into one: 'He threatened, he appealed and when his bullying did not work he tried gentleness. He was the stern police officer one moment and the sympathising kind friend the next'.[86] Waxing lyrical, the Chief Inspector promised to transport Clarke from the valley of despair, exchanging ruffians, misery and degradation for sunny uplands where he could breathe God's fresh air, regain his family's love and enjoy everything that made life worthwhile – as well as a civil service job. Even when Clarke finally terminated the encounter, Littlechild persisted, warning that his superiors would be very unhappy and urging Clarke to drop him a line at Scotland Yard if he changed his mind. Decades later Tom recalled that he had replied, 'If I were in the position where I only had to say one word to gain my freedom, I wouldn't say it, even if I had to stay here for the rest of my life'.[87]

Littlechild's breezy insincerity was equally unsuccessful with Daly, but their meeting had significant consequences. During August and September 1889, Daly was treated unsuccessfully for sores on his feet and medicine containing a tincture of belladonna led to a rapid heart rate, rashes and mental confusion. But the symptoms disappeared within three days and a doctor passed him fit and free of organic disease. Daly's illness had resulted from the prison doctor accidentally including too much belladonna in his drugs, but he was convinced that the authorities had tried to assassinate him for refusing to help Littlechild.[88] Daly was also playing perhaps his last card to publicise the Special Men's plight, hoping that accusations of state-sponsored murder would resonate in Ireland. He was not disappointed. In January 1890 many Irish newspapers headlined a pamphlet, 'The Inhumane Treatment of John Daly and other Political Prisoners in English Jails'. Then on 11 February 1890, Harris oversaw a meeting between Daly and his sister Ellen and heard Daly insist that he had indeed been poisoned ('either by accident or intention') and 'was lying at death's door; in fact I never was so near the brink of the grave before'.[89] When Daly also instructed Ellen to campaign for a full investigation into the affair, she told him that the member of parliament (MP) for Limerick, Daly's home town, was already on his case.

As concern about the prisoners' treatment mounted in Ireland, Dublin Castle requested a Home Office investigation into their conditions. But the British government only conceded special sittings of the Chatham Visitors, confident that the very committee responsible for monitoring prison conditions would hardly condemn its own record. Yet, perhaps surprisingly, the inquiry did not simply go through the motions during seven sessions of testimony between 3 March and 2 April 1890.[90] Clarke and his comrades were treated civilly and even allowed to remain in the room during the questioning of prison officers. The Visitors also accepted written complaints and Clarke entered a lengthy submission, effectively a charge sheet against Harris and the prison administration. Composed in large flowing handwriting, his

fifteen-page memorandum was impressively restrained (unlike his corus-
cating prison memoirs), well organised and detailed, though its impact
was diminished by including every grievance large and small. Impressively,
Clarke accurately pinpointed important names, events and dates; even
when uncertain – as with the month in 1883 when he was transferred from
Millbank to Chatham – he usually guessed correctly. Politely and no doubt
through gritted teeth, he signed off 'I am Gentlemen, Yours Respectfully,
Henry H Wilson'.[91]

After reading Clarke's memorandum, the Visitors cross-examined him
on 13 March 1890. McConville believes that prisoners acting without
legal advice found 'standing for hours while evidence was taken wearing
convict uniform, obliged to follow the etiquette of deference and submission, conscious of the inevitable return to a solitary cell and to prison life
at the end of the proceedings was daunting, taxing and inhibiting'.[92] But
Tom had defended himself skilfully before a Lord Chief Justice of England
and was hardly likely to be intimidated by a committee chaired by a county
court judge. And almost certainly he welcomed the opportunity to testify
because after being so long literally voiceless, he could freely denounce his
jailers. Speaking for a longer time than he had in the previous seven years,
Clarke answered questions without straying from the point and presented
his facts and arguments cogently, although without adding much to his
written submission. Daly and Egan also spoke confidently and eloquently but
similarly failed to disprove the government's contention that conditions at
Chatham were tough but fair and necessary, given the gravity of the Special
Men's offences. Furthermore, Clarke conceded that warders had not physically harmed him and indeed had never even used bad language to him. But
he can hardly have been surprised when the Visitors' report sided with the
prison authorities, apart from upholding some minor complaints. Nor did
he get transferred out of Chatham and away from Governor Harris, despite
warning the committee that 'if we are kept here after this, I firmly believe
things will be worse than ever they were for us'.[93] But at least the Visitors'
published report, accompanied by witness testimony, reminded many people
that Clarke and his comrades were still alive, thus forcing their imprisonment
back onto the political agenda. Clarke's sense of hopeless abandonment was
finally over.

It had taken a long time. Passions from the bombing campaign had
simmered for years, making it virtually impossible, McConville argues,
to 'plead on behalf of men who left bombs in railway stations or blew up
gasworks in densely populated neighbourhoods'.[94] Their explosions had also

risked reprisals against the Irish population of industrial cities in England and Scotland, made international and particularly American opinion hostile to Irish revolutionaries, and alienated even the IRB. During the 1880s almost everyone agreed that the convicted men should spend a very long time in prison and after 1886 Salisbury's Conservative government resisted Irish nationalism on every front, opposing Home Rule and instituting harsh coercion in Ireland. Home Secretary Henry Matthews denied that any prisoners were being mistreated and rejected every appeal for clemency. After Gladstone and the Liberals returned to power in 1892, the new Home Secretary, Herbert Asquith proved as unyielding as his predecessor.

It needed years to overcome official resistance. The thaw began in early 1889 when John Daly's niece Ellen initiated an amnesty campaign in Limerick. A year later it broadened into a national Amnesty Association whose Irish and English branches eventually claimed 200,000 members. Nationalist politicians then ratcheted up the pressure, badgering successive Home Secretaries in Parliament with complaints and accusations about the prisoners' treatment. On 13 March 1890 Tim Healy demanded that Matthews allow him to visit Daly, though he carefully distinguished between a person's crimes and his situation in prison: 'If a man was in prison for attempting to blow up the House of Commons, that is no reason why he should be treated like a dog'. Healy followed this up on 9 May by asking Matthews to transfer the dynamitards out of Chatham, but the Home Secretary rejected his suggestion. Thomas Sexton, MP for West Belfast, even claimed, erroneously, that prison officials had been charged with attempting to poison Daly.[95] However, the passage of time that so depressed the Irish prisoners now actually began working in their favour. As memories of the dynamite campaign faded, some sympathy developed for men who had been behind bars for considerably longer than earlier Fenians. The IRB also used the amnesty campaign to whip up anti-British sentiment and recruit new members, while prominent Home Rulers also exploited it for electoral and personal advantage; with the dynamite campaign over, they no longer feared being accused of supporting terrorism. After Parnell fell in December 1891, the various party factions competed for popular support, with both Redmond and Healy campaigning for the prisoners.

To avoid accusations of appeasement, Salisbury's government resisted immediate concessions to the amnesty campaign, but it had a face-saving way out when the Admiralty proposed to demolish Chatham Prison and build a new naval base on the site. Sir Edmund du Cane, the Director of Prisons, used this opportunity to bury Clarke and fifteen other Special Men in the obscurity of one of England's remotest convict prisons. At half an hour's notice, on 19 January 1891 they were handcuffed, linked side by side in a chain gang and escorted by rail 170 miles southwest to Portland Prison.[96] Situated on the south Dorset coast on a peninsula that was four and a half miles long, the gaol was almost inaccessible, because only a shingle beach connected it to the mainland. Portland was England's Alcatraz, surrounded by some of the most dangerous waters in the world that made escape virtually impossible. Conveniently for du Cane, Portland was also located well away from the capital's interfering politicians and amnesty campaigners, while visits by prisoners' families and friends in Ireland and Scotland were arduous and expensive.

Portland Prison was located on a mass of stone that had been used to build the Houses of Parliament and St Paul's Cathedral. Many of the 900 inmates worked, extracting the stone from nearby quarries. It was then transported in great carts to the prison's artisans' yard where Clarke worked at one time or another as a box packer, japanner, carpenter, tinsmith, woodturner and pattern maker. Despite the prison's remoteness, it was an improvement on Chatham because for most of Tom's time in Portland its governor was Captain Dawson, 'a regular gentleman'[97] who presided over a less oppressive regime. Furthermore, for a couple of years in the early 1890s, Clarke was able to establish regular contact with the outside world. Like a shipwrecked sailor sending a message in a bottle, he had dropped a note into a box destined for Woolwich Arsenal in London, appealing for someone to 'throw in a piece of newspaper – any old newspaper – and earn the gratitude of a long term prison convict'.[98] Eventually the numbered case came back full of newspapers: 'From this day onwards newspapers of various kinds kept coming into me in fairly great numbers and what a heavenly break it was on the hideous monotony of convict prison life'.[99] Concealing the most interesting sections in underclothing, he brought them to his cell. But the reports on Gladstone's Second Home Rule Bill (1893) and the associated parliamentary and public debates covered pages and Clarke needed ingenuity and daring to be able to enjoy reading this hoard at leisure. He managed to get it to his cell by secreting the pages in his boot under a piece of brown paper cut in the shape of an insole. However, Tom still had to be on his guard against a sudden search. So he ripped open the mattress, placed the newspaper pages inside, threaded a needle stolen from the tinsmith's workshop and sewed the mattress up again: 'Your old convict has always some thread hidden away somewhere in his cell'.[100] Only on Saturday evening could Clarke safely retrieve the newspaper articles, read them and make notes. He then passed the material on to Daly along with the needle in case Daly couldn't finish reading the pages in time and needed to conceal them in his mattress. After a while, Clarke trusted his Woolwich contact sufficiently to have him pass on messages to Clarke's friends on the outside, a system which worked so well that he began formulating a plan of escape. But before Tom could communicate the details, he was shifted to another work party and lost contact with his nameless benefactor.

At Portland Clarke remained in generally good health and despite his heart murmur and periodic indigestion, he felt better than he had ever done at Chatham. Nevertheless, even in his tenth year of confinement Clarke was still at best only halfway through his sentence and in a reflective mood he wrote to an old Dungannon friend:

> Here we are in 1893 with the first half of January gone. Time goes rapidly enough for you I dare say; for me it creeps slowly enough dear knows. By April 3rd I shall have been in prison for 10 years, almost a third of my lifetime. Notwithstanding it all, I am – from the heart's core to the fingertips – Irish still, proudly Irish as in the old days.[101]

Occasionally he was buoyed up by visits from family and friends, fragmentary prison records indicating that his sisters, Maria and Hannah saw him on 18 February 1892. But travelling hundreds of miles for a twenty-minute reunion was time consuming and expensive. And the meetings were held in disagreeable circumstances. Maud Gonne reported that during her visit to Portland in March 1893 she and her companion were

> taken along a passage and shown into a cage which contained two chairs. It was exactly like the cage of wild animals at the zoo, with iron bars in front giving onto a passage about four foot wide. A similar cage with its iron bars faced us. The warder who had examined the permits took his stand in this and another warder leading a prisoner came into it from a door at the side. As the door opened with much clanging and jangling of keys I saw a third warder in control of this door. The warders carried revolvers. The prisoner was dressed in faded yellow with broad arrows. I felt the horror of the place and the sufferings of the prisoners deeply affecting me, almost paralysing my thoughts. The prisoner looked apathetic and had great difficulty in articulating. He was almost unintelligible, as if he had forgotten how to speak; the silent system had this effect on some. I was glad when the chief warder said: 'Time Up', and felt guilty for being glad. The prisoner didn't want me to go; he got out the words: 'Will you help us?' as the door clanged on us.[102]

But on the outside people were now taking an interest in Clarke's cause. In December 1891 a petition for his release circulated in Dungannon, a work of fiction that described how a young man alone in New York, an innocent abroad, had been preyed upon by a bad crowd and ensnared into their 'diabolical' conspiracy. Probably reflecting his family's popularity, a surprisingly wide swathe of local society signed up, including clergy of every denomination, merchants, businessmen, magistrates, poor law guardians and even Clarke senior's former commanding officer. But Home Secretary Matthews remained unmoved. And since the petition had been on behalf of 'Mr Thomas J Clarke (alias H.H. Wilson)', it finally alerted authorities to a second identity though they assumed that Clarke was his alias. Tom had entered prison as Henry H. Wilson and that was how he would leave it. In 1892 the Amnesty Association recruited a star performer when Maud Gonne joined its campaign. From an Anglo-Irish background, this revolutionary, feminist and actress was the most celebrated beauty in Ireland. Committing herself completely to setting the Special Men free ('I could never look at an Englishman without seeing prison-bars'), Gonne's grandstanding and inflammatory language certainly incensed the main English political parties, especially when she claimed that 'there is a perpetual state of war between Ireland and England. Irishmen must hit back how and when they can'. But she was superb at attracting publicity for the prisoners' cause in America and Europe.

In May 1891 the Home Rule Party threw its weight behind the amnesty campaign when John Redmond became legal adviser to Daly, Egan, John Curtin and Henry Dalton. He visited them regularly in Portland and interviewed other Special Men as well, meeting Clarke in June 1893 and September 1894. Although rarely generous to political opponents, Clarke commended Redmond 'whose kindness on these occasions I can never forget'.[103] Disingenuously, Tom assured Redmond that he and his Old Bailey co-defendants had suffered a serious miscarriage of justice based solely on Norman's uncorroborated perjury: 'It was false from beginning to end'.[104] Having peddled this fiction in court a decade earlier, Clarke stuck with it, especially as his claim fuelled the amnesty campaign. Redmond proved himself a tenacious advocate, raising his concerns in Parliament and battling Home Office attempts to confine his discussions at Portland to purely legal matters. The new Home Secretary, Herbert Asquith remained obdurate. Even when he freed Egan in early February 1893, Asquith declared him to be an IRB member guilty of treason and stated that he was only releasing Egan because eight and a half years of incarceration had punished him sufficiently. Egan returned to Birmingham where his English wife owned two shops, but a customer boycott because of his imprisonment forced the couple to sell up and move to Dublin. There, Egan joined Maud Gonne's amnesty campaign and worked especially hard to free Daly and Clarke.

Asquith's stubbornness over releasing the Special Men stemmed partly from reassuring reports about the Irish prisoners' health from the Prison Service. One, on 28 October 1893, was submitted by none other than Tom's old Chatham adversary, Governor Harris. After Chatham's closure he had filled temporary posts and while waiting to become Governor of Dartmoor Prison, he had been put in charge of Portland for most of 1893. In his prison memoir, Clarke could not bring himself to even mention their painful reunion, probably imagining Harris gloating at once again lording it over the Special Men. In his report Harris depicted them as blissfully content: 'With regards to the statement that they are all living lives of misery they are all usefully employed at some trade or vocation, their work is performed with apparent cheerfulness and in many instances is above the average in quality'. Indeed, to his delight they had settled in at Portland very nicely indeed, and were in the pink of health. But sadly some of them still could not resist getting up to their naughty tricks: 'Many of them have from time to time feigned mental affliction but in no instance has it been found to be genuine. The prisoner Gallagher is the only man who shows the effects of imprisonment and there can be no doubt that his physique has deteriorated'.[105]

A year after Egan's release, Clarke learned that his father had died, almost fifteen years after their last meeting. Now Tom would never have a chance to explain his actions face to face and perhaps also apologise for the pain he had caused the family. For years an emotional suit of armour had protected Clarke, but this blow shattered his defences and for the one and only time in prison he broke down in tears. A visitor that year thought Clarke was 'undaunted in spirit' and 'as bright and fearless as though the last eleven years of his life had been spent on an Irish mountain instead of an English jail'.[106] But in sombre mood, Clarke confessed to

feeling dull and lonely with this wretched existence. Dull day goes on succeeding dull day; nothing breaks the monotony except 'the letter from home' or a visit. Oh, you have no idea how welcome those breaks are. They are as welcome and as cheering as a bit of God's sunshine to me. Heaven's. Life would be a terrible burden for a man fixed as I am were he friendless and forgotten. I tell you this in a cold way – but I have to. I must not give expression to the fierce indignation I feel. Strong feeling has to be sternly repressed; at least I cannot give vent to it in my letters. But well there is little danger of my heart being Saxonised.[107]

In November 1895 Maud Gonne appealed to the Home Office, urging clemency for Tom. She extolled his contribution to society as an assistant schoolteacher in Dungannon and president of the town's Total Abstinence Society. Movingly, Gonne described the devastating effect of Clarke's imprisonment on the Clarke family, unhinging his mother and confining her temporarily to a lunatic asylum: 'Since then she has been able to return but her heart is broken'.[108] Mrs Clarke had recently lost her husband and could not even fall back on his pension; it had been terminated because of Tom's conviction. Gonne promised that if Clarke received an amnesty he would look after his widowed mother; he was a wiser person now than the supposed youth led astray a dozen years earlier. However, a new Conservative Home Secretary, Sir Matthew Ridley, denied her petition.

By 1896 more Special Men were falling seriously ill. James McCullagh's heart disease was getting worse and John Duff had been diagnosed insane. To avoid them dying in Portland, Ridley opened the prison gates a little bit, freeing McCullagh in April and transferring Duff to Broadmoor Asylum. Clarke exerted more pressure by urging Redmond to demand an independent investigation into Whitehead's medical condition. But Ridley was fed up with Redmond's constant lobbying and on 3 August banned him from visiting Portland on the grounds that he was unsettling the inmates: 'These visits have a prejudicial effect on the health of the prisoners by bringing about elation and subsequent depression of spirits which has had a very serious effect upon some of them'.[109] However, when a couple of medical experts examined Whitehead and Gallagher, the Home Secretary quickly released both men in August 1896. Returning to New York immediately, Gallagher descended the gangway as a living corpse, shocking his Clan reception committee:

> Instead of the broad shouldered fine young man whom they had known in the early eighties they saw an old broken down man with hollow cheeks, grey hair and stooped shoulders. Though only forty-five years he seemed to be twice that age. He was insane and did not even recognise his old acquaintances.[110]

Pronounced incurably mad, Gallagher spent another thirty years in various asylums, violent, uncontrollably bad-tempered and suffering from a religious mania that made him wander corridors impersonating a priest. Whitehead fared no better in America. Incoherent, listless and obsessed by a fear of being returned to prison, he was convinced that spies were poisoning his food.[111]

By now Daly had had enough, especially since even political celebrity could not prise him out of Portland. In the general election of 1895, Limerick's Amnesty Association had got him elected unopposed as the city's MP, but the British government disqualified him as a felon. Not that Daly would ever have taken his seat in the British parliament. But neither could he take Portland any more. Going secretly on hunger strike to prevent the prison authorities intervening early, Daly gradually reduced his daily food intake until he collapsed in the exercise yard. Daly had not told Clarke in advance – probably because he knew Tom was opposed to hunger striking – and Tom was shaken when Daly fell down. After helping carry Daly to the infirmary, Clarke tried unsuccessfully to persuade him to give up, but Daly was adamant: he was leaving Portland – either on his feet or in a coffin. Tom was in turmoil, fearful that the authorities would let Daly die. His concern mounted as Daly refused to eat prison food and even managed to resist the tempting delicacies that Harris so considerately arranged to be left at his bedside. The Governor then resorted to force-feeding Daly, but he simply regurgitated the food. Daly only relented when the British authorities capitulated in order to avoid him dying in prison and a doctor produced a signed release order. After several weeks recuperating, he walked to freedom on 20 August 1896 and returned to a hero's welcome in Limerick. There, Daly's epic tale of captivity and survival fascinated everyone, but especially his niece Kathleen, who recalled that:

During all this time Uncle John never forgot for one moment his fellow prisoner, Tom Clarke. He talked about him continually at home, and elsewhere, and spoke about him in every speech or lecture he delivered. He fretted all the time about him and worked in every possible way to bring about his release.[112]

A couple of days before Daly's release, Home Secretary Ridley freed Thomas Devaney, another Special Man convicted in December 1883 of bombing a Glasgow gasworks. Now only Clarke and five other Irish prisoners remained in Portland. Without Daly and Egan's companionship, Clarke lapsed once again into the loneliness and melancholy from which they had rescued him, especially as none of his comrades attempted any communication. Now effectively alone, Clarke faced his greatest test in prison, one requiring all his willpower if he was to stay sane and alive. Clarke, John Curtin, Patrick Flanagan, Henry Burton, Timothy Featherstone and Terence McDermott might have been freed swiftly but for Special Branch foiling a final dynamite plot in 1896. This forced the British government to let a decent interval pass before it could act without being accused of appeasement. Ironically it could afford to wait. In January 1897 the prison doctor declared that Clarke's 'mind is perfectly sound' and he had only gained a pound during six years at Portland, and although his heart murmur was periodically present, it was 'not, at present, of a serious nature'.[113] Clarke's medical report of May 1897 noted that despite his 'irritable heart', he was in 'fair general health' and that although 'his manner during my interview with me was irritable he showed no signs of insanity'.[114] Psychologically, however, Tom just could not wait for his imprisonment to end. Just before Christmas he wrote to an old friend, Paddy Jordan that although fifteen years was

> a dreadful long time sure enough but the slow going days and hours of it never seemed to drag along as slowly as now. How I am longing for it to end! Longing – longing. Counting every moment and hour of the time as it passes – all the while longing and wishing.[115]

By 1898 the British government wanted rid of the last Special Men. And since they now had all completed long prison stretches freeing them could be spun as a humane gesture of reconciliation to Ireland in the centenary year of the 1798 Rebellion. On 1 June Ridley began a phased release and by September only Clarke and Burton were left. This made Clarke now the longest-serving Irish prisoner and – with Burton ill in the infirmary – the sole occupant of the treason-felony penal cells. With strict silence still enforced at Portland and the monotonous routine of prison life unchanged, Tom was now 'up against the dreariest spell of the entire imprisonment. I felt like my imprisonment was like the sailor's rope that had no end'.[116] As his nervous tension mounted, he feared going mad within a few years. For Clarke freedom came just in time:

> Had anyone told me before the prison door closed upon me that it was possible for any human being to endure what the Irish prisoners had endured in Chatham Prison and come out of it alive and sane I would not have believed him, yet some have done so and it has been a source of perpetual surprise to me that I was able to get through it all.[117]

On Tuesday 27 September 1898, Home Secretary Ridley began stage-managing Clarke's speedy and deliberately low-key release by transferring him from Portland to Pentonville Prison in London and simultaneously informing his family in Ireland. By Thursday morning Clarke's younger brother Alfie and John Daly were waiting outside Pentonville when Clarke stepped through its gates a free man. Momentarily disorientated by a world of bewildering colour and vitality, Tom paused to compose himself: 'Everything was so strange and new'.[118] Leaving behind a completely regimented life, he now encountered the blast of fresh air, noise and constant traffic, at liberty to go where and when he wanted. Clarke also started playing catch-up on a new world of motor cars, cinemas, home cameras, colour photography, the phonograph, escalators, wireless telegraphy, x-ray machines and a plethora of other inventions. And the London that he had terrorised was bigger than ever with the House of Commons and Scotland Yard still standing, the underground system extended, the city streets thronged and English politicians ruling over an even greater Empire. Anyone less driven than Clarke might have questioned every assumption in which he had ever believed.

Almost as an act of cleansing, Clarke jettisoned everything associated with his confinement: 'I refused to take anything away from the English jail but myself'.[119] Shedding his prison uniform, he put on clothes brought to Pentonville by the wife of an old friend, Joseph Hart. Clarke also refused to accept £3 earned in prison work and another £3 from the Prisoners' Aid Society, an organisation that he had never joined. All he wanted was his letters because of their sentimental importance. Clarke left prison just as uncompromising as when he entered and with his dignity and self-respect still intact: 'No word or act of me ever caused me any regret' and 'I asked no favours. I got none and I am proud of it'.[120]

Although he was due to leave soon afterwards for Dublin to see his mother, Clarke joined Daly, Hart and some friends at Euston Station on Friday evening to meet an Irish mail train bringing his old prison comrade James Egan to London. A single reporter who joined them on the railway platform was clearly impressed by Clarke, now attired in a smart blue serge suit and a fashionable soft hat. Despite his medium height, an emaciated face and body and a slight stoop of the shoulders, Tom dominated the gathering. With a striking presence, a force of character and an intelligent countenance, he appeared undaunted, exuding a remarkable vibrancy, high-spirited and bright-eyed, 'overjoyed and excited by the first taste of free air'.[121] Having worked in sunlight outside the prison before being released, Clarke was tanned and his health had also been bolstered by three daily doses of malt and cod liver oil. And he jauntily assured the journalist that his mind was as sound as ever. As the reporter left 'the train now steamed in and as I left I saw Mr James Egan and his newly liberated friend standing silently on the platform with their hands locked in a firm affectionate grip'.[122]

Almost every Irish treason-felony prisoner ended up physically decrepit or insane and sometimes both and despite his immense resilience even Clarke emerged from incarceration a damaged person. One friend recalled that he was

> then 41 years but looked much older. He was about 5 feet 10 inches tall, well built but so thin and spare that he looked to us as if every scrap of flesh and all material things were burnt away, as if only the vital spiritual forces of his personality remained. And in truth this was so: he had gone through a fiery furnace.[123]

Socially inept and paralysingly shy, Clarke was also filled with hatred for the politicians and system that he blamed for robbing him of the best years of his life. In his mind Chatham and Portland symbolised the British Empire which Clarke regarded as a prison house of nations that also deprived Irishmen of their liberty. And like him, for over fifteen years they had their lives shaped by servants of the British state whose orders had to be obeyed. Determined to resume full-time revolutionary struggle, Clarke's future course of action was simplicity itself: he would start all over again, the only Special Man to do so. Extraordinarily, given his lack of wealth, high educational attainment and social standing, his poor job prospects and a prison record, Clarke, in his forties, stood on the brink of the most creative, happiest and – in his own terms – successful period of his life.

NOTES

1 Thomas J. Clarke, *Glimpses of an Irish Felon's Prison Life*, p. 12.
2 There is a good description of Chatham Prison in Arthur Griffiths, *Fifty Years of Public Service*, p. 162.
3 Portland Convict Prison, 1891 Index of Prisoners, www.blacksheepancestors.com.
4 Arthur Griffiths, *Fifty Years of Public Service*, p. 166.
5 Ibid., p. 178.
6 Ibid., p. 166.
7 John Daly quoted in Louis Je Roux, 'The Life and Letters of John Daly'. There are copies of this unpublished manuscript in the Special Collections Library of the University of Limerick, P2/Folder 73 and in the National Library of Ireland, MS 44,690.
8 John Daly quoted in Louis Le Roux, 'The Life and Letters of John Daly'.
9 Thomas J. Clarke, *Glimpses of an Irish Felon's Prison Life*, p. 42.
10 Ibid., p. 14.
11 Arthur Griffiths, *Fifty Years of Public Service*, p. 162.
12 Thomas J. Clarke, *Glimpses of an Irish Felon's Life*, p. 13.

13 Arthur Griffiths, *Fifty Years of Public Service*, p. 178.
14 Thomas J. Clarke, *Glimpses of an Irish Felon's Prison Life*, p. 57.
15 John Daly quoted in Louis Le Roux, 'The Life and Letters of John Daly'.
16 Thomas J. Clarke, *Glimpses of an Irish Felon's Prison Life*, p. 53.
17 Ibid., p. 14.
18 Arthur Griffiths, *Fifty Years of Public Service*, p. 176.
19 Clarke dropped from 133 pounds to 126 pounds during his incarceration. For his weight see Clarke's medical reports of 8 November 1895 and 16 December 1896. National Archives, London, HO 144/137/A46664D/19A.
20 Thomas J. Clarke, *Glimpses of an Irish Felon's Prison Life*, p. 48.
21 Arthur Griffiths, *Fifty Years of Public Service*, p. 168.
22 Thomas J. Clarke, *Glimpses of an Irish Felon's Prison Life*, pp. 52–3.
23 Arthur Griffiths, *Fifty Years of Public Service*, p. 167.
24 Ibid., p. 168.
25 Ibid., p. 170.
26 National Archives, London, HO 144/137/A46664/1.
27 Arthur Griffiths, *Fifty Years of Public Service*, p. 175.
28 Michael Davitt, *Leaves from a Prison Diary*, pp. 171–2.
29 Thomas J. Clarke, *Glimpses of an Irish Felon's Prison Life*, p. 57.
30 John Daly quoted in Louis Le Roux, 'The Life and Letters of John Daly'.
31 Clarke Papers, Notes for a life of Tom Clarke, NLI MS 49,355/13.
32 Thomas J. Clarke, *Glimpses of an Irish Felon's Prison Life*, p. 55.
33 John Daly quoted in Louis Le Roux, 'The Life and Letters of John Daly'.
34 Thomas J. Clarke, *Glimpses of an Irish Felon's Prison Life*, p. 57.
35 Ibid., p. 58.
36 Piaras Béaslaí, 'My Friend Tom Clarke', Piaras Béaslaí Papers, NLI MS 33,935 (3).
37 Thomas J. Clarke, *Glimpses of an Irish Felon's Prison Life*, p. 15.
38 John Daly quoted in Louis Le Roux, 'The Life and Letters of John Daly'.
39 Thomas J. Clarke, *Glimpses of an Irish Felon's Prison Life*, p. 57.
40 Ibid., p. 14.
41 Ibid., p. 47.
42 Ibid., p. 21.
43 Seán McConville, *Irish Political Prisoners, 1848–1922*, p. 364.
44 Ibid., p. 372.
45 Arthur Griffiths, *Fifty Years of Public Service*, p. 300.
46 Regular devil: *Daily Independent* 30 September 1898; Pontius Pilate: Thomas J. Clarke, *Glimpses of an Irish Felon's Prison Life*, p. 30.
47 Ibid., p. 13.
48 Ibid.
49 Ibid., p. 21.
50 Ibid., p. 23.
51 Ibid., pp. 23–4.
52 John Daly quoted in Louis Le Roux, 'The Life and Letters of John Daly'.
53 Thomas J. Clarke, *Glimpses of an Irish Felon's Prison Life*, p. 16.
54 Arthur Griffiths, *Fifty Years of Public Service*, p. 166.
55 Thomas J. Clarke, *Glimpses of an Irish Felon's Prison Life*, p. 27.
56 National Archives, London, HO 144/137/A4664C/1.
57 Thomas J. Clarke, *Glimpses of an Irish Felon's Prison Life*, p. 12.

58 Ibid.
59 Ibid., p. 30.
60 Ibid.
61 Ibid.
62 Ibid., p. 27.
63 Ibid., p. 48.
64 Ibid.
65 Lecture on Clarke by John Kenny, *Gaelic American*, 12 January 1924.
66 Thomas J. Clarke, *Glimpses of an Irish Felon's Prison Life*, p. 60.
67 Ibid., pp. 40–1.
68 Ibid., p. 41.
69 Ibid.
70 Ibid., p. 21.
71 Ibid., p. 45.
72 Ibid., p. 43.
73 Clarke's lecture to Dublin's '98 Club, NLI MS 49,354/6.
74 Kathleen Clarke, 'A Character Sketch of Tom Clarke', Clarke Papers, NLI MS 49,355/12.
75 Thomas J. Clarke, *Glimpses of an Irish Felon's Prison Life*, p. 21.
76 Arthur Griffiths, *Fifty Years of Public Service*, p. 175.
77 Thomas J. Clarke, *Glimpses of an Irish Felon's Prison Life*, p. 16.
78 Ibid., p. 17.
79 Ibid., p. 14.
80 Clarke's lecture to Dublin's '98 Club, NLI MS 49,354/6.
81 Thomas J. Clarke, *Glimpses of an Irish Felon's Prison Life*, p. 16.
82 National Archives, London, HO 144/137/A4664C/1.
83 William (Billy) Kelly, BMH WS 226.
84 National Archives, London, HO 144/137/A4664C/1.
85 Thomas J. Clarke, *Glimpses of an Irish Felon's Prison Life*, p. 24.
86 Ibid., p. 25.
87 Piaras Béaslaí, 'My Friend Tom Clarke', Béaslaí Papers, NLI MS 33,935 (3).
88 National Archives, London, HO 144/137/A46664/30.
89 Harris Report, 11 February 1890. National Archives, London, HO 144/137/A46664/36.
90 Report of the Visitors of Her Majesty's Convict Prisons as to the treatment of certain prisoners convicted of Treason Felony. Presented to both Houses of Parliament 1890. PP 90 xxx vii (C6016). There is a copy in Clarke's Papers, NLI MS 49,354/1.
91 National Archives, London, HO144/115/A46664/C.
92 Seán McConville, *Irish Political Prisoners, 1848–1922*, p. 374.
93 National Archives, London, HO144/115/A46664/C.
94 Seán McConville, *Irish Political Prisoners, 1848–1922*, p. 364.
95 HC Deb 18 February 1890 vol 341 cc 571–2.
96 Louis Le Roux, 'The Life and Letters of John Daly'.
97 *Daily Independent*, 30 September 1898.
98 Thomas J. Clarke, *Glimpses of an Irish Felon's Prison Life*, p. 31–2.
99 Ibid., p. 33.
100 Ibid., p. 29.

101 Clarke to Paddy Jordan, 17 January 1893. Clarke Papers, NLI MS 49,425.
102 Maud Gonne, *Servant of the Queen*, pp. 128–9.
103 Thomas J. Clarke, *Glimpses of an Irish Felon's Prison Life*, p. 16.
104 *Irish Weekly Independent* , 25 May 1894.
105 Harris Report, 28 October 1893. National Archives, London, HO 144/137/A46664/183a.
106 A journalist and IRB member, Fred Allen in the *Irish Weekly Independent*, 25 May 1894.
107 Ibid.
108 Maud Gonne's letter, 5 November 1895. National Archives, London, HO 144/136/A4664C/220.
109 Redmond Papers, NLI MS 15,222.
110 *Gaelic American*, 12 December 1925.
111 Seán McConville, *Irish Political Prisoners, 1848–1922*, p. 393.
112 Kathleen Clarke, *Revolutionary Woman*, pp. 22–3.
113 National Archives, London. Prison doctor report, HO 144/925/A46664D/24.
114 National Archives, London. Medical report, 27 May 1897, HO144/925/A46664C/24a.
115 Clarke to Paddy Jordan, 21 December 1897, NLI MS 49,425.
116 Thomas J. Clarke, *Glimpses of an Irish Felon's Prison Life*, p. 61.
117 Ibid., p. 11.
118 *Daily Independent*, 30 September 1898.
119 Ibid.
120 Ibid.
121 Ibid.
122 Ibid.
123 Sean Carroll in an essay on Tom Clarke in the Clarke Papers, NLI MS 40,355/13.

3

Exile:
America 1900–1907

On 1 October 1898, Clarke, Daly and Egan were back at Euston, this time to catch the Irish mail train. A farewell party of prominent London-Irish republicans saw them off, wrongly persuading Dublin Castle's Crime Special Branch that already Tom 'must be looked upon as an important man'.[1] Next day he reunited with his widowed mother and brother Alfie at their home in St Anthony's Road, Kilmainham, so beginning his quest for the material, emotional and social security that had as yet eluded him. This would not be easy in a country which he had not seen for almost twenty years and might well dismiss him as an irrelevant reminder of dreadful past times. First he reconnected with Egan and Daly, who since their earlier release had rebuilt their lives. Egan was now Dublin Corporation's sword-bearer and Daly was a successful businessman, bakery-owner and leader of the Limerick Labour Party which controlled that city's corporation. They now accompanied him on an Amnesty Association victory tour of Ireland, whose collections and donations subsidised Clarke's living expenses, while its busy programme demonstrated his speedy rejuvenation. At a torchlight procession on 24 October in his home town of Dungannon, he proclaimed his undiminished revolutionary fervour and stated that 'as far as the past is concerned I was then an Irish Nationalist of the old type, that I am still and shall ever remain'.[2] But Clarke's old political world had vanished and with dynamiting discredited as a policy, he had to adjust to a new order. Although never expressing any remorse for past actions, Clarke now dedicated himself to the traditional republican policy of an armed uprising and he used the tour to determine whether the IRB was seriously preparing for one. But all he discovered was a demoralised organisation with only around 5,000 subscribing members and a leadership which could not even boost recruitment during the centenary year of the 1798 Rebellion.

A Dublin detective who watched Clarke trying to stir up the IRB, regarded him as 'a really clever fellow, very bitter in disposition and holds views about promoting outrages that are intelligible, and during his brief residence in Dublin he has put the sincerity of certain persons to the test'.[3] And Tom's reported avowal that 'he did not believe in speeches but in work' led one county inspector to predict that 'somehow he anticipates trouble from this man'.[4] Reportedly, Clarke even criticised his old mentor at a banquet hosted by 'Daly and a number of Daly's most subservient followers'. The police, who still knew Tom as Wilson, noted that 'the affair did not appear to impress Wilson who observed that Daly was not backed by the right men. Notwithstanding the apparent friendship between Daly and Wilson the latter is said to distrust Daly'.[5] The police also recorded Clarke claiming that Daly's 'whole conduct since his release has been that of a selfish man'.[6] Quite possibly an incorruptible Tom did suspect that wealth, fame and position had softened this once fiery individual.

Already a better conspirator than the entire Supreme Council, Clarke was infuriated by the IRB's stagnation. After over fifteen years evading surveillance, hatching plots and conducting secret communications, he had developed his own blueprint for reviving the organisation. Tom believed an effective secret society had to concentrate power in a small, hermetically sealed elite that could react swiftly to events and neutralise spies and informers – a vision which antici-pated the cell system of modern revolutionaries. Inevitably it would marginalise the IRB's rank and file and extinguish a long tradition of Fenian democracy, but it reflected the distinctive personality of a security conscious person who now trusted only a small circle of intimates – in effect a junta. Clarke's authoritarian political mentality also manifested itself in a hatred of political enemies and his belief that ordinary IRB members should unquestioningly obey their leaders' orders. Moreover, Clarke's preference for actions rather than words reflected his distaste for the messy compromises and political stalemates of democracy. Clearly he was fearful that the Irish people might settle for material comforts and shrink from what he considered to be its destiny. And believing as he did that the ends justified the means, Clarke, like Lenin, was prepared to manipulate dupes and figureheads, 'useful idiots' who could be casually tossed into the political gutter once their usefulness had been exhausted.

Despite his busy schedule, Clarke had not forgotten Burton, the only Special Man still languishing in Portland and whom he was determined should not be left behind. On 3 January 1899, Tom wrote to the prison governor asking permission to see him, 'knowing from experience how much the friendly face and cheering words of a sympathising visitor mean at this season to an Irish prisoner behind the bars of an English prison and knowing how very few of such visits poor Burton has ever had'.[7] Although the request was denied, Burton was soon released at the end of February. Clarke then put him up for a few weeks in Kilmainham but quickly realised that yet another Irish prisoner had mentally disintegrated. By now Burton was

> an extremely peculiar and eccentric fellow. He sometimes forgets that I had ever been in prison and tells me some awful and monstrous things that have happened in prison. I am simply reduced to a state of speechless astonishment at the terrible sufferings he has endured and the heroic courage he displayed.[8]

Clarke was also joined by his favourite sister Maria, whom he and Daly had met at Queenstown on 18 November 1898 when she returned from America. With his other sister Hannah also living in Dublin, the Clarke family was as close to being reunited as it had been since Tom's departure for America eighteen years earlier.

After Daly became Mayor in February 1899 his first act was to grant Tom the Freedom of Limerick. On 2 March, Corporation members, local dignitaries and the entire Daly clan packed into the gilded council chamber for a ceremony that Clarke found even more nerve-wracking than handling nitroglycerine. What he later called his anxiety 'not to make a mug of myself'[9] increased during Daly's long rousing introduction and when he came to reply Clarke dissolved into a 'wooden-headed duffer'.[10] Ever afterwards he cringed at the memory of a tongue-tied debacle and his stumbling apology for not being able 'to make a coherent speech here tonight. I feel quite knocked out over it'.[11] Yet, briefly, Tom did manage to speak from the heart and encapsulated powerfully what he was and what he stood for, the roots of his rebelliousness, and what he believed lay at the heart of the conflict between Ireland and England:

> I am like John Daly, a man who will always stand by the cause and never flinch from doing my duty by it. It is true that I was fired in my early boyhood by what I knew of the past of my country and what I could see of the misgovernment that was going on through the country around me. It is true the history of our country in the past is the history of the struggles of the victim enveloped in the folds of the boa constrictor – the victim too strong to be crushed outright but not strong enough to free itself from the reptile's clutches unless the reptile is afraid to do so when danger threatens in the distance. Truly it has been said, 'the reptile's difficulty is Ireland's opportunity'.[12]

Clarke's vivid imagery reveals his conviction that the Irish people were engaged in a life-and-death struggle with a bestial enemy that was intent on crushing them. For him the IRB's mission was about something more fundamental than separatism and an Irish republic – it was the very survival of the Irish nation. His life was committed to saving it, not from physical extinction but from the Irish people being sapped of their unique identity and turned into a country of contented West Britons. For Clarke the stakes could not have been higher. Whether 'to be or not to be' was the question he was determined to answer.

Tom partly blamed his 'disastrous' performance on the effect of one of Daly's nieces closely scrutinising him. This was a young lady fascinated by her uncle's reminiscences about 'a noble, courageous, unselfish character, one who showed unwonted sweetness and restraint under the most terrible provocation'.[13] The third of nine children, 20-year-old Kathleen Daly was from a prominent republican family in Limerick. As a young man her own father Edward had been imprisoned for Fenian membership, an experience that Kathleen believed contributed to his premature death in 1890. Since her mother was 'prostrate with grief' and Edward's elder brother John had been imprisoned at Portland, 'this forced on us responsibilities not normally placed on children's shoulders'.[14] Kathleen grew up in a hurry, maturing into a capable and strong-minded young woman, and when another uncle crushed her dreams of a musical career by refusing to fund piano lessons, she established her own dress shop. At 18 years of age, Kathleen faced down family protests about being 'too young and not experienced enough and that people would not have confidence in one so young. I ignored all they had to say and went on with it'.[15] Stubbornly defending her independence against age and seniority, Kathleen even defied her Uncle John. After being freed from prison he assumed responsibility for his late brother's widow and children and

> tried to induce me to give up the dressmaking business and go into the bakery. I would be under the control of two elder sisters. Furthermore I was making a lot more money than the bakery could pay me and I felt I had worked too hard to establish my business to give it up. Uncle John was very angry with me.[16]

Kathleen's photographs show a striking rather than a conventionally pretty young woman though one – appropriately for a successful dressmaker – who was always immaculately turned out in fashionable clothes. Unusually serious for a teenager, she was steeped in politics and history, revelling in her grandmother's stories about Irish rebels:

She was a grand woman whose sorrow for her son's [i.e Uncle John's]
suffering was deep but whose pride in the fact that he could, if necessary,
die for Ireland's freedom was greater. She was a very devout Catholic and
took great pleasure in teaching us our prayers. At bedtime we knelt around
her and repeated the prayers after her. The first was always for Ireland's
freedom and when Uncle John was imprisoned the second was for his
release. She could see good in everyone and everything but England.[17]

Strongly republican, Kathleen admired anyone who made sacrifices for
Ireland and her own father's death at 41 must surely have resonated when
another former prisoner of the same age, Tom Clarke, visited Limerick. But
it was not – on her side at least – love at first sight: 'I was keenly disappointed.
His appearance gave no indication of the kingly, heroic qualities that Uncle
John had told us about; there was none of the conquering hero which I had
visioned. He was emaciated and stooped from the long imprisonment and
hardship'. However, 'as I came to know him his appearance receded into the
background and the man Uncle John had portrayed was revealed. By the
time he left Limerick to join his mother and sister in Kilmainham we had
become intimate enough to agree to correspond with each other'.[18] Tom
and Kathleen's tentative early letters combined formal greetings such as
'Dear Mr Clarke', 'Your sincere friend Kathleen' and 'Your very good friend
Thos. J Clarke' with pleasantries about family, local politics and the weather.

   In his letters Clarke also described his efforts to land a well-paid job as clerk
to the Rathdown Board of Guardians. These were party politicians responsible
for maintaining workhouses in south Co. Dublin and their votes would elect
the new clerk. Clarke and his republican supporters campaigned strongly for
their support. By 4 May he was 'out every day now "on the war path" after that
clerkship – flying hither and thither through the South Co. Dublin attending
to everything that must be attended to'.[19] Tom knew that it would be tough
winning support from a Board dominated by conservative Home Rulers:

> These so-called Nationalists on the Board of Guardians are for the most
> part unprincipled. I am afraid and need to be very carefully looked after
> or they'll play the 'duck' on me. Recognising this I am bound to work
> for all I am worth now that I am into the thing.[20]

Working into the early morning hours, Clarke tried pressurising the Guardians
('popular opinion is strong – very strong – for me'[21]) by importing Daly to
address his meetings and declare Limerick Corporation's endorsement of

him. By the end of May Tom was optimistic of victory ('If I win — and there seems every prospect') and had begun familiarising himself with his future responsibilities: 'I am reading up everything bearing upon the duties of a clerk of the union so that if I do get the job I will be able to know my way about without depending on others'.[22]

Clarke gave the campaign everything he had, but in the end it wasn't even close: 'I lost — in fact I was badly beaten', though he had 'the satisfaction of knowing I did my level best to win and my friends did far more than I could expect to help me'. Like many defeated candidates, Tom claimed he was robbed, only denied victory by machine politics, corruption, and the Board's connivance with Dublin City Hall's ruthless patronage system: 'We had public opinion right through the whole district running strong in my favour but the blackguards of Guardians quietly defied it. But they haven't heard the last of it'.[23] However, he was always an unlikely winner, mistakenly assuming that Amnesty Association parades, Limerick Corporation's distant endorsement and generalised sympathy for a former political prisoner would carry this prosperous, conservative area of south Co. Dublin. But although angry and disappointed, Clarke was hardly crushed. Recovering rapidly, he luxuriated in 'first class health and now that I am free from that cursed election, am able to indulge in long country walks and it is indeed glorious weather for strolling'.[24] He now intended to achieve financial security by emulating Daly's money-spinning American tour and wrote to John Devoy — once again Clan leader — proposing a series of talks about his prison experiences. Confidently preparing for the lecture circuit, Clarke delivered a vivid handwritten account to Dublin's '98 Club on 25 April, basking afterwards in his audience's enthusiastic response and telling Kathleen his only problem was 'what to omit for I had such a stock of material to work out of that had it been required I might, once I got started, go on forever'.[25]

While awaiting Devoy's presumably formal approval, Clarke concentrated on getting to know Kathleen better. Despite exchanging letters for three or four months, they were still just friends when in the first three weeks of July 1899, he joined the entire Daly family at Uncle John's lodge on the Atlantic coast of Co. Clare. Kathleen recalled that 'Tom and I hailed this as a golden opportunity to meet'.[26] During his stay, Clarke fell in love with the beautiful scenery and the lakes on which the Dalys went boating; he also fell in love with Kathleen. Evading watching eyes, they rose very early each day, went on long country walks and had many heart-to-heart conversations. Within a week they were secretly a couple. Yet Tom almost missed out.

Customarily a man took the initiative, but if Kathleen rebuffed him he risked accusations of preying on a young woman – under an unsuspecting Uncle John's roof. But Tom longed – needed – to know if he had a chance, perhaps his last one, of personal happiness. In the event – as he later confessed to Kathleen – he acted spontaneously:

> You wonder how it came that I took to you. Oh I'll tell you that. I couldn't help it. Do you recollect the morning in the dining room I astonished you by tossing your hair? That was done on impulse and my own astonishment was far greater than your own – even yet when I think of it I can't understand how it came about – I couldn't help it. But I think it was that morning I got a clutch on hope – the hug and kiss was lost sight of in my lady's concern about her hair being touched – and that gave me heart and lo I got yours and that's all I care about.

Clearly he also spoke of his love for her: 'I never made the confession to any woman that I made in your ear – I couldn't'.[27]

For Kathleen and Tom this was almost certainly their first serious relationship with the opposite sex, because in her memoirs Kathleen mentions no previous boyfriends, while Tom's sister Maria once joked about how he 'used to hate the girls'.[28] But the ties binding them together were unbreakable. For Kathleen this was no adolescent infatuation but rather the love of her life. Tom's age and physical appearance were rendered unimportant by his seemingly epic tale of a young man gone to war and taking many years to return home. Despite a wounded heart and fifteen years of suffering etched on Clarke's face, the man standing before her was unbroken and entirely devoid of self-pity, a fighter who was determined to return to battle. With the high moral purpose of someone whose principles were more important to him than life itself, Tom seemed to Kathleen 'in many ways an extraordinary character, being the most selfless and unselfish man I ever met'.[29] In her presence – as well as in his letters – Tom was modest, gentle and honest, entirely devoid of the professional conspirator's reticence and deviousness in which he habitually concealed his real feelings and intentions. With Kathleen he could be himself, revealing an honesty and vulnerability that he would never have shown to the outside world. In him she saw the strength of character of someone for whom retreat and surrender simply did not exist. While any life with him would be hard and probably dangerous, Kathleen sensed it would also be exciting and fulfilling, a prospect that drew her irresistibly on. If Clarke was a gambler, then so was she.

Tom was overjoyed that after so many silent years, an intelligent young woman was listening attentively as he unburdened himself, entrusting her with his innermost thoughts. Tom loved Kathleen's intensity, boldness and pursuit of anything she wanted. Realising she was mature beyond her years, he told Kathleen, 'You are a woman and not a chit of a schoolgirl'.[30] She believed 'it was always a matter of surprise to him what a girl as young as his wife was could see in him to attract her and to find her ready to marry him'.[31] Clarke had long wanted a happy and loving family just like the one of which he was now head and his father-figure role probably appealed to Kathleen. But in another way she was more mature than Tom, his social development having been arrested at the age of 26 when he had entered a monastic existence of shrivelled emotions, cut off from everyday social interaction. Kathleen was touched by Tom's shyness and his awkwardness in navigating the social obstacle course of sitting in an easy chair, using cutlery and dining with her family: 'For a time, he found difficulty in sitting at an ordinary table'.[32] Clarke's lack of sophistication appealed to her as did his disarming innocence: 'Big in every sense of the word though simple and as easily pleased as a child'.[33]

Unlike many older men and younger women, Tom and Kathleen had much in common, being two passionate, strong-willed individuals with republican politics in their blood. She made him laugh once after a local council pledged loyalty to Queen Victoria by joking that 'the pity is they didn't toast her the right way'.[34] They also shared a love of books and newspapers as well as long walks in the Irish countryside, revelling in its colours, flowers, fresh air, mountains and lakes. As their love bloomed, they communicated more affectionately. Clarke's letters went to 'My dear Kattie', while Kathleen wrote to 'Dear Tom' even though 'it does seem very strange to be addressing you this way'.[35] Physically separated by over a hundred miles, they longed for each other. He wrote, 'I only wish you could have heard all the nice things I whispered to myself about you'.[36] She replied that 'the morning you left I felt as if I'd like to run after the train and bring you back. As I couldn't do that I had a smart walk by myself to work off the bad humour'.[37] Even her love of boating offered Kathleen little distraction: 'I enjoy it very much but keep all the time wishing you were with me'.[38]

Anticipating hostility, they kept their relationship secret, especially from Kathleen's mother and Uncle John, a self-centred, manipulative bachelor patriarch waited on hand and foot by Daly females and reluctant to lose even an unbiddable Kathleen. Increasingly impatient, Tom awaited Devoy's approval of his American tour, though confidently assuring his transatlantic friends that he would see them soon. He wrote to Kathleen: 'I have been pegging away with

the pen all day writing over to America turning off letter after letter. I haven't
yet heard from Devoy and I am feeling a bit anxious at the delay'.[39] This was the
happiest time of his life. Then in the first week of August everything fell apart
when Devoy finally replied, turning down Tom's tour proposal without any
explanation. Clarke buckled, fearful of penury cheating him and Kathleen of
their life together, and he was also emotionally devastated by the sheer injustice
of it all. He could handle rejection by the Rathdown Guardians – strangers
who owed him nothing – but Tom had never imagined his own political family
spurning him with such apparent ingratitude. Feeling utterly abandoned he
broke the news to Kathleen:

> I took it for granted I would go on a lecture tour and that tour would
> be successful – on the strength of that I built my hopes of having a
> home and the means that would justify my going down to see you on
> my return and ask you to give me your hand and leave your own home.
> I never anticipated such a decision on the part of the Bosses on the
> other side. I was living in a fool's paradise all the while for I took it for
> granted those people would willingly – enthusiastically – co-operate,
> as they co-operated with John to make a lecture tour a success for
> me but alas hopes and plans and fairy castles are knocked smash in a
> moment by that New York letter.[40]

Without money to marry and establish a home, Clarke feared losing Kathleen.
But he was determined to act honourably and gave her an opportunity to back
out of their relationship, once again gambling everything on her decision:

> When I read that letter and realised what it meant Kattie my first
> thought was about you and thank God I am strong enough to act fair
> and square with you no matter what the cost to myself may be.
>   But now Kattie you must think over what I am going to say and
> decide for yourself and for me – no, no only for yourself – that lecturing
> tour being knocked on the head my future is uncertain. I shall have to
> go to America and get employment of some sort. Maybe I shall have
> to start at the bottom of the ladder to knock out a living for myself.
> God in Heaven only knows when I shall be able to get firmly upon my
> legs … You have given me no promises – from my point of view you
> are now as free as if you had never seen me at all – free if you so wish
> to stop writing to me. But Kattie My Darling I love you and I am out
> to be honest.[41]

Tom's anguished letter shook Kathleen just as much as Devoy's had crushed him, but when she tried writing comforting words 'half the things I wanted to say have got so muddled up in my head that I'll have to let them stand till the next time'.[42] However, she did manage to sweep aside Tom's fear of financial insecurity devaluing him in her eyes. Kathleen did not care about money or material possessions; she just wanted him:

> It's ridiculous for you to think that because a lecturing tour fell through my love for you must change. Things may look black at the moment but if they looked as black again I cannot take back what I gave. As it is I am very glad it happened the time it did for if you had not high hopes you would not I know speak to me you'd go off to America leaving me to the humiliating thought I had given my love unasked unsought. So you see there's a bright side to everything if we could only see it … For myself I'm no worse off than before. I have all I care about, your love and as long as I have that I'm all right.[43]

To Clarke's immense relief, the danger had passed. He had never wanted Kathleen to leave him and she did not. Indeed at this critical moment it was the younger woman who had steadied the older man. On 8 August Tom told Kathleen:

> God bless you for this brave loving letter. Tis but a few moments ago that I got it. But I'm happy now. Fate may do its worst my Kattie's heart is safe in my own keeping for good and all now and I can face the worst and feel confident that I'll succeed. After all now that I think the prospect for me is not by any means so dark − oh yes I'm happy and stronger. You have no idea I think what it cost me to write that last letter to you − it wrung my heart lest you might misunderstand me or that understanding me you would do what I apparently wished you to do. But Kattie I'll tell you now I dreaded your answer − dreaded you would be 'wise' but in my heart of hearts I had hopes you would do and say just what you have − God bless you for it my brave girl.[44]

Once the crisis passed, Tom and Kathleen grew ever closer despite the distance between them. From Dublin he wrote that 'you say you wish I was down there with you, that you could talk to me about everything. Oh yes I'll echo that wish, were I down there beside you or you here beside me now, time would not hang so heavily on my hands then'.[45] And though he could not see it at the time, Devoy had really done him a great favour. Clarke could never have attracted the huge pay-at-the-door audiences that flocked to see Daly who was box-office magic in Irish-America and whose lectures were really political show-business. Performing like an old Vaudeville trouper, Daly always kept the customers satisfied, making them laugh and cry through his commanding presence, with his resonant voice, humorous anecdotes and heart-rending stories. Socialising afterwards into the early hours, he oozed charm and Irish blarney while downing glasses of beer, and his legendary reputation as a womaniser did him no harm either. But Tom was a minor half-forgotten figure, introverted and prone now to stage fright. Lacking his mentor's oratorical ability, this once enthusiastic actor could never have carried the lead role, let alone a solo show. Clarke believed none of this mattered, that his compelling story alone was enough, just as it had been with Dublin's '98 Club. But reciting a one-hour prepared speech verbatim would never have worked in New York, Boston and Chicago. Lecturing in those cities Daly had taken flight; Tom would have crashed and burned. And this inhibited teetotaller entirely lacked the social dexterity for glad-handing and small-talking into the early morning hours. Devoy had probably saved him from the ultimate theatrical indignity of opening and closing on the same night and Clarke's reluctant acceptance kept their relationship intact. In time that would change his life.

Although nothing could now drive them apart, Tom and Kathleen would soon be separated by thousands of miles after he suddenly decided to leave for America in late September. A year in Ireland since his release from Portland had only left him politically disillusioned, especially by a decrepit leadership that was seemingly navigating the IRB into terminal decline. It had squandered the opportunity of a rising in Ireland presented first by the 1798 centenary celebrations and then by the coming of war in South Africa between Britain and the Boers. And after missing out on the Rathdown clerkship's financial security and social respectability, Tom felt himself stagnating, still living at home and still unemployed. Perhaps he might have aimed lower and settled for a manual labouring job, but Clarke was talented and ambitious and probably felt entitled to some material recognition for the sacrifices he had made. Unable to turn his life around in Ireland, Tom felt impelled to break free and had no fears about starting afresh in America. But he had to make the journey alone. Although he wanted Kathleen to join him eventually in New York and become his wife, Clarke first needed a job, money and a home. A delay also suited her as she had a business in Limerick to wind up and needed to overcome Daly family resistance to their relationship. After receiving Devoy's letter, Tom had told John Daly about his love for Kathleen, probably hoping he would intercede with the Clan leader about approving Tom's proposed lecture tour. He couldn't have been more wrong. Uncle John immediately informed Kathleen's mother, who vainly tried to change her mind.

As the clock counted down to Tom's departure, Kathleen became increasingly despondent. But then at the end of August 1899 came the possibility of a breakthrough: James Egan told Tom that Councillor John Clancy, chairman of Dublin Corporation's markets' committee, intended dismissing the Corporation's abattoir superintendent for swindling and was informally offering Tom the job on an annual salary of £150 along with free housing, coal and gas.[46] As Corporation sword-bearer, Egan was tight with Clancy, a former IRB man who protected his formidable patronage system at City Hall by cultivating both republicans and Home Rulers. Subject to a committee vote, Clancy planned to have everything settled within a month, just before Tom departed for America on 21 September. Although the post was less attractive than the Rathdown clerkship, Clarke's chances this time seemed better as Clancy was a power broker whom many councillors would be reluctant to cross. So at the last moment Tom might not have to leave Ireland – and Kathleen – after all. On 1 September he told her that within a few days Clancy intended introducing a motion to dismiss the superintendent, and though this did not happen he remained confident there would soon be a vacancy to be filled. In the meantime he attended a party in Blackrock, Co. Dublin for James Stephens, founder of the Fenian movement. It was a surprising gesture, as Stephens' reputation had never recovered after his attempt to stop the 1867 Rising, and although Stephens returned from exile in 1891, he had lived thereafter in obscurity and relative poverty. Perhaps Clarke sympathised with someone who, like himself, had been forced to live so many years away from his homeland; possibly out of curiosity he also wanted to gaze upon the face of a man whose organisation had decisively shaped his own life.[47]

With time running out, Kathleen scoured the newspapers in vain for Tom's appointment as abattoir superintendent. On 14 September she told him, 'Why it's only a week from the 21st. My goodness think of it. One little week and you may be putting the Atlantic between us'.[48] Next day he broke the news that the post was on hold until a number of lawsuits concerning the suspended superintendent were settled and so he had booked tickets for himself and his sister Maria on a liner out of Queenstown on 27 September. Clancy had promised that once the legal problems were resolved the job was his for the taking if he came back from America.[49] Kathleen replied that his imminent departure 'gave me a bit of a shock though I fancied I was quite prepared for it'.[50] However she was cheered that his sailing out of

Queenstown, Co. Cork meant they could meet one last time and Clarke had already promised, 'I need you. I'm not going to leave without seeing you again'.[51] After a final stay in Limerick, Clarke left to join his ship: 'I am feeling rather lonely and feel more like a man going off to jail'.[52]

When Clarke arrived in New York on 3 October he was effectively starting all over again. Only a few old acquaintances still lived in the city and his former best friend, Billy Kelly, had returned permanently to Ireland. Initially homeless and jobless, Tom and Maria stayed at the Vanderbilt Hotel, which despite the grandeur of its name was actually a modest establishment on the corner of 42nd Street and Lexington Avenue in east Manhattan, one block from Central Station. Its owner, Matthew Clune, was a Clan member who kept open house for anti-British revolutionaries from around the world. A week later Tom and Maria transferred to a boarding house on West 94th Street, but after a month moved into an apartment on West 36th Street. For the first time in his life Clarke had a home of his own, furnished by Maria, pleasurable and comfortable. In a snug front room that Maria grandly christened the 'parlor', Clarke loved to sit at a desk on which stood Kathleen's photograph, writing letters to 'my Guardian Angel', 'my loving Irish girl'.

Having worked once before in a New York shoe shop, Clarke now dreamed of owning one himself. Adapting easily to American capitalism, he proposed financing his business venture by selling shares to members of Irish-American organisations. He would start out as manager, but buy back the shares and become sole proprietor once the shop was profitable. At public meetings in Brooklyn during November 1899, he canvassed investors whose enthusiastic response made him hopeful about opening soon. But the scheme petered out amidst Clarke's complaints about powerful individuals – probably political bosses – wanting to be 'owning my soul and making a tool of me'.[53] Instead, he resumed his old prison trade of a pattern maker in a foundry, supplementing his weekly wages of $15 by bookkeeping a couple of hours a night at home.[54] In his letters Clarke was deliberately discreet about the clerical work which he was doing at the Clan's New York headquarters, where was also acting in a secretarial capacity to John Devoy. Two jobs and long hours exhausted him, but despite suffering a heavy cold in late November and early December 1899, he struggled into work every day. In January 1900 a far worse infection, a combination of flu and catarrh that verged on pneumonia, left him unable to eat or smoke for days on end. This time Clarke gave up the bookkeeping, though he stuck at his foundry job, going straight to bed afterwards, fortified by quinine, whiskey, brandy and spray inhalers. Despite being a lifelong teetotaller, Clarke drank Maria's medicinal alcohol: 'The finest dose she gave me was a noggin of best brandy made into punch. I don't recollect ever tasting brandy before and I don't want to taste it again, it is a most nauseating drink, but the whiskey she later gave me was far easier to drink'.[55]

Regardless of these illnesses, Clarke was increasingly confident about succeeding in America, having achieved more there after three months than during an entire year in Ireland. By January 1900 he intended 'making my home here and that nothing would induce me to return to Ireland except it was going to fight something or somebody – meaning John B'.[56] He was now living the American Dream, the belief that anyone – irrespective of background – could achieve success and wealth through hard work and enterprise. Clarke's restless self-improvement also manifested itself in an upward social mobility that had him and Maria shifting regularly to more affluent districts. Even his comfortable apartment on West 36th Street soon left him dissatisfied, located as it was in 'a rather bad neighbourhood. There are any amount of niggers living here about and we Irish as a rule don't care for coming too much in contact with the coloured folks'.[57] Despite such abhorrent language being then commonplace, Clarke was clearly indifferent to racial equality and neither in America nor in South Africa did the systematic discrimination inflicted on black people trouble him much. Seeing everything through the prism of his hostility to British imperialism, he empathised instead with fellow strugglers such as the Boers of Transvaal and those white colonists who had created America. Clarke's apathy towards racism was hardly unique among Irish republicans, many of whom had fought as Confederates during the American Civil War, while Kathleen, a true daughter of Limerick, then a bastion of social and religious conservatism, sympathised with Tom's plight: 'I suppose those niggers were too much for you. I must say I've an objection to them myself'.[58] In early March 1900 Clarke and Maria fled to a newly built apartment on Second Avenue. It had many modern features – though not steam-heated rooms – and the district was more congenial and situated near a station of the electric railway that brought him to work in fifteen minutes. Even in this urban setting there was much for a passionate lover of nature to enjoy, with an abundance of trees and flowers in parks and along many streets. Almost every Sunday Clarke loved to stroll through nearby Central Park and watch squirrels scampering along the ground and up trees. And after so many years of terrible prison food, he indulged himself in the city's famous street markets, becoming for a while effectively a vegetarian: 'I live largely on fruit and such fruit! Peaches, plums, pears, bananas and such as I never saw before. The fruit of all sorts has been wonderfully improved since I left America last'.[59]

Despite occasional illnesses, Clarke adapted well to American weather, which he assured Kathleen suited most people better than the damp Irish climate and could even cure invalids. He coped much better than Maria with New York's extreme temperatures which ranged from 90°F in the summer shade to 'very cold and disagreeable' winter blizzards: 'I find I can stand the cold so much better now than I could when last in America'.[60] Some winter days were mild, 'as balmy as an Irish May day', though Clarke actually enjoyed very cold frosty weather. Socially, Clarke lived inside an Irish-American bubble. He sat on New York's United Irish Societies Committee and frequently accompanied Maria to functions of the Tyrone Ladies' Association. Although he couldn't dance, Clarke joined in the singing. He also organised Tyrone Men's Association's excursions and submitted articles about them to the newspapers. But despite keeping busy, Tom told Kathleen that 'I feel very lonely at times in this big city and keep longing to have you and the happiness it would mean to me were you at my side. In truth I don't care to go on confessing how much I keep thinking of you and longing to see you again – you are everything to me and before everyone to me'.[61] However, he also knew she needed time to win over her mother and Uncle John. Leaving unilaterally would have caused a family schism, distressed Kathleen's mother and sisters and brought her great unhappiness. At Christmas 1899 Kathleen optimistically assured Tom that she did not anticipate either Uncle John or her mother preventing her going, though he chided himself for not making his case to her mother before leaving Ireland: 'You see this is my first experience in that sort of thing and I really didn't know how to go about it'.[62]

But Kathleen's mother and especially Uncle John soon disabused her and Tom of any illusions. Despite being an irascible egocentric, determined that he alone would decide Kathleen's future, John Daly also shared her mother's doubts about Tom's suitability. His straitened finances, poor job prospects and the significant age difference between himself and Kathleen hardly made Tom an irresistible catch. Furthermore, Uncle John probably regarded Tom's behaviour as insufficiently respectful. After deferring to his authority for twenty years, Clarke for the first time – and in Daly's own home – had seemingly gone behind his back to court Kathleen – for whom Uncle John acted as guardian. Uncle John deemed Clarke's actions as an abuse of his hospitality because he had brought Tom to Limerick to recuperate and made him a Freeman of the City in recognition of his suffering, not as a prelude to marrying into the Daly family. And Clarke's refusal to back down must have shaken him. By asserting his authority, Uncle John had become an immovable obstacle that Kathleen would have to win over or wear down. But Daly was cunning, intent on gaining time by stringing Kathleen along with endless excuses and promises, hoping that her long-distance relationship with Tom would gradually wither and die.

In March 1900 Clarke asked Kathleen's mother and Uncle John to release her within four months. But Mrs Daly was possessive and wouldn't contemplate her daughter moving thousands of miles away to live with someone whose nomadic existence troubled her. And John Daly wanted Kathleen to wait a year since she was so young, a delay that Tom told her, 'horrifies me as the prospect of twelve months inside prison walls never did ... I'm all the time longing to hear from you and all the time I may say, thinking of you and yearning for you'.[63] On 10 April Kathleen confirmed she was not coming because, although she could argue with her mother, Uncle John was beyond reason. In May Tom tried to force the issue by urging Kathleen to set her own date for departure. This was a decision that would decide their future as her family's opposition had set him pondering a shift to the Transvaal. Shaken, Kathleen promised to present Daly with an ultimatum and come to him as soon as possible, her resolve immediately lifting Clarke's spirits: 'There are very few in this big city who feel as satisfied and content as myself for the last couple of days'.[64] But Uncle John's intimidating presence and his frequent absences on political business during the summer of 1900 prevented a speedy resolution. By early August Kathleen was sick of Uncle John's dodging and warned unless he agreed to a date for her departure she would go anyway.

However, everything was put in flux again when Dublin Corporation finally advertised the abattoir superintendent's post. Applicants needed good commercial knowledge and either a practical background in the cattle and butchery trade or a qualification as a veterinary surgeon, conditions that Crime Branch Special assumed killed off Clarke's candidacy. But Egan's superior knowledge of City Hall's internal machinations had him confidently summoning Tom back from New York. Having left Ireland disenchanted, Clarke was ambivalent but out of loyalty to his supporters there he reluctantly made the journey. Leaving New York at very short notice on 18 September, Tom told Kathleen the election for the job was expected in ten days and so he intended travelling straight from Queenstown to Dublin. If he got the job their future together lay in Ireland, but otherwise he would return immediately to America and expected her to join him on the voyage.

In Dublin Tom reunited with Egan, his campaign leader. He had been organising public meetings in support of Tom's candidacy and assiduously canvassing councillors ahead of an election that was now finally fixed for 1 October. At a large gathering in Phoenix Park, Maud Gonne endorsed Clarke, who declared that he could only be truly happy living in Ireland. Egan claimed a big majority of councillors was supporting a man who had 'done his duty for Ireland' and 'would be in hands down'[65] if open voting were used. But Crime

Branch Special thought 'it is not likely he will get the appointment',[66] and certainly Councillor Clancy's influence had waned at City Hall after a falling out with the Lord Mayor. At the selection meeting, Clarke's supporters packed the galleries and side benches as the Town Clerk – who clearly knew his duty – waved him through as one of thirty qualified candidates. But the turning point came when a councillor's motion to suspend standing orders and allow open voting was carried by only 33 votes to 20 – short of the required two-thirds majority. Secret voting prevented Egan collating councillors' promises of support for Clarke against their actions on the day and some clearly double-crossed him during the first round of voting when Clarke's 16 votes put him in second place, three votes behind the leader John Fagan. On a second and final ballot of the top three candidates, Fagan won by 29 votes to Clarke's 18. The police reported pandemonium among Tom's supporters, with 'a great outburst of groans, boos and cries of "To Hell with you"', three cheers for Clarke, Egan and Maud Gonne and the singing of 'Who fears to speak of '98'.[67]

Afterwards Tom told Kathleen rather unconvincingly, 'It's over and I feel easy once more. Truth to tell I am very little disappointed'.[68] But dashed hopes, wasted effort and an expensive journey over thousands of miles clearly rankled as Clarke emphatically warned Egan never to mention Dublin Corporation again. Still, he could at least look forward to a reunion with Kathleen before escorting her to America now that she had wound up her business in Limerick and let Uncle John and her mother know she was leaving. Finally realising that Kathleen was serious, Daly invited Clarke to stay at his house in William Street, Limerick where, face-to-face at last, they settled their differences. Despite both men's determination to get their own way, neither had ever pushed matters to the point of no return. They were held back by their long-standing friendship, mutual respect, years of shared suffering and a judicious fear on both sides of the consequences of seeking complete victory. Uncle John now sanctioned a marriage in January 1901, when Kathleen would accompany him to America where he had another lecture tour lined up. In return, Tom abandoned months of encouraging Kathleen to leave Ireland and persuaded her to wait until the New Year, arguing 'January wont be long till its here anyway and then you'll be here with me surely and no more disappointment'.[69]

Once again, his optimism was sadly misplaced. Hoping to cheer up Kathleen, Uncle John arranged a holiday for her in Dublin with the Egans. As she and Mrs Egan waited for a tram in the city centre, a *Freeman's Journal* van glanced off Kathleen and knocked Mrs Egan into the road where another newspaper van ran over her. At first Kathleen thought Mrs Egan was dead but then got her to Jervis Street Hospital with severe injuries to the hip and spine. Writing jocularly to Tom, Kathleen feigned disappointment about not being more seriously hurt and liable for compensation of £500 or £600. Equally jovial, he sympathised that 'you weren't fat enough to be in luck's way and seen the chance of coming in for 500 or 600 pounds – as you put it'.[70] But Tom soon stopped laughing. Intent on suing for heavy damages, Mr Egan insisted that Kathleen was a vital witness in a case that might last a very long time. When she remained adamant about going to America, Egan's solicitor pronounced himself hopeful everything would be settled by the end of January, probably without even going to court. Egan also advised her not to hurry, dangling a Corporation post that was coming up and which was a 'certainty' for Tom. Trusting and rather naïve, Kathleen was still learning about men stringing her along, but Tom quickly grasped the legal implications. Although sympathetic to the Egans, he dreaded their arrangements falling apart at the last minute, because even if Egan won, the verdict could be appealed for years. Ultimately Tom was helpless and all he could do now was hope for the best.

To Clarke's chagrin, his second stay in America was very different politically from two decades earlier when he had joined a vibrant Clan's bombing campaign against England. This time the organisation was simply unable to satisfy his craving for action. By 1900 Devoy himself had climbed back up the greasy pole to become Clan leader once again, but the organisation itself was still debilitated. After resigning from the Revolutionary Directorate in August 1881, Devoy had to wait patiently for seven years until Alexander Sullivan finally ruined himself by breaking with the IRB's Supreme Council over his bombing strategy and then being accused of pilfering Clan funds. But even after Sullivan stood down, Devoy's insistence on totally crushing his defeated rival resulted in another decade of internal strife that eventually reduced the Clan to impotence. For most of the 1890s Devoy's faction had only 4,000 members and it was not until June 1900 that the Clan finally reunited at an Atlantic City convention which appointed Devoy as Secretary.

Devoy spent the next ten years and more rebuilding the Clan, reviving moribund branches, attracting new members and boosting its depleted finances. But this concentration on organisational reform prevented the Clan playing an active role in Irish politics or taking advantage of any English involvement in a foreign war. And Tom had reached New York in October 1899 just as one such conflict broke out in South Africa. He wanted the Clan to help the Boers as well as urge the IRB to rise in Ireland where there was considerable pro-Boer sentiment. In Clarke's eyes it was too good an opportunity to miss, to strike while a distracted England had almost 200,000 soldiers – the largest force it had ever sent abroad – deployed on another continent. Yet to his disgust nothing happened. Only one IRB member played an important role in the Boer war – and even then entirely on his own initiative. The 32-year-old John MacBride was originally from Westport, Co. Mayo but had worked for a Dublin wholesale chemist company before leaving for South Africa in 1896. Working as a gold assayer, MacBride created the Irish Transvaal Brigade of 500 Irish and Irish-American commandos just days before the conflict began. They fought alongside the Boers whose government commissioned MacBride as a major.

Devoy wanted to help the Boers by sending 1,000 fighting men to South Africa and stopping the supply of American horses to the British Army. He envisaged his expeditionary force turning the tide of war by acting as shock troops and storming enemy fortresses such as Ladysmith, something the Boers avoided because of a shortage of men. However, equipping his contingent would cost $150,000, more than twice the Clan's entire reserves. And a freelance group of Clan members mopped up public subscriptions for a bogus Ambulance Corps whose members defected to MacBride's Brigade immediately they reached South Africa. Devoy was reluctant to expel the organisers in case it split the only recently reunited Clan.

Standing on the sidelines never came easily to Tom and in January 1900 he complained to Kathleen about Irish-America's political stagnation:

> Things here are not satisfactory – by no means. I am sick of a good deal of what I see. The same demoralization has taken place here as on your side and here we are 'getting ready', making preparations when we should be acting. But where's the good. A fellow can do nothing but keep on churning his wrath.[71]

Tom attended rallies supporting the Boers and avidly followed newspaper accounts of their impressive military successes, including the sieges of British garrisons at Ladysmith and Mafeking. Full of admiration, he rapturously praised the Boers' daring and courage: 'Holy God but aren't they surprising the world! Yes almost as much as they are surprising the English. Talk of Washington and the American patriots of the Revolution! These Boers and their Oom Paul [i.e President Kruger] are knocking them completely into the shade'.[72] However during 1900 the tide turned. By May the British had relieved Ladysmith and Mafeking and the conflict became a guerrilla war, forcing Clarke to reluctantly accept that the British Army would eventually win. All he could hope for now was that the Boers would inflict as much damage as possible and that 'Johnny Bull may get enough before the Boer War is over yet'.[73]

During the summer, MacBride's brigade fought a rearguard action, fatally weakened by a growing shortage of horses. By the autumn they had retreated to the border with Portuguese Mozambique, crossing over on 23 September 1900.[74] After a brief internment, they chartered a ship to Trieste from where most dispersed to Ireland, Holland and Germany. But over a hundred went on to New York, arriving homeless, jobless, penniless and friendless. Devoy rescued them, smoothing their way through immigration, providing them with accommodation at the Vanderbilt, and re-clothing those men still wearing their brigade uniforms. Clarke also made MacBride's men welcome, spending time with them at the Vanderbilt where he enjoyed listening to their war stories. Soon most of them left for mining camps in California, New Mexico and Nevada, travelling on rail tickets provided by the Clan. In January 1901, Tom finally met MacBride himself during a Clan-sponsored American lecture tour. Unlike the dashing warrior of Clarke's imagination, the major initially seemed rather unimpressive, a small unassuming man with reddish hair, a high forehead and quick eyes: 'But the more one knows him the better you like him. He is a first class fellow. All the fellows who served with him in Africa speak of him as having great pluck'.[75] Despite the dramatic story he had to tell, MacBride's tour was a disappointment, netting only $3,000 in two months. MacBride was nervous addressing audiences, a disability with which Clarke could empathise; at one New York meeting that Tom attended, the hall was only half full despite the luminous presence of Maud Gonne. Clarke and MacBride got on very well.

In early December 1900, Kathleen told Egan she was leaving in six or seven weeks and urged him to hurry up.[76] This delighted Tom who was now living at Brook Avenue in the Bronx in an apartment that Maria was furnishing in anticipation of Kathleen's arrival. But Egan rejected a generous offer by the *Freeman's Journal* and went to trial on 12 January 1901. And although he won, the paper could still appeal, forcing Kathleen to remain in Ireland. This left Tom in suspended animation, railing at both the *Freeman's Journal* and an English legal system that had only ever brought him misery: 'I'd like to bundle them all up and send them – well, to Jerusalem'.[77] When a Daly finally arrived in New York, it was Uncle John, rolling into town on 27 February 1901 for his lecture tour and an appearance as principal speaker at New York's St Patrick's Day parade. Tom offered him accommodation at Brook Avenue but that was 10 miles from the city centre and unsuitable for Daly to hold court and meet the Mayor, city politicians and prominent Irish-Americans. Staying instead at the Vanderbilt, Uncle John's round-the-clock carousing exhausted Tom who was on leave and acting as his minder. Never a party animal, he watched with a horrified fascination as Uncle John 'blarneyed' his many admirers and hangers-on while alcohol flowed without apparently affecting anyone. Clarke never got to bed earlier than 2 a.m. and it was sometimes as late as 4 a.m. before he retired: 'The worst of it he stays up too long at night sometimes till three in the morning. And I'm in the same boat too'.[78] Accompanying Daly to sell-out speaking engagements in cities like Boston and Philadelphia, Tom also marvelled at a seductive power not confined solely to powerful oratory:

> He proclaimed off every platform he spoke from that he was a bachelor –
> of course proclaimed that after saying some nice things about the Irish
> American ladies and at the same time twirling that handsome Mayor's
> chain though his fingers. I have seen quite a number of ladies hug him
> and kiss him.[79]

By now Tom had taken to calling Daly a 'rogue', denouncing his vanity: 'He ought to remember the centre of the universe is not at all times himself'.[80] Tom raged at his insufferable interference and frequently wanted to give him a mauling: 'I'd like to hit him in the head with a big knotty blackthorn stick'.[81] Yet despite all his exasperation with Daly and the aggravation he had caused, Tom ruefully acknowledged him as a unique character, someone who for good or ill had decisively influenced his life and whom he would always respect. As the poison drained out of their relationship and mutual respect returned, Tom relaxed and assured Kathleen after Uncle John departed on 20 March that he had really 'enjoyed John's stay here and feel so proud of his successes – he has carried everything before him and has won the admiration of all our people here'.[82]

Anticipating Kathleen's imminent arrival, Tom had told her on 11 March 1901 that he had invited MacBride and Maud Gonne 'to be at the wedding as Best Man and Best Woman or whatever they call it. They are both delighted with the idea and pledge themselves to be there if you are over in time'.[83] But, infuriatingly, Egan's legal problems went on complicating his and Kathleen's lives: 'I feel savage with Egan for the way he treats both you and myself in this matter. Not a single word have I got from him ever since I came'.[84] In mid-April 1901 he wrote, 'Kattie in my heart of hearts I feel very discontented over these disappointments. I say nothing to nobody but I tell myself all about it when alone. How unfortunate things have turned out'.[85] Then on 6 May when Kathleen thought Egan's case had been definitively settled, Clarke's spirits soared in the expectation of her arriving within a few weeks:

You can't come too soon for me and surely now after the awful delay there can't be anything else to prevent an early start. Kattie for God's sake start as soon as ever you can, perhaps something else might crop up like the Egan case to keep you back were you to stay for any length of time ... I won't be sure of you till I have you in my arms.

This proved to be a false dawn of hope and by 31 May he was 'back to the tedious and tiresome waiting for the end but doesn't seem to be anywhere in sight yet'.[86]

Egan had now replaced Uncle John as Clarke's punching bag: 'Egan has been doing or rather he has not been doing a great many things which he ought to have done and I'd like to kick the careless fellow ... I feel mad with him when I think of it'.[87] Perhaps Tom reflected bitterly on the irony that the two men who had helped him survive prison had subsequently done most to blight his freedom. On 11 June he told Kathleen, 'I am not going to say one word in this about Egan's case and the long continued disappointments – what is the use of railing over it, matters won't change for the better because of that'.[88] At last, just over a fortnight later, Kathleen announced that the case really was finished. And since Egan wanted his wife recuperating in America, he offered to chaperone Kathleen as well. After a very rough passage they reached New York on 15 July and were met by Tom and Maria, both of whom brought Kathleen to Clarke's Bronx apartment.

A marriage had been arranged for the following day but by next morning Kathleen's luggage, including her wedding clothes, had still not been delivered from the docks. So the ceremony was postponed until the evening and when the luggage had still not arrived, Kathleen insisted on going ahead in white clothes borrowed from Maria. Major John MacBride was Tom's best man and Maria, John Devoy and the Egans were among the congregation. Despite a short honeymoon in Atlantic City being called off when her luggage took a week to arrive and Tom's leave from work ran out, Kathleen still found New York exhilarating and loved their spacious Bronx apartment. But marriage changed her life overnight. From sharing a large, noisy house crowded with siblings, Kathleen now lived with a solitary man who worked twelve-hour days, was frequently silent at home and rarely indulged in small talk, while even the smallest noise had agitated neighbours banging on walls, floor and ceiling, forcing Kathleen to wear soft slippers around the apartment.

Tom's foundry job was exhausting but the money was too good to give up, so he reduced his travelling time by shifting with his family to an apartment in Greenpoint, Brooklyn and also stopped doing clerical work three nights a week. In this new location Clarke became president of the Clan's Celtic

Club. He encouraged Irish music and dancing and classes in the Irish language, organised summer picnics and was in charge of the Club's official publication, *The Clansman*. Tom also joined the Brooklyn Gaelic Society and arranged a series of autumn and winter lectures that boosted membership. In 1902 Kathleen gave birth to their first child, a son whom Tom insisted on christening John Daly, proof that the breach with Uncle John was truly healed. But probably to avoid confusion, they always addressed their son as Daly. Eight months later Tom's Irish foreman at the Cameron Pump Works was dismissed along with every employee he had taken on. Unemployed, with a wife and child to provide for and rent to pay, Clarke's prospects seemed bleaker than ever, especially after he and Kathleen raided their savings to open an ice cream and candy store.[89]

Soon afterwards Tom caught the lucky break that changed his life. Because New York's four Irish-American publications generally supported Redmond's Home Rule party, the Clan decided in late 1902 to establish its own weekly newspaper, the *Gaelic American*, and once Devoy was unanimously elected editor he recommended his protégé Clarke as managing director. Devoy surely saw how much he and the younger man resembled each other. They had the same deadly seriousness and self-control as well as a capacity for surviving vicissitudes that would have finished off lesser men. Steeped in Irish historical literature and filled with admiration for outstanding orators, they knew how the spoken and written word could inspire and believed especially that newspapers had the power to influence their readers. A talented writer, Devoy had already tried journalism and even launched his own – unsuccessful – publication. Clarke also was a former reporter and newspaper proprietor – though his paper had only circulated among three inmates in Chatham Prison, including himself. With the *Gaelic American* Tom had an impressive title and social status, having finally escaped from manual labour and intellectually deadening clerical work into a job that, for the first time, used his creative energies. Furthermore, Devoy's time-consuming commitments as Clan Secretary allowed Clarke considerable independence, and during 1903 he proved his organising ability by getting the *Gaelic American* ready for its September launch. Thereafter he effectively ran the paper, commissioning articles, reproducing stories from the Irish press, and selecting book excerpts on Irish history, politics and literature, as well as designing each issue's layout and composing headlines.

During Clarke's three years as managing editor, the *Gaelic American* survived and prospered in a very competitive environment with circulation eventually climbing to 30,000.[90] It became New York's second most popular Irish-American publication and despite sales being concentrated along the eastern seaboard and in the Midwest, the newspaper was read throughout the United States. Devoy and Clarke's winning formula lay in the *Gaelic American*'s distinctive appearance and its successful tailoring of content and political message to educated, middle-class Irish-Americans. Their subscriptions and ordinary Clan members buying shares kept the paper afloat, insulating Devoy and Clarke from commercial pressures (such as an interfering proprietor demanding big profits) and giving them freedom to produce their own kind of paper.

Whereas its Irish-American press rivals helped immigrants assimilate into American society and the mainstream press provided daily news and muck-raking sensationalism, the *Gaelic American*'s sole purpose was propaganda. Merging fact and opinion into a political message, the paper reflected Clarke's obsessions with Irish history, politics and literature, and while its columns were serious and intelligent, their tone was stridently partisan. Although Tom did not consider the pen mightier than the sword, the *Gaelic American* was a highly effective launching pad for his weekly literary offensives against England. Along this newly opened American front, Tom inflamed readers' emotions with a simplistic but satisfying explanation for Ireland's past and America's present troubles: England's desire for world domination. Dripping Anglophobia, the *Gaelic American* campaigned against Anglo-American rapprochement, Anglo-Saxon cultural imperialism and British misrule in Ireland. With zeal and inventiveness, Clarke produced endless variations on the theme of English perfidy and cruelty. The *Gaelic American*'s extensive coverage of Europe, South America and the Pacific demonstrated Clarke's knowledge of international relations and his insistence that Irish affairs could only be understood in a global context. For him England's enemy was Ireland's friend. However such *realpolitik* sometimes landed Clarke in excruciating ideological contortions. After the Anglo-Japanese alliance of 1902, the *Gaelic American* accurately predicted a Russo-Japanese war in which it sided with a Czarist autocracy despised by every European liberal while simultaneously lambasting England for helping a coloured Asiatic people challenge white European – and American – interests in the Far East. One *Gaelic American* headline ran 'The Yellow Peril'.

The responsibility of creating and managing a newspaper boosted Clarke's self-confidence and a friend observed in him a new air of authority:

His face was refined, deeply marked with lines of suffering and endurance yet humorous and kindly. His eyes were quick, alert and his whole personality gave the impression of strength, decisiveness and intelligence. To his friends he was generous, kind and full of fun and humour but in general he had a quick decisive manner, a way of coming to the point in a most direct manner.[91]

But Tom's transformation owed most to John Devoy. In the Broadway offices
shared by the *Gaelic American* and the Clan, their regular discussions about
politics, history and news from Ireland gradually led to a close relationship.
As Devoy's leading confidant, Tom was entrusted with his correspondence
when he was away and also acted as an envoy to Clan leaders in other
American cities. Devoy, for his part, supplanted John Daly as the most
influential person in Clarke's life. Dominant, manipulative and skilled in
accumulating power, Devoy showed Tom how to control a revolutionary
organisation. And beneath an austere and scholarly exterior lay an intolerant
political brawler with a take-no-prisoners mentality, someone adept at
crushing opponents and running them out of the Clan. Devoy heightened
qualities already present in Tom, who emulated his vitriolic diatribes and
whose language acquired a semi-hysterical quality laced with highly person-
alised abuse of his enemies. Politically, Clarke was now a bare-knuckle fighter
who willingly hit below the belt if it helped him land a knock-out blow.

   Tom's position on the *Gaelic American* allowed him and Kathleen to sell their
shop and move into an apartment on 99th Street, just off Broadway and close to
where Devoy lived with his sister. But an unspecified illness that afflicted Kathleen
in 1904 forced another shift to a more healthy semi-rural part of Brooklyn. There,
Clarke established the Brooklyn Gaelic Society which organised weekly classes,
lectures, debates and social evenings in support of Irish culture. Then in the
late spring of 1905 young John Daly contracted diphtheria. Refusing hospital
treatment, Tom and Kathleen were quarantined along with their son for six weeks
and despite a visiting doctor's warning to prepare for the worst, they saved Daly's
life. But the illness had left John Daly a physical wreck and drained Kathleen as
well, so Clarke insisted they recuperate at the Dalys' home in Limerick. However,
short of cash, he had to remain in New York, thus compelling him between late
July and November 1905 once again to conduct a transatlantic correspondence
with Kathleen. Tom's letters show his transformation into a devoted family man,
deeply in love with his wife and missing her keenly:

> Say Kattie. I miss you very much. Life wouldn't be worth living if I had
> to face the future 'free and unfettered'. God Almighty how fond I am of
> that chain that binds us to each other – Yes you are my first thoughts in
> the morning and my last at night are of you. God bless you darling and
> send you back safe and strong to me.[92]

He also worried constantly about her weight loss, face sores, neuralgia, poor
appetite and kidney trouble, all of which slowed Kathleen's recovery and

prolonged her stay in Ireland. Clarke also emerges as a proud and doting father. He loved hearing Kathleen's description of how everyone – but especially her mother and Uncle John – loved their son: 'I am delighted to know Daly is such a pet. They can now see for themselves that our description of our little lad was not the overdrawn picture of a fond father and fond mother'.[93] Despite warning Kathleen not to let them spoil Daly, Clarke himself could not avoid indulging the boy, writing that 'you and I are great friends and I am going to have twenty nine pieces of candy for you when you come back'.[94]

During the summer of 1905 Clarke showed his devotion as a family man when he became embroiled in his sister Maria's troubled life. Once level-headed and well ordered, she had descended into chaos after vacating Tom's apartment and marrying Ed Fleming, a feckless, lazy drunkard by whom she had a son. Tom's rage at Ed's dissipation culminated in mid-August when he arrived home and found a frantic begging letter from Maria. Next morning Clarke brought a borrowed $10 bill round only to discover Ed – who had rolled in at four o'clock in the morning – lying on a bed in an alcoholic haze: 'I felt very mad but had common sense enough to realise that the fellow was too degraded a wraith to risk getting into trouble with. If he were only half decent I think I would have tried to give him a good walloping'.[95] This was the end of the line for Tom. Trying to bulldoze her out of the marriage and as far away from Ed as possible, he persuaded Maria to write home asking Hannah for a loan so that she and her son could settle in Ireland. But even if Hannah could not raise the money, Tom promised to protect Maria:

I would stand by her and borrow whatever was needed. This was after she told me she wouldn't dream of coming to live with us. I also told her if she was in any difficulty about anything where a friend was needed to send me word and I would be with her. She had decided to auction off the furniture as soon as possible and have done with that degenerate once and for all.[96]

But a month later Maria reconciled with Ed 'who has made her any number of holy and religious promises as to his future conduct'.[97] Begging forgiveness, he swore that this time it would be different; he would change, stop drinking, get a job, become a better person and never let her down again. That his sister swallowed such worthless assurances infuriated Clarke, but while he had promised to stand by Maria she was standing by her man. Perhaps Tom more than most should have remembered how love could bind two very unlikely people together.

As Kathleen put on weight again and Daly's health improved, Clarke worked on giving them a better life when they returned to America. By taking out American citizenship in September 1905, he was able to sit a civil service examination for the coveted post of city inspector, whose holders supervised New York's schools, restaurants, waste disposal, construction industry and transport system on a generous annual salary. When Kathleen arrived back in November and learned that Tom had passed the exam she was delirious with joy, thinking that they and John Daly were set up for life. But after a friend warned Tom that the authorities would deport him if they discovered his prison record, he overrode Kathleen's protests and turned the offer down. In the spring of 1906 Kathleen became ill again and a doctor advised her to swap New York for the country life. Resigning from the *Gaelic American*, Tom moved his family to a 60-acre Long Island farm bought with money gifted by Uncle John. Although inexperienced, Kathleen loved working on the land, enjoyed having her husband around all the time and would gladly have stayed there permanently. Nevertheless, during 1907 she could see how much Tom wanted to return to Ireland. After three absorbing years on the *Gaelic American*, a farmer's life was unappealing, especially as Irish independence was becoming less of an impossible dream to him. Always a close observer of the international scene, he now saw Europe divided into two armed camps with the Triple Entente of England, France and Russia confronting a Triple Alliance of Germany, Austria-Hungary and Italy. And the naval and economic rivalry between England and Germany was intensifying. Kathleen

> could see that this talk of England being engaged in war in the near future was having an unsettling effect on Tom. Night after night, sitting down when work was done, he would revert to it, and the tragedy it would be if Ireland failed to avail itself of such an opportunity to make a bid for freedom. If she failed to do so, it would break the tradition of generations, and might end in Ireland becoming resigned to her fate as part of the British Empire. The thought of such a thing happening was to him intolerable; to avert that fate from the country he loved he was ready to sacrifice everything, self, wife, child.[98]

Unlike most Europeans who dreaded a continental conflict, Clarke longed for a war that would open the way for an Irish rising and he could not bear the thought of missing out if and when one actually came.

Tom had other compelling motives for returning. Although he loved America, it could never replace a homeland whose people and landscape were all etched in his memory:' 'Tis nice warm weather here now and the parks and green spots of the city look lovely. I have caught myself over and over again as I admired the beauty of them asking myself "Is Ireland lovelier than this?"'.[99] Then he would remember the old country and realise that nothing he saw in America had the same pleasurable hold on him: 'Even in my busiest moments here in the whirl of busy New York memories of those times, those places and that girl steal in on me and won't let me alone'.[100] Furthermore, a fiftieth birthday had reminded him of his own mortality and having already lost over fifteen years, Clarke was now a middle-aged man in a hurry and it might soon be too late to uproot his family. Kathleen loved America, resented her husband's treatment in Ireland on his return from prison, and feared for his safety if he again troubled the British government. She also recalled that when Daly was born, 'the idea of having a son to follow him to carry on the fight for Ireland's freedom was almost too good to be true. At times he would say, "God, Katty, wouldn't it be wonderful if he could grow up in a free Ireland"'. [101] But in the near future 5-year-old Daly might think of America as his home and begrudge leaving it for the distant land of his parents. And Tom had come close to settling permanently in America himself. He was already a citizen and one of the great imponderables of Irish history is what might have happened if he had taken up the lucrative city inspector's post that would have given his family the good life of economic security, social prestige, a spacious apartment, material comfort and a decent school for his son. Even had he wanted it, it would have been difficult for Clarke to ask Kathleen and Daly to give up all these for him.

Tom was also motivated by his awareness of changing attitudes in Ireland, where organisations such as the Gaelic League reflected a rising generation's disenchantment with constitutional nationalism's political and cultural domination. This view was shared by the National Council and the Dungannon Clubs, both of which supported the separatist policy of Sinn Féin advocated by Arthur Griffith. And two young Belfast republicans, Denis McCullough and Bulmer Hobson, were re-energising the IRB in Ulster by clearing out dead wood such as McCullough's own father. Born into a Quaker family and educated at Friends' School, Lisburn in Ulster's Protestant heartland, Hobson's study of Irish history had led him towards militant nationalism and finally revolutionary republicanism. By the time he left school in 1899, Hobson's political hero – just like Clarke – was Wolfe Tone, and after joining the IRB Hobson – again like Clarke – dedicated his life to breaking the connection with England. Quickly developing into a talented journalist and political organiser, he regarded Sinn Féin's policy of passive resistance and separatism as sufficiently progressive to warrant republican support. But unlike Griffith, Hobson was also a fine platform speaker, tall, imposing, fluent and emotionally powerful, and Devoy invited him to articulate Sinn Féin policy to American audiences. Since Clarke's ties to Devoy and the Clan had been unaffected by his resignation from the *Gaelic American*, Devoy entrusted him with arranging Hobson's two-month lecture tour of New England and the Midwest. Beginning on 16 February 1907 with a packed meeting at New York's Grand Central Palace, Hobson's triumphant journey bore all the hallmarks of Clarke's meticulous preparation. Hobson later spoke in many cities, including Philadelphia, Indianapolis, Chicago, Boston and St Louis, and despite being still in his mid-twenties, he impressed audiences everywhere with his poise, confidence and showmanship. Declaring war on Redmond's Home Rulers,

> he accused the Irish Parliamentary Party of betraying Ireland by taking their seats in the Westminster parliament, thus recognising the right of a foreign government to rule their nation. He assured the audience that a new generation, dedicated to bringing 'the people of Ireland, North and South, Catholic and Protestant' together as 'Irishmen', was engaged in combating this situation.[102]

Hobson's message delighted Clarke who knew that next time in Ireland he would not struggle single-handedly but have young, talented allies as determined as him to set the IRB on the road to revolution.

Once again Clarke was asking Kathleen to uproot her settled life, travel thousands of miles away to another country and start all over again. Having always given Kathleen time and space to make important decisions about her future, Tom did not try to impose his will on her. Instead he worked hard to dispel her fears about returning home, especially those concerning unemployment and poverty. He proposed purchasing a newspaper and tobacco shop in Dublin using their savings and money from selling the farm. His sister Hannah was in the same business and was willing to help Tom establish himself. Finally Kathleen gave in:

> He moved me so much one night that I had to respond 'Well', I said, 'how about going back?' He became very excited and said, 'Katty, do you mean that? I want to go, but feared I would never get you to agree'. I told him that I did not want to go but if it would make him happier to go back I would reluctantly consent. His happiness came first with me.[103]

Whatever her fears about Tom's future and how their lives together might unfold, Kathleen knew that ultimately she could never stand in the way of his destiny.

Spurred on by Kathleen's announcement that she was expecting another child, Tom sold the farm and booked tickets on a transatlantic liner before she had a chance to change her mind. Spending their final days in America at Maria's apartment in New York, Clarke surprised Devoy with the news of his impending departure. But the Clan leader quickly realised that Clarke might be just the man to revive Irish republicanism and he drew up credentials introducing Tom to the IRB's leaders. Devoy's action made it clear that offending Clarke would mean alienating him and jeoparding the American subsidies on which the IRB depended. At the end of November 1907, the Clarke family arrived at Queenstown and were met by Uncle John and Kathleen's sister Madge. The Dalys encountered a very different Tom to the former prisoner of almost a decade earlier. In America the Clarke familiar to future generations had become recognisable, a charismatic, self-confident and brilliant conspirator. In 1898 he had returned to Ireland hoping to help revive the IRB and bring about a revolution, but had failed. This time Clarke was determined to effect great changes; this time he would achieve Irish freedom or die in the attempt.

NOTES

1 Home Office, Crime Department Special Branch. Precis of Information on Secret Societies. 19132/S. 117529/S 21 October 1898. National Archives of Ireland.
2 *Dungannon News*, 27 October 1898.
3 Home Office, Crime Department Special Branch. Precis of Information on Secret Societies. 19132/S. 13 April 1899.
4 Ibid., 17828/S. 10 November 1898.
5 Ibid.
6 Ibid.
7 Clarke Papers, NLI MS 49,354/4.
8 Clarke Papers, Tom to Kathleen, 1 April 1899, NLI MS 49,351/1/1.
9 Tom to Kathleen , 5 September 1899, NLI MS 49,351/1/1.
10 Ibid.
11 *Limerick Leader*, 3 March 1899.
12 Ibid.
13 Kathleen Clarke, *Revolutionary Woman*, p. 23.
14 Ibid., p. 18.
15 Ibid., p. 20.
16 Ibid., p. 22.
17 Ibid., p. 15.
18 Ibid., pp. 24–5.
19 Clarke Papers, Tom to Kathleen, 4 May 1899, NLI MS 49,351/1/1.

20 Ibid.

21 Ibid.

22 Clarke Papers, Tom to Kathleen, 21 May 1899, NLI MS 49,351/1/1.

23 Clarke Papers, Tom to Kathleen, 5 June 1899, NLI MS 49,351/1/1.

24 Ibid.

25 Clarke Papers, Tom to Kathleen, 26 April 1899, NLI MS 49,351/1/1.

26 Kathleen Clarke, *Revolutionary Woman*, p. 25.

27 Clarke Papers, Tom to Kathleen, 5 November 1899.

28 Clarke Papers, Tom to Kathleen, 7 October 1899, NLI MS 49,351/1/1.

29 Kathleen Clarke, *Revolutionary Woman*, p. 69.

30 Tom to Kathleen, 20 April 1900.

31 'A Character Sketch of Tom Clarke' by Mrs Kathleen Clarke, Clarke Papers, NLI MS 49,355/12.

32 Kathleen Clarke, *Revolutionary Woman*, p. 25.

33 'A Character Sktech of Tom Clarke' by Mrs Kathleen Clarke, Clarke Papers, NLI MS 49,355/12.

34 Clarke Papers, Kathleen to Tom, 12 April 1899, NLI MS 49,352/1/1.

35 Clarke Papers, Kathleen to Tom, 1 August 1899, NLI MS 49,352/1/1.

36 Clarke Papers, Tom to Kathleen, 3 August 1899, NLI MS 49,351/1/1.

37 Clarke Papers, Kathleen to Tom, 10 August 1899, NLI MS 49,352/1/1.

38 Clarke Papers, Kathleen to Tom, 15 August 1899, NLI MS 49,352/1.

39 Clarke Papers, Tom to Kathleen, 3 August 1899, NLI MS 49,351/1/1.

40 Clarke Papers, Tom to Kathleen, August 1899, NLI MS 49,351/1/1.

41 Ibid.

42 Clarke Papers, Tom to Kathleen, Undated, August 1899, NLI MS 49,351/1/1.

43 Ibid.

44 Clarke Papers, Tom to Kathleen, 8 August 1899, NLI MS 49,351/1/1.

45 Ibid.

46 Clarke Papers, Tom to Kathleen, 27 August 1899, NLI MS 49,351/1/1.

47 Clarke Papers, Tom to Kathleen, September 1899, NLI MS 49,351/1/1.

48 Clarke Papers, Kathleen to Tom, 14 September 1899, NLI MS 49,352/1/1.

49 Clarke Papers, Tom to Kathleen, 15 September 1899, NLI MS 49,351/1/1.

50 Clarke Papers, Kathleen to Tom, 14 September 1899, NLI MS 49,352/1/1.

51 Clarke Papers, Tom to Kathleen, 8 August 1899, NLI MS 49,351/1/1.

52 Clarke Papers, Tom to Kathleen, Saturday after 15 September 1899, NLI MS 49,351/1/1.

53 Clarke Papers, Tom to Kathleen, 5 November 1899, NLI MS 49,351/1/1.

54 Clarke Papers, Tom to Kathleen, 21 November 1899, NLI MS 49,351/1/1.

55 Clarke Papers, Tom to Kathleen, 21 January 1900, NLI MS 49,351/1/2.

56 Ibid.

57 Clarke Papers, Tom to Kathleen, Undated, March 1900, NLI MS 49,351/1/2.

58 Clarke Papers, Kathleen to Tom, 1900, NLI MS 49,352/1/2, NLI MS 49, 352/1/4.

59 Clarke Papers, Tom to Kathleen, 22 July 1900, NLI MS 49,351/1/2.

60 Clarke Papers, Tom to Kathleen, 18 July 1900, NLI MS 49,351/1/2.

61 Clarke Papers, Tom to Kathleen, 29 August 1900, NLI MS 49,351/1/2.

62 Clarke Papers, Tom to Kathleen, 9 February 1900, NLI MS 49,351/1/2.

63 Clarke Papers, Tom to Kathleen, 20 April 1900, NLI MS 49,351/1/2.

64 Clarke Papers, Tom to Kathleen, 8 June 1900, NLI MS 49,351/1/2.

65 *Independent and Nation*, 1 October 1900.

66 Home Office, Crime Department Special Branch. Precis of Information on Secret Societies. 22517/S, 14 August 1900.

67 For a detailed report on the meeting see *Freeman's Journal*, 2 October 1900.

68 Clarke Papers, Tom to Kathleen, Undated, early October 1900, NLI MS 49,351/1/2.

69 Clarke Papers, Tom to Kathleen, 22 October 1900, NLI MS 49,351/1/2.

70 Clarke Papers, Tom to Kathleen, 15 November 1900, NLI MS 49,351/1/2.

71 Clarke Papers, Tom to Jim Bermingham, 28 January 1900, NLI MS 49,351/1.

72 Ibid.

73 Clarke Papers, Tom to Kathleen, 25 November 1900, NLI MS 49,351/1/2.

74 For MacBride's Brigade, see Donal McCracken, *MacBride's Brigade: Irish Commandos in the Anglo-Boer War* (Dublin: Four Courts Press, 1999).

75 Clarke Papers, Tom to Kathleen, 15 April 1901, NLI MS 49,351/1/2.

76 Clarke Papers, Kathleen to Tom, 8 December 1900, NLI MS 49,352/1/2.

77 Clarke Papers, Tom to Kathleen, 11 March 1901, NLI MS 49,351/1/2.

78 Ibid.

79 Clarke Papers, Tom to Kathleen, 21 March 1901, NLI MS 49,351/1/2.

80 Clarke Papers, Tom to Kathleen, 22 January 1901, NLI MS 49,351/1/2.

81 Clarke Papers, Tom to Kathleen, 18 July 1900, NLI MS 49,351/1/2.

82 Clarke Papers, Tom to Kathleen, 21 March 1901, NLI MS 49,351/1/2.

83 Clarke Papers, Tom to Kathleen, 11 March 1901, NLI MS 49,351/1/2.

84 Ibid.

85 Clarke Papers, Tom to Kathleen, 15 April 1901, NLI MS 49,351/1/2.

86 Clarke Papers, Tom to Kathleen, 31 May 1901, NLI MS 49,351/1/2.

87 Ibid.

88 Clarke Papers, Tom to Kathleen, 11 June 1901, NLI MS 49,351/1/2.

89 Kathleen Clarke, *Revolutionary Woman*, p. 30.

90 For the growth and character of the *Gaelic American*, see Mick Mulcrone, *On the Razor's Edge: The Irish-American Press on the Eve of the First World War*.

91 Clarke Papers, Essay on Tom by Sean Carrol, NLI MS

92 Clarke Papers, Tom to Kathleen, 18 August 1905, NLI MS 49,351/1/2.

93 Clarke Papers, Tom to Kathleen, 22 August 1905, NLI MS 49,351/1/2.

94 Clarke Papers, Tom to John Daly, 15 August 1905, NLI MS 49,351/1/2.

95 Clarke Papers, Tom to Kathleen, 15 August 1905, NLI MS 49,351/1/2.

96 Ibid.

97 Clarke Papers, Tom to Kathleen, 19 September 1901, NLI MS 49351/1/2.

98 Kathleen Clarke, *Revolutionary Woman*, p. 35.

99 Clarke Papers, Tom to Kathleen, 11 June 1901, NLI MS 49,351/1/2.

100 Ibid.

101 Kathleen Clarke, *Revolutionary Woman*, p. 30.

102 Marnie Hay, *Bulmer Hobson and the Irish Nationalist Movement in Twentieth Century Ireland*, p. 69.

103 Kathleen Clarke, *Revolutionary Woman*, p. 36.

4

Climbing to Power:
1908–1914

Initially Clarke and his family lived in Limerick with Uncle John and the Daly family who urged them to stay on permanently. But Tom was determined to settle in Dublin, now indisputably the centre of Irish politics. His sister Hannah's offer to help him open a tobacco and newspaper shop would make that possible. While Kathleen remained in Limerick with young Daly for the rest of her pregnancy, Tom moved into rooms that his mother and sister shared above Hannah's Parnell Street shop. Immediately he began reconnoitring central Dublin for suitable business premises. Trudging streets that were figuratively paved with gold, Tom told Kathleen that Hannah was 'making money hand over fist', her shop takings often exceeding £10 in a couple of days – a revelation that 'nearly took my breath away'.[1] In early January 1908, he signed the lease on an empty property at 55a Amiens Street. Partitioned from a drapery shop, the premises included a back room, yard and a garden with a toilet. Along that side of the street were the substantial North Star Hotel, two large public houses and a line of mixed businesses and shops. Behind lay inner-city tenements and a notorious red-light district. Close by across the street was the Great Northern railway station, a terminus for main lines to the north and the south-east, the latter including nearby Kingstown with its mail-boat connection to Great Britain. A constant passing trade made Clarke confident about eventually transforming his small, dilapidated premises into a 'bright, clean and up to date little concern'.[2]

During January and early February 1908, Clarke got the shop ready for opening. Realising that his family's future depended on its success, he committed himself totally, removing old posters and cleaning out the premises, supervising tradesmen doing the painting and paper-hanging, laying linoleum, installing gas appliances and fitting fixtures. With his talent for visual display, Tom also re-designed the shop's appearance inside and outside in order to attract customers. Ignoring Hannah's warning that American brashness was alien to Dublin shopkeepers, he placed a large gold '55' on the front window, anticipating that soon 'everybody will be talking about it'.[3] But for all his drive and vision, Tom couldn't have done it without his sister. Hanna secured a tobacco licence and her reputation alone sufficed to get him a supplier, while she advised him on which newspapers and periodicals he should stock. Clarke promoted the shop opening energetically, printing 2,000 cards and getting IRB contacts to distribute them among Dublin Corporation employees and as far away as the towns of Ulster. He also used an electoral roll for the North Dock ward to send voters a promotional leaflet, advertised in the *Sinn Féin* newspaper and *Gaelic American*, and installed a public telephone inside the shop. As the stock arrived Tom prepared methodically for opening day. He practised standing behind the counter and cutting tobacco, memorised publication titles, prices and location on the shelves and was confident that 'my being able to chat intelligently on any subject'[4] would put his customers at ease.

As Tom's optimism swelled, he reassured Kathleen – and probably himself – about the wisdom of returning to Ireland. The tobacco trade's many success stories had made him

> more confident than ever that we will be able to build up a good business in that shop. Everyone who is competent to judge says if a person can get over the first twelve months without going under it means success. We appear to have almost everything in our favour at the start off and I am full of hope and confident that we can make it go – at least we are going to get a 'look in' at the money-making game.[5]

But renovating the shop was exhausting and Tom quickly abandoned his original intention of offering a hairdressing service: 'There would be too many strange irons in the fire'.[6] Besides, having already hired a boy assistant, Clarke could not afford any more staff, especially as he was already uncomfortable about being dependent on Uncle John's generosity. With so little time for socialising, Tom rarely went out at night. And while his mother and Hannah did 'everything in their powers to make me comfortable, they can't understand me sitting for long stretches without a word'.[7] Missing his wife and young Daly, whom he saw only briefly during a trip to Limerick, he told Kathleen that:

There is a very lonely feeling over me all the time that won't be shaken
off no matter where I am or to whom I am talking. At the bottom of it
all is my being separated from you. There is no getting away from the
fact. I could not feel happy or even easy if you were not by me.[8]

Tom also longed to hear Kathleen's opinions about reshaping the shop
premises. She was his confidante, the person who understood him best and
'the habit of chatting things over with you has grown so strong upon me that
I don't feel easy if I haven't the opportunity of getting your advice'.[9]

On 14 February 1908 the shop opened to a fairly brisk trade, taking £1 0s
12d. Tom considered this a promising start and more than twice what most
'greenhorns'[10] managed to bring in. After a quieter couple of days, business
picked up again on Saturday and Sunday and in all the first week yielded over
£7. But it was hard graft, especially since Tom was now living and sleeping
in the shop's back room. Despite having hardly any customers until about
8.00 a.m., Tom opened up at 6.30 a.m. every morning. Vans delivered newspapers early, his boy assistant needed to put headline posters on billboards,
and he had to clean out and wash the shop. As well as serving customers,
Tom had to re-stock, pay for goods, do his accounts and supervise the boy's
work. Hannah sometimes gave him a break, but in mid-April she dismissed
her own shop assistant, forcing Tom to stay on his premises all day every
day: 'So I am as immoveable here now as the everlasting mountains'.[11] After
closing up at 11.30 p.m., he was often 'so tired I often fall asleep taking off my
shoes or when undressing'.[12] Battling on through sleeplessness and influenza
also took its toll. But 'the encouragement of seeing the shop "go" gives me
the strength to stick it. I'm delighted to stand at the door here and hear
the comments of the people as they pass by on the "fine bright shop"'.[13]
And Clarke was a quick learner, soon developing a knack for cutting and
weighing tobacco, systematising newspaper returns and introducing many
efficiencies: 'I'm building up and doing well but am doing so mainly because
I'm attending with scrupulous attention to everything that is calculated to
make for the building up of the business'.[14] Gradually his hard work paid off.
The week ending 27 March 1908 was his best yet with takings of £7 0s 18d.
The republican grapevine was encouraging support for Clarke's shop, he had
secured newspaper contracts with libraries, and by stocking 'Protestant' titles
had attracted Unionist and English customers. By mid-April Tom's takings
were £75 in two months and four days.[15]

On 3 March 1908 Kathleen gave birth to a second son, whom she
named Thomas. Since he could not visit Limerick, she wanted to join

Clarke permanently in Dublin, but the Dalys persuaded her to stay on with them until July. Even then Uncle John convinced Kathleen to leave the new baby behind until she and her husband found better accommodation. In Dublin, she spent a month house-hunting until Tom became dangerously ill with typhoid fever, forcing Kathleen and her 17-year-old brother Ned to take over running the shop. After being discharged from the Mater Hospital, Tom convalesced in Limerick. From there in September 1908, he reassured Kathleen that he was eating, sleeping and feeling well, taking plenty of fresh air as the Daly family helped build him up again. When Clarke had fully recovered he returned to Dublin but confessed in January 1909 that he was not nearly as strong as before his illness. Running a shop meant 'the whole job has kept me going at as strenuously a pace as a rushing New Yorker'.[16] And both Egan and John Daly had been seriously ill as well. Tom said the former had come close to 'passing in the checks',[17] while for a couple of days Uncle John had been close to death before pulling through but had been left feeling very weak and shaken up.

Besides providing for his family's upkeep, the Amiens Street shop was Tom's political base, an innocent public front for subterranean activities. He had quickly discovered that the IRB's continued decline meant his mission was not so much about reinvigorating as resuscitating the organisation. By 1907 Redmond's reunited Home Rule party dominated Irish politics to such an extent that Dublin Castle believed no secret society was active in Ireland and wanted the police to concentrate instead on open organisations like the Gaelic League, the Gaelic Athletic Association (GAA) and Sinn Féin. The Irish administration even contemplated abolishing Crime Special Branch, the detective organisation that monitored subversives. Obscurity also enveloped the death in March 1907 of John O'Leary, a Fenian elder statesman who had participated in the abortive rising of 1848, served five years in prison in the 1860s and then spent fourteen years in exile in France. Despite being IRB President, he died an almost forgotten figure whose funeral had none of the trappings of great Fenian funerals of the past, not even a graveside oration at Glasnevin cemetery where O'Leary was hurriedly interred during a torrential downpour. As Clarke immersed himself once again in the IRB, it must have seemed that time had stood still for seven years. Demoralised and steeped in apathy, the organisation was literally dying away as older members passed on and few recruits replenished its ranks, while the political dinosaurs whose leadership had driven Tom out of Ireland still contentedly roamed the landscape.

A trio of long-term survivors dominated the IRB's Supreme Council. Its secretary, P.T. Daly, was a former newspaper compositor who had become a member of Dublin Corporation and President of the Dublin Trades Council. Active in many political and cultural societies, Daly radiated bonhomie and was a much-in-demand speaker, but he had acquired a reputation for financial dishonesty. Fred Allan was a Methodist, a former railway clerk and journalist who in 1900 had become personal secretary to the Lord Mayor of Dublin, Thomas Pile, an English Methodist and Home Ruler with an extensive property portfolio in the capital. During a royal visit to Ireland in March 1900, Pile agreed to tender a loyal address to Queen Victoria, so committing Allan to attending a reception for the monarch and organising a children's fete in her honour. On debating his dilemma, the Supreme Council agreed that Allan should participate rather than lose his livelihood. But many members never forgave him and he owed his survival largely to the staunch support of John O'Hanlon, Chairman of the Leinster Executive. An associate recalled that O'Hanlon 'ruled the Dublin organisation with a rod of iron. His vision was limited and he had an inordinate admiration for Allan but for which Allan would never have been on the Council'.[18] Passionless and timid, these three men 'were all impregnated with just one idea about the organisation and that was just "to keep the spirit alive" as O'Hanlon put it'.[19] Clarke would have to winkle these leaders out of the bailiwicks in which they had been so comfortably ensconced for decades.

· Despite being a ticket-of-leave man, Clarke absolutely refused to report regularly to a police station and so Crime Branch Special placed him on its suspects' register and watched his shop constantly. During 1908 they observed many politically active young men visiting it, including Bulmer Hobson who had moved from Belfast to Dublin where he became a newspaper sub-editor and now began consolidating the relationship with Tom which had started in America. Hobson's intelligence, oratory, social poise and literary mien somewhat dazzled Clarke, who envisaged him as another John Mitchel, the nineteenth-century Ulster Protestant journalist and revolutionary. Tom also visualised himself grooming Hobson and other Young Turks and guiding them down the path to revolution. But he had failed to grasp that Hobson was perhaps the leading revolutionary in Ireland and already beyond his tutelage. Tom also failed to recognise the younger man's stubborn independence, arrogance and self-righteousness and it would take him years to realise that ultimately Hobson was unbiddable. But initially Hobson was Clarke's invaluable channel to other young radicals like Pat McCartan, Diarmuid Lynch, Piaras Béaslaí and Sean MacDermott, whom Tom regarded as

a splendid set of young fellows – earnest, able and energetic – around
Dublin, with whom it is a pleasure to work, fellows who believe in
doing things, not gabbling about them only. I'm in great heart with this
young, thinking generation. They are men; they'll give a good account
of themselves.[20]

McCartan was a 28-year-old medical student at University College Dublin
and Hobson's fellow lodger. A farmer's son from Tyrone, he loved the Irish
language and music and had become increasingly fascinated by Irish history,
especially the story of Wolfe Tone and the 1798 Rebellion. Upon learning
about Fenianism's continued existence in America, McCartan impulsively
emigrated to Philadelphia in 1900, worked as a barman for five years and
joined Clan na Gael before deciding to return to Ireland and become a
doctor. On his way home, he called at the *Gaelic American*'s New York office
where he met Clarke for the first time and received credentials from Devoy
that transferred him to the IRB. In Dublin, P.T. Daly allocated McCartan
to an IRB circle; he also became active in Sinn Féin, where he worked
with Hobson and McCullough. Staying in contact with Devoy and Clarke,
he contributed articles to the *Gaelic American* and it was McCartan who had
suggested Hobson's successful American tour. On Tom's return to Ireland,
McCartan recalled him as

a lean or thin type of man who wore glasses and smoked many cigarettes. If he did not know a person he pretended to know nothing
about Ireland or Irish organisations and seemed just a businessman.
To those he knew well – mostly IRB men – he talked freely and liked
a joke and could enjoy one heartily. He knew what was taking place in
all Irish organisations as the IRB had members in all, but to the stranger
he knew nothing outside the news in the press. He looked straight into
a customer's eyes if one spoke to him and seemed to study them with
those piercing eyes of his.[21]

Another young visitor to Amiens Street was a talented 27-year-old reporter,
Piaras Béaslaí who had been born in Liverpool to Irish parents but settled
early in Dublin where he worked for the *Freeman's Journal*. In 1908 the
paper's editor commissioned him to write an article on a former political
prisoner just back from America. In fact Béaslaí had already known about
Clarke's imminent return which McCartan had announced at a meeting of
the IRB's Teeling circle: 'We were all interested in this news. We had heard

him mentioned before – a Fenian who had endured fifteen years of imprisonment in England and every kind of hardship and punishment'. At Clarke's
shop Béaslaí encountered

> a thin slim middle-aged man – more than 50 years of age. He had a very
> high forehead, which was very broad in comparison with his sunken
> hollow cheeks and his narrow chin. Some say that he had the face of a
> fanatic. I'd prefer to say that it was clear from his countenance that he
> was a man who would hold vehemently, closely, faithfully, and earnestly
> to the basic opinions and principles which were dearest to him, that he
> would direct his life accordingly, and that no one would be able to make
> him retreat, deviate, desist or abstain from that, irrespective of whatever
> obstacles might be put in his way. I recognised him as a man who had
> suffered a great deal over many years, that he'd spent the flower of his
> youth in prison suffering bodily and mental torment which had left
> a mark on his life afterwards, but which had done no more than to
> strengthen his courage and steadfastness, and his will to fight.[22]

Clarke's calm and controlled demeanour, his steely determination also
impressed Béaslaí:

> Thomas had a quiet kindly way with him, and usually kept his tongue
> in check, but I felt that he had something fierce inside him. He used to
> express his opinions boldly without fear. He was always deadly serious
> and his mind was focused on one point only – the cause of Ireland.[23]

A close relationship developed rapidly between the two men who shared a
love of journalism and conducted regular conversations in Tom's shop.

Sean MacDermott was a 24-year-old farmer's son from Co. Leitrim. First
moving to Glasgow and later Belfast, he had worked successively as a gardener,
tram-conductor and barman. Starting out politically as a Home Ruler,
MacDermott then graduated to revolutionary conspiracy and in 1906 Hobson
swore him into the IRB. MacDermott demonstrated a formidable energy, self-
discipline and organising talent. Charismatic and handsome with jet-black hair,
he was gregarious and charming but also manipulative and cagey, never for a
moment lowering his guard even when among people he trusted completely.
MacDermott's own girlfriend conceded that 'secrecy was his watchword;
he never talked of the business he did with others'.[24] When Charles Dolan,
the Home Rule MP for North Leitrim, resigned to contest a 1908 by-election

for the newly established Sinn Féin party, Hobson appointed MacDermott as Dolan's campaign director. Both sides employed numerous dirty tricks and MacDermott proved himself adept at the dark arts. Although the Home Rulers won comfortably, Dolan's performance had prevented them strangling Sinn Féin at birth. Like Hobson, MacDermott had moved from Belfast to the capital and Kathleen Clarke recalled that:

> When he returned to Dublin, he came to the shop to see Tom and tell him all about the election. He was full of fun and laughter, relating all the tactics they had resorted to win the election. When he had finished Tom turned to him and said, in a very severe tone, 'Seán, I would rather lose an election than resort to tricks to win it. Our cause is too sacred to be sullied with electioneering tricks. No matter who else, we should not, neither should we participate in an election to the British Parliament'. Opening his big beautiful eyes and looking startled, Sean said, 'Tom, I never looked at it that way before. I see now you are right'. He held out his hand to Tom, saying, 'There's my hand on it'. They shook hands. 'I promise you never to take part in such proceedings again'. He kept his word, and later resigned his position as organiser for Sinn Féin.[25]

Superficially Clarke and MacDermott were very different people. Separated in age by more than a quarter of a century, one was suspicious and introverted, the other sparkling and loquacious. Yet they complemented each other perfectly and Clarke could see as well how useful was MacDermott's willingness, as a single man, to travel throughout Ireland on IRB business. Tom's family and business commitments tied him to Dublin, while his ticket-of-leave status meant that at any time Dublin Castle could return him to prison if it considered that he had become too dangerous politically. From this point on Clarke and MacDermott began forming what eventually became the most important political relationship of their lives.

Thirty-year-old Diarmuid Lynch had been a post office clerk in his native Co. Cork, but in 1896 he emigrated to New York to work as a shipping clerk in his uncle's company that exported farm machinery.[26] While living in Manhattan, Lynch met Clarke with whom he picketed theatres staging plays they considered anti-Irish. But despite his republican sympathies, Lynch did not join the Clan; as President of New York State's Gaelic League he did not want to alienate its Home Rule supporters. In March 1908 a homesick Lynch returned to Ireland without a job lined up, though he eventually secured employment with a Dublin firm selling farm foodstuffs and machinery.

He also transferred to the governing body of Ireland's Gaelic League and
finally discovered that the IRB was still functioning. Within days he visited
Tom in Amiens Street.

Twenty-eight-year-old P.S. (Patrick) O'Hegarty was another post office
clerk from Co. Cork.[27] After transferring to London in 1902, he had joined
both Sinn Féin and the Gaelic League and discovered accidentally that
the IRB had not, as he believed, died out. In rapid succession, O'Hegarty
joined the organisation, became a circle head and then in 1907 was elected
Southern England's representative on the Supreme Council. But he was
shocked at having metaphorically stumbled into a cobweb-infested museum
whose aged curators' sole ambition was to prevent it being closed down and
boarded up. Craving change, O'Hegarty endured constant frustration at
the inaction of 'men of another generation'.[28] They included the chairman
Neil John O'Boyle, a Co. Antrim farmer and a deaf Scottish treasurer, James
Geraghty, both of them men in their sixties and 'quite beyond effective
political work of any kind'.[29] At meetings O'Boyle would glowingly recite
membership figures for the Ulster counties, numbers that everyone else
round the table knew were pure fantasy. Major John MacBride represented
Connaught but rarely saw the west of Ireland, preferring to live in Dublin.
O'Hegarty thought MacBride 'was no good as an organiser and didn't
pretend to be and he only retained the position because there was nobody
else to take it up'.[30] Although there were 800 men in Dublin, no real
organisation existed in Leinster outside the capital. The IRB in Munster
was just recovering from a split, while O'Hegarty considered Bennett,
the North of England representative, absolutely useless: 'His men never
materialised and he never tried to materialise them'.[31] Indeed Bennett and
the rest resembled aged, deluded field marshals manoeuvring phantom
armies while completely oblivious to their soldiers having already melted
away. Secretly they were glad that no battles would actually happen because,
as O'Hegarty soon realised, they had no stomach for a fight and lacked any
interest in arming the IRB or devising military plans: 'All they could vision
was a secret society meeting month after month, collecting subscriptions
which were used in organising and expenses and just keeping together'.[32]
Disgusted, O'Hegarty saw only defeatism, a Supreme Council convinced
'that all that could be done was to keep the principle alive and hand it on,
that there was no hope of a rising in our time'. Apart from MacBride, who
did at least support change, O'Hegarty's proposals for procuring arms and
fighting were unanimously rejected. O'Hanlon argued they would 'only be
getting chaps into trouble'.[33]

O'Hegarty's scathing description of decay and stagnation laid bare the great challenge facing himself, Clarke and other reformers. Daly, Allan and O'Hanlon were running the Supreme Council as a closed shop, resistant to change and buying off discontent with minor concessions. In 1908 they co-opted Denis McCullough on to the Supreme Council while continuing to exclude the far more able – and dangerous – Hobson. Perhaps at his most frustrated, Clarke dreamt about bypassing not just the Council but also the IRB itself, letting it slowly die like the Fenian Brotherhood. As yet he lacked the clout and anyway the IRB was too deeply embedded in republican consciousness. So far from raising the standard of revolt, Clarke played a long game, patiently cultivating the IRB leadership in the hope of eventually being admitted to the inner circle. And he started well. In January 1908 the Supreme Council invited Clarke to be the keynote speaker at an Emmet Commemoration in the Rotunda. But, reluctant now to address large gatherings, he declined. Just as Clarke and his allies were wrestling with the problem of winning over the Supreme Council, T.P. Daly undermined the ruling triumvirate by delivering himself gift-wrapped into his enemies' hands.

Daly's downfall was rooted in both his reputation for misappropriating money and the Supreme Council's financial dependence on America. Twice annually the IRB received subsidies of £300 from the Clan and when Daly attended its 1908 convention he collected a contribution. Just like Daly himself, it immediately went west. Daly successfully evaded the Supreme Council's fitful efforts to locate the money until the spring of 1910 when Devoy dispatched a Colonel Keating to Ireland. Since Keating could confirm to IRB leaders that the Clan subsidy had indeed been handed over, Daly realised the jig was finally up. On a Sunday evening the Supreme Council convened behind the closed doors of Clontarf Public Library for a conference with Keating. But half an hour before his arrival, Allan shocked them all by reading out a letter that he had received in the morning post. From his refuge in a Newry hotel, Daly confessed to holding the Clan's money all along – but only, he claimed, to help his indebted family and the sick children who needed medical treatment. After trying unsuccessfully to repay it, Daly now threw himself on the mercy of the Supreme Council. O'Hegarty recalled that 'everybody was flabbergasted'.[34] Although Daly's offence warranted his expulsion from the IRB, he could well have taken the entire Supreme Council down with him; after all, it had given Daly the power and responsibility that facilitated his misconduct in the first place. According to O'Hegarty, 'it was a thunderbolt to O'Hanlon and Allan who represented to us that if that got out the Organisation in Dublin would break up'.[35] So with only thirty minutes left before they met Keating, the Supreme Council hurriedly improvised a cover-up, leaving Daly still in the IRB but 'resigning' him as Secretary and co-opting Tom Clarke in his place on the Council. They also sanitised the accounts by awarding Daly a £300 gratuity, supposedly in recognition of the losses his printing firm had suffered when he was away on IRB business.

The Council's solution to Daly's embezzlement was cynical but masterly. And by recruiting Clarke – Devoy's ally – it had guaranteed that the Clan's subsidies would continue while reassuring the Americans they were not being squandered. The final hurdle was a 'rather mystified and disturbed' Keating who wanted to question Daly about the missing money. But all he found was an empty chair, like a head-office auditor whose prime suspect had just retired early with a handsome compensation package. Instead, Keating was told that because of Daly's personal problems, the Council had granted him a lifetime sabbatical to spend more time with his 'distressed' family. O'Hegarty recalled that Keating 'accepted all that without argument, though it was plain enough that the Colonel was nobody's fool'.[36] In a scene of low comedy, the Council had lied through its teeth to him, Keating knew its members were lying and they knew that he knew they were lying. But nobody wanted another transatlantic schism and Keating could at least report back favourably on the Supreme Council's changes.

Thirty-two years after John Daly swore him into the IRB, Clarke had at last reached the top. This was not as a reward for long service or sacrifices made, or because the Supreme Council wanted someone of his ability. Tom's promotion was entirely accidental and only because of a cosmetic exercise by IRB leaders desperate to placate their American counterparts. But if O'Hanlon and Allan believed that some minor tweaking meant business as usual, with Clarke a pliant puppet, they would soon be confounded. Clarke was on the rise. His leap from the fringes to the heart of the IRB coincided with the acquisition of a second tobacconist and newspaper shop in Parnell Street. These premises were located in the city centre just off the northern end of O'Connell Street. Ideal for meeting political associates and contacts, Tom shifted there and hired staff to run the Amiens Street business. One visitor described the new shop as being

of a size that did not permit more than half a dozen men to stand in front of the counter at a time. There was just about enough space between the counter and the wall for two men to walk in together. Along the wall were arranged all of the important Dublin and Irish newspapers, weekly and monthly periodicals, and so forth. Behind the short and narrow counter was a large assortment of brands of tobacco, cigars, pipes and cigarettes, with a sideline of stationery. The window was occupied mainly by a cardboard representation of an Irish round tower, advertising the Banba brand of Irish tobacco. Both the window and the store itself were brilliantly lighted, and the whole place suggested care and attention and spotless cleanliness. But the store and its attractiveness were forgotten after the first glance at the man who stood behind the counter. Of medium height, with grey hair thinning away from the temples, dark blue eyes deeply sunken under shaggy brows and high cheekbones standing up in startling prominence from thin, sunken cheeks, the general appearance of the man was keenness personified. Seemingly nearing his seventies, he was, nevertheless, possessed of a force and vigour that might well have been envied by men in their early thirties. The truth was that the man was in the prime of life. Brutality and confinement, however, had left on his features a mark that death alone could remove but had been powerless to subdue the fire that glowed within and animated every thought and action of his life.[37]

By 1910 Clarke had vindicated his decision to return to Ireland. A happily married man with two young sons, he owned two successful shops. Of the Parnell Street property Tom said that 'this place is "going" in great'.[38] His situation became even better when he shifted the Amiens Street business to larger premises at No. 77 that had overhead accommodation for his growing family. This was visible proof that Tom had left economic hardship and unemployment behind him and that the social status and material comforts of middle-class life were finally within his reach. Politically, too, this was Clarke's moment. With a seat at the IRB's top table, he could now envisage expelling an aged leadership from power and setting the organisation on an entirely new course.

Change at the top happened even faster than Clarke could have anticipated after a newspaper was launched to disseminate the IRB's philosophy and political opinions. This was a pet project of younger radicals keen on emulating the *Gaelic American*'s success. Tom supported them, but the IRB leadership had always baulked at such innovations. O'Hanlon had a 'morbid fear of publicity', dreaded 'letting anyone outside the movement know we were there'[39] and had prevented the Supreme Council ever discussing the idea of a newspaper. Only when an exasperated Hobson threatened to establish his own publication did Clarke skilfully pose as a conciliator and offer to broker a compromise, thereby ingratiating himself with Allan and

O'Hanlon. They were convinced that someone like Tom who looked of the same generation as themselves also shared their traditionalist opinions and would always side with them. Aware that both men could drop him from the Supreme Council just as easily as they had co-opted him, Clarke still needed to conceal his wider ambitions, lulling them into a false sense of security. And Allan and O'Hanlon gladly reciprocated Tom's apparent loyalty by appointing his protégé MacDermott as a national organiser for the IRB. Tom now persuaded O'Hanlon to bend a little and approve a monthly publication, *Irish Freedom*, but he indicated that O'Hanlon would be able to control the project by appointing Allan as its manager and Pat McCartan as the editor. With O'Hanlon's unsuspecting co-operation, Clarke had initiated a silent coup at the top of the IRB, one that would eventually sweep aside everyone there who stood in his way.

McCartan recalled that while 'Fred Allan thought I would be a tool in his hands', the radicals secretly 'laughed at how Allan was going to be fooled'.[40] McCartan, Clarke and their supporters wanted an Irish version of the *Gaelic American*, a serious, lively journal that appealed to intelligent, educated, politically interested readers. But McCartan was a newly appointed resident surgeon at the Mater Hospital and settled for correcting proofs and delivering *Irish Freedom* to the printers. It was Hobson who commissioned articles and along with P.S. O'Hegarty wrote much of the paper's content. The paper's first issue in November 1910 badly jolted Allan who had his proposed editorial replaced by one from Hobson. Then in early 1911, the Supreme Council's balance of power tilted slightly towards the radicals. First, McBride told Clarke he was resigning his Connaught seat, allowing time to get MacDermott chosen as his successor. Next McCullough was elected in his own right for Ulster and O'Hegarty stayed on to represent Southern England. When Clarke was co-opted again and replaced the departing Geraghty as Treasurer, a nucleus of reformers finally existed at the top of the IRB. By now Tom had accumulated considerable power. As Treasurer he sat on the three-man Executive that ran the organisation between meetings of the Supreme Council and he was clearly being groomed to take P.T. Daly's place in the ruling triumvirate in O'Hanlon's misguided belief that he would be a bulwark against the 'hot-headed young fellows'.[41]

With *Irish Freedom* slipping out of his control, O'Hanlon tried unsuccessfully to secure a Supreme Council deadline for the paper to make a profit. But the inevitable showdown came about somewhat accidentally. In February 1911 Clarke and McCartan began organising opposition against King George V's royal visit to Ireland in July. *Irish Freedom* announced that an Emmet Commemoration at the Rotunda in March 1911 would debate resolutions opposing Dublin Corporation presenting a loyal address to the monarch. However, the Wolfe Tone Memorial Committee, which organised this meeting, was a front for the IRB's Supreme Council and O'Hanlon instructed Clarke to get McCartan to drop resolutions that would only create party political controversy. McCartan remembered that 'both he [i.e Clarke] and I were disgusted'.[42] But despite the leadership's desire for a quiet life, the Rotunda gathering proved to be anything but sedate. Holding the audience spellbound, Patrick Pearse proclaimed that 'Dublin would have to do some great act to atone for failure to produce even one man to dash his head against a stone wall in an attempt to rescue Robert Emmet'.[43] His peroration profoundly moved McCartan who immediately drafted a resolution against the royal visit and showed it to Clarke in the front row:

> Tom said he could not advise me as he was at the meeting at which no resolutions were decided upon. The band was then leaving the platform and though I knew I was dashing my head against a stone wall of discipline I went over the footlights and proposed my resolution. To my surprise Tom jumped up beside me and seconded it and of course it was passed with enthusiasm.[44]

For Clarke this was a defining moment. Bound by collective responsibility, he had toed the official line until almost the end when he could no longer contain his natural instincts. Perhaps McCartan reminded him of his impetuous younger self and he felt that someone risking his superiors' wrath in a just cause should not have to stand alone. But for the old guard this was mutiny. Observing Clarke defy the Supreme Council of which he was a member, Allan and O'Hanlon suddenly realised that he was never really 'one of us', had indeed taken them for a ride and now threatened to tear the IRB apart. McCartan knew that 'from this moment on Allan did not trust any of us. And Tom was blamed as much as any of us ... Tom and I were guilty of a breach of discipline and we knew it. John Devoy on hearing the facts from Tom thought in the interests of discipline we were wrong'. Yet 'no immediate action was taken. It would have been easy to expel me but not Tom Clarke. Besides to expel me on such an issue was dangerous. I was known in America and the story would get there'.[45] Instead Allan and O'Hanlon stayed their hand, deciding to wait for the next Supreme Council elections when they could quietly drop Clarke into political oblivion. The strain on Clarke was considerable. In mid-June 1911 he spent a week at Woodenbridge in Co Wicklow and reported 'I have improved

immensely. For some time past I have had a bad tension in my nerves —
all wound up like. I am eased very much after this rest — loafed and slept and eat
all the time — that and nothing more'.[46]

Until they could eliminate the Young Turks, Allen and O'Hanlon had
to put up with *Irish Freedom*'s increasing popularity with the rank and file
and watch a paper that they wanted to be uncontroversial become loudly
and uncompromisingly separatist. In particular, Allan regarded its campaign
against the royal visit in July as an implicit rebuke of his behaviour towards
Queen Victoria. Clarke and his followers ratcheted up the pressure by
establishing a committee to lobby Dublin Corporation, while MacDermott
arranged for a streamer to hang across Grafton Street proclaiming 'Thou
art not conquered yet dear land'. Determined as always to symbolically
connect the present and past through marches, commemorations and funerals,
Clarke devised a republican pilgrimage to his hero Wolfe Tone's grave at
Bodenstown. At the cemetery, a large protest coincided with a spectacular
military reception for King George V in Phoenix Park. Returning afterwards
to the city centre, soldiers and sailors saw an *Irish Freedom* billboard outside
Clarke's Parnell Street shop proclaiming 'Damn your concessions, England,
we want our country'. Kathleen recalled how:

> They started using threatening language, and one of the sailors took
> the poster off the hook it was hanging on and threw it into the shop.
> I walked out of the shop with the poster board and replaced it on its
> hook. Then I turned to the crowd and announced I would have anyone
> who touched the board again arrested. The poster remained untouched
> after that. But the angry demonstration continued. Tom was a welcome
> sight when he walked into the shop on his return from Bodenstown,
> though by then the demonstration was over.[47]

Instead of letting the situation settle down, McCartan just could not keep
his mouth shut. Criticised months later at his IRB circle, he protested that
he was being censured when a man who had stolen IRB funds was being
feted. When the Supreme Council learned that McCartan knew about
P.T. Daly's misconduct — a closely guarded secret — 'this gave Allan, as I
presume he believed — the chance to get rid of Clarke and myself'.[48] Moving
first against McCartan at an emergency Executive meeting, Allan and the
chairman Mulholland overrode Clarke, dismissed McCartan as editor of *Irish
Freedom* and temporarily suspended both him and Hobson from the paper.
They also threatened Clarke with an IRB trial if he did not resign from

the Supreme Council. And since December's *Irish Freedom* was already at the printers Allan took it over, intending to close the paper down later. He also raided the paper's small office and ejected Hobson from the premises. With the radicals seemingly cornered, Hobson wanted to start a new paper but McCartan refused to simply walk away. Set on producing a rival version of *Irish Freedom*, McCartan found another printing firm, only for it to demand a £100 guarantee when Allan and O'Hanlon threatened legal action. Since Hobson and most of his other friends were virtually broke and he could barely scrape together £20, McCartan turned to Clarke. As IRB Treasurer, Tom had the funds in his own account but even he was nervous about bankrolling McCartan's insurrection. Any sudden financial emergency might reveal a shortfall and expose Clarke to the same disgrace that had ruined his predecessor Daly. Desperately, McCartan

> begged Tom to give me the £80 and if necessary I would go up to Tyrone next day and get it from my father. His reply was 'Don't talk like that Pat, it hurts', and turning round, he lifted the keys, came out and locked the door after him. He went down to the bank and got the money, which he handed over to me. We lodged the £100 with the solicitor.[49]

In a way, McCartan had shamed Clarke into helping, but after initially hesitating, Tom had once again felt driven to stand beside him. Had he not, Tom would have found it difficult afterwards to live with himself.

Indeed having funded a rival *Irish Freedom*, Clarke now seemed ready to declare war. Arriving in Dublin, O'Hegarty discovered Tom and McCartan 'had made up their minds to resign from the Organisation altogether as they had decided it was quite useless so long as O'Hanlon and Allan ruled it and to come out quite openly about the matter in the next issue of *Irish Freedom*'.[50] But O'Hegarty and Hobson persuaded them to stay in the IRB and fight behind closed doors. Consequently, two broadly similar *Irish Freedoms* appeared, puzzling a rank and file unaware of a power struggle at the top. Playing for time, O'Hegarty secured a special Supreme Council meeting for early January 1912 to hear McCartan and Hobson's statements and cross-examine them about the happenings at *Irish Freedom*. But while Allan and O'Hanlon envisaged a speedy show trial ending in immediate expulsions, their opponents were determined to spin the proceedings out. Bamboozling their inquisitors and treating every accusation with outraged innocence, they dragged investigation out from 11 a.m. to 5.30 p.m., as hour after hour Clarke, Hobson and MacDermott sowed confusion and created reasonable doubt. But while Clarke asked 'some very clever leading questions' and MacDermott gave 'some very clever answers', it was Hobson who stole the show. Defending himself 'with the most consummate skill', he floated like a butterfly from one complicated argument to another until Allan and O'Hanlon 'found themselves agreeing to whitewash everybody concerned on the ground that the whole business was a misunderstanding'.[51] The one weak link was McCartan, who when questioned under oath about his source for Daly's theft, dragged Clarke once again to the edge. If he confirmed that Tom had betrayed his oath and breached Supreme Council security by leaking the information – as McCartan's memoirs all but say he did – it would have destroyed Clarke. He must have held his breath until McCartan finally offered up the name of a Clan leader who was far beyond the Supreme Council's reach: 'When I answered "from Joseph McGarrity of Philadelphia" Allan's plans collapsed and Tom was left untouched'.[52]

Outmanoeuvred, Allan and O'Hanlon felt angry and humiliated, certain in their hearts that for them it would never be 'glad confident morning again'. Clarke and his fellow tormentors would just go on making their lives a misery, constantly striving to impose on them their radical vision of the IRB's future. In the end it was not even a fight to the finish. Ironically, the very listlessness and passivity against which the dissidents had railed caused the old guard to simply give up and fade away. Allan had served continuously on the Supreme Council since 1883, the year when Hobson and MacDermott were born, O'Hegarty was 4 years old and both McCartan and Lynch had celebrated their 5th birthdays. O'Hegarty recalled an exultant mood at the next Supreme Council meeting: 'I shall never forget how happy and cheerful we were the day O'Hanlon and Allan resigned. Tom Clarke was like a boy. "By God" said he "now if we don't get something done, it'll be our own fault"'.[53] To the victors went the spoils. MacDermott replaced Allan as Supreme Council Secretary and manager of *Irish Freedom* while another radical, Seamus O'Connor, took over from O'Hanlon as Leinster representative and Hobson was co-opted in Allan's place. O'Hegarty said that when Diarmuid Lynch was elected for Munster, the clear-out was finished: 'For the first time we had the men who meant business in complete control of things'.[54] But in fact it still took a year after the convulsions for the IRB to settle down. The upheaval astonished many members, especially in Dublin, Allan and O'Hanlon's power base. But if the two men anticipated a counter-revolution there restoring them to power, they had badly miscalculated; after Clarke brought in O'Hegarty to restore calm in the capital, only twenty of O'Hanlon's personal friends seceded.

McCartan asserted that 'after Allan and O'Hanlon resigned this made Tom Clarke the real leader of the Republican movement'.[55] In a coded acknowledgement of his new status, *Irish Freedom* serialised 'Glimpses of an Irish Felon's Prison Life', an expanded version of Clarke's lecture to Dublin's '98 Club. The Supreme Council also began meeting in his living quarters above the Amiens Street shop.[56] Tom was now acting like a leader and his younger followers treated him as one. In him they saw an iconic figure, living proof that the republican ideal could never be extinguished. They also recognised the suffering he had endured and that he would never demand of them something that he had not already done:

> Tom Clarke's friends used to come to the shop in Parnell Street at night before closing time. There, they often used to surprise Tom sitting on a chair in the same position as, when a convict, he used to sit on a stool in his cell, trunk erect, gazing into the distance, his eyelids hardly moving, his hands resting on his knees. Nothing resembled a prison cell more than this small shop in Parnell Street, for it was so narrow that there was hardly more room to sit on the public side of the narrow counter than on the other side.[57]

Yet Clarke showed no self-pity. Habitually reluctant to talk about – far less trade on – his prison experiences, he articulated instead an inspiring vision of a free and independent Ireland and imbued his inner circle with a certainty that ultimately they would reach the Promised Land. With one exception they would follow him to the end. Only Hobson, hugely self-confident and independent of mind, did not succumb to the hero-worshipping of Clarke. After succeeding McCartan as editor of *Irish Freedom* in January 1912, he had serialised Tom's prison memoirs but did not treat the text as sacrosanct. Hobson excised some passages, infuriating Kathleen and hurting Tom who wrote that 'for the first time Katty disputed friend Bulmer's word in matters of that kind. Bulmer's idea is that I was too "gushy" in that passage. Maybe I was, yet God knows it was "gush" straight from the heart'.[58] While relatively trivial in itself, the episode demonstrated Hobson's refusal to defer to anyone, even Clarke, and one day soon this would drive him and Tom apart forever.

That Clarke had perfected his conspiratorial skills is evident from the way he deceived Allan and O'Hanlon. Needing their support to reach the Supreme Council, Tom had played a long game, posing as a loyal subordinate and patiently cultivating them, pandering to their complacency and gullibility while disguising his contempt through dollops of insincere flattery and outright lying.

The sting had demanded a masterly performance, but Tom was equal to the task. Betraying the trust of anyone whom he considered had betrayed the cause of Ireland, caused him neither anguish nor regret. Indeed he regarded Allan and O'Hanlon's downfall as poetic justice for them having brought the IRB to the brink of extinction and if they were stupid enough to fall for his dissembling, then in Clarke's eyes they had no one to blame but themselves.

Keeping his nerve for months on end, Clarke had gone for broke and victory over the old guard boosted both his self-confidence and that of his followers in him. Although now supreme in the IRB, Tom's authority did not derive from the posts he held. Desiring power far more than position, Clarke never wanted to become President of the Supreme Council or even be elected to a seat on it in his own right, preferring automatic co-option instead. Rather it was Clarke's personal qualities – his charisma, dynamism and commitment to transforming the IRB – that explain his ascendancy. Members realised immediately that fundamental change was under way as Clarke acted quickly to make up for so much lost time, creating in effect a new organisation that was infused with his own vitality and seriousness. Under Clarke it was clear that things would happen.

In America Clan na Gael also endorsed Clarke's elevation to leadership and for the first time there was complete harmony between it and the IRB. Devoy was gratified that 'the IRB inspired by his resoluteness and singleness of purpose, began to assume new life and vigour and became an active force'.[59] Both men communicated regularly, posing as family members for security reasons. But in addressing Devoy as 'Dear Uncle', Clarke also conveyed the closeness and warmth of their friendship. He also kept the Clan informed about political developments in Ireland by dispatching trusted envoys to Clan conventions, Sean MacDermott in 1912 and Diarmuid Lynch two years later. Devoy reciprocated by significantly increasing American subsidies, never allocating less than £1000 a time to the Supreme Council.

During 1912 and 1913 Clarke's political relationship with Sean MacDermott deepened into the most important friendship of his life, surpassing even those he enjoyed with Daly and Devoy. From early on, when MacDermott was in his eyes just 'one of Hobson's school', Tom believed he would 'make a name and a reputation for himself that any Irishman might envy'.[60] Quickly the younger man won his trust and a shared love of conspiracy drew them ever closer as they manipulated people, traded intelligence and gleefully hatched plans. Clarke fast-tracked MacDermott into key IRB positions – Secretary to the Supreme Council, a seat on its three-man Executive and manager of *Irish Freedom*. As an unmarried man able to freely travel the country, MacDermott became Clarke's talent spotter and his liaison with provincial republican leaders. Madge Daly, Kathleen's eldest sister, also recalled Tom using him as his troubleshooter and that 'wherever there was a row, a misunderstanding Seán was sent to clear the air and make peace'.[61] As their friendship developed, Tom relaxed in MacDermott's easy-going company, treating him almost as a fourth son. This was especially true after September 1911 when Seán contracted polio and spent four months in the Mater Hospital. When he finally emerged looking somewhat aged, lame in his right leg and using a walking stick, Clarke brought him to Limerick for a fortnight's recuperation. In the following years both men's exhausting activities would require regular holidays at the Daly residence.

Clearly MacDermott liked Clarke, but his charm concealed the icy calculation and nose for power of an intensely ambitious man, one set on being Tom's closest confidant but for the furtherance of his own aims. This meant deliberately cultivating Clarke, manipulating this master of manipulation while simultaneously climbing over anyone who stood in the way – even Bulmer Hobson, his former patron. Initially Clarke envisaged both younger men working harmoniously together and even unsuccessfully tried establishing them as partners in a shop. But in MacDermott's eyes, Hobson was already surplus baggage. With subtlety and remarkable ingratitude, he began isolating Hobson from both Tom and the Supreme Council, quietly setting him up for a fall. MacDermott also fostered good relations with Kathleen Clarke, who thought him 'full of charm and magnetism and very handsome' and like many women, wanted to mother him after his polio attack. Adoring his company ('he was a very lovable character'[62]), she helped him win over her husband. Kathleen's attitude to Hobson was more ambivalent. She claimed to have liked him, but thought Tom had mistakenly put Hobson on a pedestal: 'I had warned him more than once that he was idealising the man too much'.[63] Coming from a background very different from her own, his rather grand literary manner and cultured accent probably irritated her. And Hobson had a superior air unwarranted in someone who lacked a decent job and was permanently broke. Hobson could see for himself that his influence was waning. O'Hegarty too noticed that his 'relations with Tom Clarke and Sean MacDermott had been deteriorating for a couple of years'.[64] Clarke blamed the widening gulf on Hobson's anger at the Supreme Council's refusal to help him buy a printing press and start up a weekly newspaper. As long as these personal tensions were confined to a small inner circle they mattered little, but soon enough they would ripple through the IRB and then into the entire political system, poisoning friendships and ultimately changing the course of modern Irish history.

The trigger was the Third Home Rule Bill that Asquith's Liberal government introduced in April 1912 after two general elections had left Irish Nationalists holding the balance of power at Westminster. The possibility that a devolved parliament in Dublin with Redmond as prime minister might result in Ireland accommodating itself peacefully within the United Kingdom worried Clarke and the IRB. But the prospect of a smooth transition to this situation was greatly reduced when Ulster Unionists opposed the Bill. This rapidly became an organised militant campaign of resistance led by Sir Edward Carson, an outstanding lawyer and orator who was passionately committed to the Union. Unionists regarded him as their saviour, someone able to articulate brilliantly their often inarticulate emotions. On 28 September 1912 ('Ulster Day') over 218,000 men signed a Solemn League and Covenant – some in their own blood – while 228,000 women signed a similar Declaration. Even more significantly, in January 1913 the Ulster Unionist Council started a new military organisation, the Ulster Volunteer Force (UVF) that attracted over 60,000 recruits in just four months. In these developments Clarke could see that the time of opportunity he had been waiting – living – for was coming.

Publicly, the Home Rule movement dismissed the UVF as a feeble, last attempt to stop the inevitable. It suggested that the organisation was physically ineffective and that nationalists could always cripple Unionist resistance by boycotting Ulster's industrial goods. One paper declared that 'the first shot fired by the Ulster rebels will mean the commercial ruin of Belfast'.[65] Furthermore, Joseph Devlin, the province's most prominent Home Ruler, refused to take 'Carson's stage army' seriously, declaring himself 'not in the slightest fear of their civil war. It is all arrant nonsense and bluff. It is a picturesque and well-organised masquerade'.[66] But for other nationalists the UVF was like a fire-bell in the night, demanding the creation of a volunteer force to defend the Home Rule Bill and protect Ulster's Catholics. IRB circles in and around Dublin sent resolutions to their Centres Board urging action. In fact they were pushing at an open door. Seán T. O'Kelly remembered 'often seeing Tom Clarke rubbing his hands with glee when speaking about the reports of Ulster Volunteer activity. "Let them fire away, the more they organise the better", he would say, "Aren't they setting us a splendid example? Soon, very soon, we will be following in their footsteps"'.[67] In a backhanded compliment, Hobson even credited Carson as 'the founder of the Irish Volunteers, for they were the logical and necessary outcome of the Volunteer movement he organised in Ulster'.[68]

Despite his increasing isolation on the Supreme Council, it was Hobson who set the pace. He was still a major IRB figure, indeed officially the capital's leading republican as chairman of the Dublin Centres Board and editor of *Irish Freedom*. But while longing to harness nationalist unease about Ulster, Hobson also knew that timing was everything: 'We saw our opportunity coming, but we must wait till it came. Time must be given for the situation to develop. We must not move too soon – or wait too long'.[69] Yet a lengthy delay might surrender the initiative to rival nationalists. So in July 1913 the Dublin Centres Board decided in principle to establish an Irish Volunteer Force but wait a few months for nationalist opinion to be radicalised. Meanwhile Hobson secretly began drilling IRB members at a hall in Parnell Square so that officers would be ready when the time came. By October Hobson thought it had arrived but that he still needed a frontman who was acceptable to conservative nationalists. Then, on 1 November 1913, the Gaelic League's journal published 'The North Began', an editorial on the Ulster crisis written by Professor Eoin MacNeill of University College Dublin. He argued that while remnants of a reactionary feudal aristocracy had created the UVF to protect their selfish interests, the Protestant farmers and workers in its ranks were really 'Home Rulers in principle and essence' who had been duped into supporting the 'Crown', 'Empire', and 'Union'. And by threatening force against the British Army, MacNeill asserted that the UVF had exposed the shallowness of Protestant loyalty to Britain. Finally, in demonstrating the British government's powerlessness to stop drilling in one part of Ireland, the UVF had opened the way for a nationalist force in the rest of the country.

By publicly proposing an Irish Volunteer Force, MacNeill had set great events in motion and even though not himself an IRB member, the Supreme Council had found its man. Hobson believed 'MacNeill's value to us lay in the fact that he was an important intellectual figure, able, clear-headed, sincere and well-liked, that he quarrelled with nobody and could throw oil on the most troubled waters. These qualities made him an ideal chairman'.[70] MacNeill also looked the part, a dignified man with a distinguished face, high forehead, clear, thoughtful blue eyes and a blond beard.

Afraid that his own radical political reputation might put off MacNeill, Hobson first approached Michael O'Rahilly, the somewhat theatrical manager of the Gaelic League's journal *An Claidheamh Soluis*. Now styling himself as The O'Rahilly, he agreed to act as Hobson's intermediary with MacNeill and persuaded him to chair a meeting about establishing a nationalist Volunteer movement. Hobson then booked a room for the meeting at Wynn's Hotel in Lower Abbey Street on Tuesday 11 November. Intent on keeping a low profile, Hobson decided to stay away but he invited members from his own Teeling circle, including the journalist Piaras Béaslaí and Éamonn Ceannt, an accountant in Dublin Corporation's finance department. But significantly Hobson ignored MacDermott who only learned about the event when Béaslaí asked him along.[71] Everybody present at the discussion was an Irish-Irelander and most of them spoke in Gaelic, something that highlighted the need for a broader membership to prevent them being dismissed as cranks and factionalists. At a second gathering a few days later, they formed themselves into a Provisional Committee dedicated to establishing an organisation called the Irish Volunteers that would 'secure and maintain the rights and liberties common to the whole people of Ireland'.

Almost every newspaper ignored this low-key start and Dublin's Home Rule Lord Mayor rejected the Provisional Committee's application to use the Mansion House for an inaugural meeting on 25 November 1913. Instead it was held in the Rotunda at the northern end of O'Connell Street. The IRB instructed every Dublin member to attend, but many more Home Rulers and Sinn Féiners were among the 7,000 men present. Organisers employed the larger Rotunda Rink but still had to pack an overflow audience into a nearby hall. Speakers like MacNeill, Pearse and MacDermott shuttled between both venues. On the night about 4,000 people enrolled in the Irish Volunteers, including Clarke himself. Immediately a rudimentary Volunteer organisation began taking shape. Offices were rented at 206 Great Brunswick Street and six days later the first assembly of Irish Volunteers took place. After Dublin was divided into four battalion areas, Tom joined the First, one of the few recruits who could actually fire a weapon. In America he had been a regimental adjutant in the Clan's military wing, also known co-incidentally as the Irish Volunteers. On 7 February 1914 a monthly journal, *Irish Volunteer*, appeared, edited by Larry de Lacy, an IRB journalist.

Within weeks the Provisional Committee expanded to thirty people. Among the newly co-opted members was Sir Roger Casement, a 49-year-old Protestant who had been born near Dublin but raised by relatives in Co. Antrim after his parents died. As a British consular official, Casement had exposed colonial cruelties in the Belgian Congo and Peru, experiences that turned him strongly against imperialism. Increasingly attracted to Irish nationalism, he joined the Gaelic League and Sinn Féin and after retiring in the summer of 1913, he settled in Dublin. Persuaded by his friend MacNeill to involve himself in the Volunteers, he joined an informal executive consisting of MacNeill, The O'Rahilly, Sean Fitzgibbon, Colonel Maurice Moore (to be Director of Military Operations) and Hobson who acted as

Honorary Secretary. Sixteen of the thirty Provisional Committee members were in the IRB, while others were Sinn Féiners or followers of Redmond. Although not in any political party himself, MacNeill was publicly identified – not entirely accurately – with the Home Rule movement.[72]

As 1913 ended Clarke reported satisfying political progress to Devoy: 'The Volunteer movement has caught on in great style here in Dublin. Such an outpouring of young fellows was never seen'.[73] According to Kathleen, Tom envisaged the Volunteers as 'the open arm of the IRB',[74] but he wanted to control them secretly in order to avoid arousing British suspicions. Consequently, the Supreme Council had prohibited IRB members from occupying high positions in the Volunteer leadership – an instruction Hobson immediately ignored by becoming Honorary Secretary. Kathleen recalled that this 'came as a complete surprise to Tom, who had believed that Hobson was in agreement with all their decisions. It shook the complete faith he had in Hobson'. So from the Volunteers' early days, Clarke suspected that Hobson regarded the Volunteers as his pet project. Hobson again displayed his independence when the Provisional Committee advertised for a paid secretary who had to be conversant in Irish and shorthand. A subcommittee vetted applicants and on 3 February 1914 the full Provisional Committee gathered to make an appointment. Before the meeting, Béaslaí noticed Hobson with a large entourage of 'the old Fenian boys' who were primed to shoo in a young IRB man from Belfast. Béaslaí regarded this as a blatant stitch-up, especially since Hobson's choice had no Irish or shorthand – unlike one person recommended by the subcommittee majority. Béaslaí recalled that 'Sean MacDermott whispered in my ear: "Hobson is going to make a mess of it. This will antagonise all the others. They'll see it's a put-up job"'.[75] MacDermott then spoke up and with Béaslaí's support persuaded the meeting to postpone a vote. Subsequently in the office of *Irish Freedom*, Béaslaí attended a meeting of IRB members of the Provisional Committee at which the Supreme Council President, Seamus Deakin, instructed them to veto Hobson's candidate. In his diary Béaslaí recorded, 'Contest between Bulmer Hobson and Seán MacDiarmada'. Decades later he gave his opinion that 'this was, I think, the early symptom of an estrangement which was to have very important consequences'. While MacDermott regarded Hobson's manipulation as amateurish and no doubt suspected him of trying to establish his own power base inside the Volunteers, Hobson can only have resented being side-swiped by a former political apprentice.

MacDermott must have used the episode to fuel Clarke's suspicions of Hobson. Tom envisaged the Supreme Council controlling the Volunteers by instructing

IRB members on the Provisional Committee to vote as a monolithic bloc. But
Hobson believed that the Supreme Council should settle for being able to block
any policies inimical to IRB interests and beyond that the Volunteer leadership should represent every shade of nationalism. The Provisional Committee
should be a broad national front operating by consensus, one in which IRB
members should freely express their own opinions and not have to obey the
Supreme Council's orders. Hobson demonstrated his vision in action when as
chairman of a Volunteer committee selecting ex-British Army men as instructors, he ignored Clarke's wishes and chose recruits purely on merit, irrespective
of party affiliation. At ease with people like MacNeill and Casement, Hobson
increasingly regarded Clarke and MacDermott as narrow, partisan and blinkered.
Tom on the other hand began to see in Hobson only egotism and a wilful
refusal to listen, someone whose enthusiasm for political diversity and intellectual ferment at Volunteer headquarters belonged to a literary salon rather
than the engine room of a revolution. More and more, Clarke viewed Hobson
as a self-indulgent dilettante who had gone soft and seemed more comfortable
around people like Moore, a Sandhurst graduate who had fought on the British
side in the Boer War, and Casement, a knight of the realm whom Tom had
once suspected of being a British spy. But Hobson had a strong power base in
the IRB, and lacking a clear-cut issue on which to confront him, Clarke had
to make the best of it. Furthermore, an early split – even if he had then really
wanted one – would only have threatened the existence of the Irish Volunteers.

By the spring of 1914, the Volunteers still had only 18,000 members.
The so-called 'Curragh Mutiny' in March dramatically changed that situation
when 57 British officers at the Curragh army camp in Kildare indicated they
would resign rather than obey orders to forcibly impose Home Rule on Ulster.
The crisis was only defused when the Secretary of State for War, Sir John Seeley,
pledged that it would never instruct them to do so, a humiliating concession
that robbed Asquith's Liberal government of the power to extract concessions
from Ulster Unionists. Then, on the night of 24–25 April 1914, in defiance
of an Arms Proclamation of December 1913 forbidding arms importation to
Ireland, the ship *Clyde Valley* smuggled 30,000 rifles and 100,000 rounds of
ammunition into Larne harbour in Co. Antrim and UVF lorries distributed
the weapons throughout Ulster. As a consequence, the question of partitioning
Ireland came to dominate the political agenda, seriously undermining the
influence of Redmond, who had constantly assured nationalists that the British
government would not let them down. But Clarke's happiness only rose with
every setback that Redmond suffered. *Irish Freedom* mockingly tendered its
'thanks to Sir Edward Carson and the gallant British officers who have helped

their beloved Empire on to the slope above the precipice'. The paper even welcomed Larne's rifles going to the UVF:

> It is essentially a good thing in itself to put guns into the hands of any Irishman, no matter from whom they come or what the intention of the donors may be. For once guns begin to flow into Ireland sooner or later Ireland will stand armed and erect and the evil days of an unarmed and decrepit Ireland will be gone forever. The inevitable effect of an armed Ulster will be an armed Ireland.[76]

These were heady days for Clarke. He told Devoy that:

> The country is electrified with the volunteering business – never in my recollection have I known in any former movement anything to compare with the spontaneous rush that is being made all over to get into the movement and start drill and get hold of a rifle.[77]

Tom also believed that Wolfe Tone's vision of Irishmen of all creeds uniting ('Catholic, Protestant and Dissenter') might finally become reality after he learned UVF leaders had supposedly indicated that they would welcome Irish Volunteer support if the British army attacked them:

> This is an extraordinary change in the attitude of the one-time Orangeman when he even allows himself to entertain the thought of himself and the papists fighting together in any circumstance. However seeing with what lightning-like rapidity things are developing in various directions, one needn't be surprised at anything now.[78]

And, after worrying for years that the Irish peoples' national spirit might be rotting away, Tom claimed they were now standing tall and proud:

> The change that has come over the young men of the country who are volunteering! Erect, heads up in the air, the glint in the eye, and then the talent and ability that had been latent and is now being discovered! Young fellows who had been regarded as like wastrels now changed to energetic soldiers and absorbed in the work and taking pride that at last they feel they can do something for their country that will count. 'Tis good to be alive in Ireland these times.[79]

After the Curragh 'Mutiny' and the Larne gunrunning, the Irish Volunteers grew to over a 100,000 members. Such a rapid expansion convinced Redmond that he could no longer leave an organisation containing so many nationalists outside his control. So during late April and May 1914, he began secretly negotiating with MacNeill about replacing the Provisional Committee with a new and smaller executive. MacNeill was comfortable with the idea of co-opting Home Rule party nominees since he believed that he and Redmond had a common interest in defending the Third Home Rule Bill. But whereas MacNeill envisaged a genuine partnership, Redmond in fact wanted to gain control of an unpredictable Volunteer movement and leave MacNeill in place as a powerless figurehead. Furthermore, Redmond thought mistakenly that the entire Provisional Committee had authorised MacNeill's discussions with him when in reality only a small inner circle knew about them. This group consisted of MacNeill himself, Colonel Maurice Moore, Sir Roger Casement, The O'Rahilly and Sean Fitzgibbon, while Hobson was also told at the end of April after returning from a two-month American tour.

Clarke of course was alert to the danger of Redmond snatching control of the Irish Volunteers away from him and the IRB and turning them into a tame adjunct of the Home Rule movement. On 29 April 1914 he wrote to John Daly that 'Redmond and Co are thoroughly alarmed at the wild-fire spread of the Volunteer Movement'.[80] Tom's two main intelligence sources on the Provisional Committee could tell him nothing about the contacts between Redmond and MacNeill. Hobson had frozen MacDermott out from the start and now he shunned Béaslaí as well. Béaslaí recalled that he was 'never approached though Hobson was my "Centre". I was too much in the confidence of Seán MacDiarmada'.[81] But Tom managed to glean 'scraps of evidence here and there'[82] about the negotiations between Redmond and MacNeill. He told Daly that MacNeill was standing firm against Redmond's demand for a controlling majority on the Provisional Committee in return for agreeing to finance the Volunteer movement. But just to make sure, Tom decided to make it constitutionally impossible to secure a controlling majority. He told Daly that the Supreme Council had quietly decided to allow more options on the Provisional Committee, a decision that could not be overridden as long as its IRB members remained united on the issue. Eventually news of the negotiations between MacNeill and Redmond began leaking out. On 2 June MacNeill admitted at a Provisional Committee meeting that he had agreed to form a small central committee but that he and Redmond were deadlocked on its membership. The revelation caused uproar and Béaslaí 'left the meeting confident that the Committee would never agree to the control of a political party'.[83] But talks actually continued unproductively until Tuesday 9 June 1914 when MacNeill reluctantly announced their complete failure. Next day Redmond stepped up the pressure with a letter in the morning newspapers condemning the Provisional Committee as unrepresentative of a membership that consisted overwhelmingly of Home Rulers. He demanded the right to nominate 25 members to the Provisional Committee and threatened that otherwise his followers would establish their own local Volunteer committees which would be independent of central control.

When the Provisional Committee convened hurriedly that evening, a surprisingly relaxed MacNeill announced his proposed solution – one that Casement had actually sold to him. Naïvely accepting at face value Redmond's complaints about an unrepresentative Provisional Committee, he proposed co-opting one new member from every county, elected by Volunteer conventions. Since most Volunteers were Home Rulers, county elections would give Redmond a majority on the Provisional Committee while maintaining the principle of Volunteers controlling their own affairs. In MacNeill's opinion, this allowed everybody to save face and a delighted Casement thought it had 'cut the ground from under the feet of our critics'.[84] Béaslaí was incredulous: 'It was an ingenious argument which only a learned professor could have thought of. I knew that politicians do not think on those lines'. But Béaslaí saw that MacNeill's supreme confidence had infected others, who backed his plan in the apparent belief 'that Mr Redmond did not mean what he said'.[85] In reality, an infusion of grass-roots democracy that would make the Volunteers even more uncontrollable was the last thing Redmond wanted. Two days later on 11 June, Redmond rejected MacNeill's proposal and repeated his demand for 25 nominees, an ultimatum that The O'Rahilly grudgingly acknowledged was 'a most brilliant coup', a 'master stroke'[86] that finally cornered the Provisional Committee.

Nevertheless MacNeill did not summon a special meeting of the Provisional Committee, preferring to wait until one already scheduled for 16 June. Confident as always of victory, Clarke urged defiance. He believed Redmond was bluffing and that popular opinion was running strongly against an increasingly discredited Home Rule leader. Tom began mobilising opposition with a Supreme Council order that every IRB member should oppose Redmond's demands and followed this up on 15 June by appearing with MacDermott at Buswell's Hotel, intent on persuading Casement to lead resistance on the Provisional Committee. Inside they found Casement ill in bed, surrounded by copious documents and talking with Moore and Hobson. On the previous day Casement and MacNeill had agreed that resignation from the Provisional Committee was probably the only honourable course, but Hobson had just convinced Casement that they had at any cost to save the Volunteers from disruption 'and I did not think disruption could be averted except by accepting Redmond's demands for the moment'.[87] Casement then floored Clarke and MacDermott by urging surrender, maintaining that otherwise Redmond would destroy the Provisional Committee. Tom recorded that after Casement brushed aside his animated protests,

> Shawn [i.e MacDermott] sailed in and argued and reasoned with him along similar lines but all to no purpose. Hobson kept quiet all the time till Shawn had finished – Moore only broke in once in an angry tone to resent something I said about the treasonable betrayal of the Volunteer organisation by the Provisional Committee were they not to stand up to Redmond.[88]

When Hobson endorsed Casement's position, Clarke and MacDermott gave up and left. By now, as Tom recollected, they were certain that:

> A junta was intriguing behind the backs of the majority of the members of the Provisional Committee, entering into negotiations with Redmond, Devlin etc and arranging matters to the material satisfaction of both parties to the intrigue. When we got outside we could have cried, we realised what was going to happen and we were then powerless to do anything.[89]

On the morning of Tuesday 16 June, Hobson returned to Buswell's where he and Casement began formulating a policy statement for that evening's meeting of the Provisional Committee. Casement then sent Hobson to bring MacNeill to the hotel and the professor arrived still in a state of deep depression and threatening not just to resign from the Provisional Committee but to leave politics altogether. However, Hobson, Casement and Moore finally persuaded MacNeill to carry on and the four men agreed a statement reluctantly accepting Redmond's ultimatum since defiance would simply cause the Home Rule leader to establish a rival organisation. Hobson also believed that in the long run the original Provisional Committee could stay effectively in charge of the Volunteers by accepting Redmond's nominees and then frustrating them through its control of key subcommittees. But his argument was very unlikely to sway Tom Clarke who had never bent for anyone and had no intention of starting now.

The statement was typed up by 6 p.m. and two hours later the Provisional Committee convened at Volunteer headquarters in Great Brunswick Street. MacNeill read out its recommendation to accept Redmond's demands 'as a lesser evil and to avoid having our organisation split into two rival factions'.[90] Hobson wound up the ensuing debate by powerfully endorsing MacNeill's policy and urging everyone to preserve Volunteer unity. His intervention caused consternation. Béaslaí recalled that 'to some of us in view of his high position in the IRB his attitude came as a bombshell'.[91] When MacNeill's motion was carried by eighteen votes to nine, one person vowed never to shake Hobson's hand again. Eamonn Ceannt remonstrated furiously with The O'Rahilly and later that night sent him an anonymous, taunting poison pen letter.[92] Afterwards the dissidents, including Patrick Pearse, Eamonn Ceannt, MacDermott and Sean Fitzgibbon, gathered in Wynn's Hotel where Béaslaí drafted a resolution for the newspapers opposing the Provisional Committee's decision. When MacDermott finally gave Clarke his undoubtedly lurid account of Hobson's actions, a friend Seán McGarry witnessed Tom's incandescent reaction:

> I had never seen him so moved. He regarded it from the beginning as cold-blooded and contemplated treachery likely to bring about the destruction of the only movement in a century which brought promise of the fulfilment of all his hopes. During his life he had had many, very many grievous disappointments but this was the worst and the bitterness of it was increased by the fact that it was brought about by a trusted friend.[93]

Clarke's rancour towards Hobson was driven not just by his feelings of betrayal but a conviction that Hobson was a dangerous menace who might soon ruin everything. Tom now realised they were locked in a power struggle that he had to win.

Clarke got his chance to confront Hobson sooner than he anticipated when he travelled next evening to a holiday cottage in Dalkey where John Daly was recovering from a recent stroke. Soon afterwards, Hobson and Casement arrived. Knowing that Tom normally worked late at his shop, they believed mistakenly that the coast was clear and hoped to secure Uncle John's mediation. Instead the antagonists now stood face-to-face. Madge Daly recalled that there was 'calm on the surface but the atmosphere was electric' with 'an undercurrent of violent emotion'.[94] And when an agitated Uncle John suddenly accused Hobson of treason, she feared an 'explosion' until Clarke terminated the discussion. After Hobson and Casement left, Tom and Madge travelled back into Dublin on a tram. During the journey she suggested that Hobson had simply made a young man's error of judgement, but Clarke insisted he could never forgive his unconcealed disdain for collective responsibility. For years the IRB leadership

> had worked loyally together, meeting to discuss anything of national importance, and after free expressions of opinions, agreeing to take unanimous action. But when the question arose Hobson could not be got to discuss it with his old comrades, that he avoided them and used his position as a well-known Irish Republican to influence men inside and outside that organisation to vote with him.[95]

As Clarke discovered more about the Provisional Committee meeting, his rage at Hobson only mounted. MacNeill's statement to the Provisional Committee recommending acceptance of Redmond's demands had been typed up by the daughter of a friend of Tom's and she revealed that Hobson had written 'the betrayal manuscript'.[96] Furthermore, Hobson had admitted deliberately positioning himself to be the last speaker, so swinging at least five votes behind acceptance. Since Clarke had calculated beforehand that a majority of five existed against Redmond, Hobson and his converts had apparently turned victory into defeat. Tom told Devoy that:

> The O'Rahilly and others made no bones about it and say it was only Hobson's attitude that swayed them at the last moment. They believed he spoke for and represented the virile section of the Volunteer movement. They now recognise the terrible mistake they made and are full of regrets. Hobson expresses no regret. On the contrary he boasts of the part he played.[97]

Clarke claimed that anger at the surrender was sweeping the country and he regretted that Redmond's 'blackmail' had not been resisted:

> Had the Provisional Com. only stood up to Redmond he would have been smashed inside of three months – the brains and youth of the country are in the Volunteer movement – the best men from amongst the A.O.H. [Ancient Order of Hibernians] had joined and were streaming into it and no more violent opponents to Redmond control had we than most of the former A.O.H. men.[98]

Clarke and MacDermott hit back immediately by dumping MacNeill as main speaker at the Wolfe Tone commemoration that was to be held in Bodenstown on 21 June. But dealing with Hobson required careful planning. A Supreme Council court martial would have risked splitting the IRB while allowing Hobson to exploit his unrivalled capacity for marshalling facts, exploiting loopholes and dazzling audiences. Having once before witnessed Hobson confound Allan and O'Hanlon, Clarke and MacDermott decided to ambush him on Monday 29 June when the Executive Committee of *Irish Freedom* met at its offices in Findlater Place.[99] Shunning reasoned argument in favour of vitriolic tirades, they accused Hobson of working for Redmond and even being paid by Dublin Castle, verbal brutality of a kind with which the fastidious Hobson was unfamiliar:

> I had expected disapproval of the action I had taken, but I was met with a storm of hysterical abuse and accusations of having betrayed the movement. It was impossible to argue or state a case in such an overcharged atmosphere, and, when I made a little attempt to do so, this seemed to increase their fury.[100]

Strikingly, nobody at the meeting spoke up in his defence, ample proof that to know Hobson was not necessarily to like him. For years his reputation for arrogance, preening self-importance and ignoring unwelcome advice had alienated many republicans and even his friend O'Hegarty, who was also present, recalled how:

> From the start of the Volunteers we had trouble with him. He was a man of very great ability, earnestness, single-mindedness and patriotism; who made very heavy sacrifices for the cause but he was never able to subordinate his own judgement to the combined judgement of his associates. He had to boss everything and get his own way in everything. He was never coopera-tive unless when he was laying down policy and giving instructions.[101]

Clarke, of course, was just as driven and often prickly and dictatorial, but at least he could distinguish between being single-minded and single-handed. Tom understood the importance of a talented inner circle and loyal followers and he never forgot to consult and persuade others. Unlike Hobson, Clarke was never a one-man band.

Physically and emotionally exhausted, Hobson resigned from the Supreme Council and as editor of *Irish Freedom*, the two IRB offices that brought him into contact with Clarke and MacDermott: 'I was quite well aware that my action would leave the direction of the IRB in their hands and I was also aware that my resignation was exactly what Clarke and MacDermott wanted'.[102] Having just narrowly prevented a Volunteer rift, Hobson wanted to avoid more confrontations that he feared would only split the republican movement. However, what Hobson had not yet grasped was that a split already existed, brought about not just by personal antagonisms and arguments over political tactics but because of two irreconcilable visions of the Volunteers' future. Hobson believed that recent developments had exposed the Volunteers' institutional fragility as well as their puny military and financial resources, dooming to failure any rebellion in the near future. Instead both they and the IRB should play a long game, strengthening their organisations, training and arming members while building a broad national front. Eventually they could both lead a united people into a guerrilla war against England. In advocating patience and delay, Hobson also had the IRB constitution on his side since it specifically forbade the Supreme Council initiating a rising without first having the support of a majority of the Irish people. Hobson's vision then reflected the man himself, cautious and evolutionary, confident that time was on his side. However, Clarke and MacDermott were impatient, romantic gamblers, fearful that time might soon run out if Redmond began accommodating a Home Rule Ireland comfortably and permanently inside the British Empire. They were convinced that only quick decisive action could save the separatist ideal of complete separation from England and saw in Hobson a defeatist who lacked the appetite for war, someone whose policy amounted to postponing revolution indefinitely. And whereas Hobson's approach was inclusive, seeking a broad nationalist coalition, Clarke and MacDermott were elitists, certain that they alone could realise Ireland's destiny. Unwilling to share power, they had a compulsive need to control any organisation within their orbit; they drove out of the IRB anyone opposed to their course of action. Hobson, in turn, regarded them as 'narrow partisans, inclined to distrust anybody who was not a member of our small organisation. They were very suspicious of my co-operation with men like MacNeill who belonged intellectually and socially to a different world'.[103]

Hoping to finish Hobson off completely, Clarke had got Devoy to dismiss him as the *Gaelic American*'s Irish correspondent, depriving Hobson of the paltry $10 a month salary that was his only regular income. Tom probably hoped that unemployment would force him out of Dublin, but at the least Hobson's resignation from the Supreme Council and *Irish Freedom* seemed proof that the danger had passed. It was 'Bulmer, R.I.P.'[104] Clarke proclaimed:

His connection with the paper completely severed – the friendship of all his old colleagues gone too. He will be before long an outcast. Even his standing on the Provisional Committee will be a more or less impossible one. 'Tis a great pity. He with his great ability and in some respects he has ability in greater measure than any one in Ireland. But it is some satisfaction to know that in spite of all his ability and popularity he was promptly put in his place when he showed the cloven hoof.[105]

Having now demonised Hobson, Clarke never spoke to him again.

But Hobson refused to be cast into darkness. Despite fearing that financial hardship would drive him out of politics and possibly Ireland itself, he somehow scraped up enough money to stay in the capital. The Teeling circle then reaffirmed Hobson's leadership, the Dublin Centres Board re-elected him chairman and the Leinster Board vainly implored Hobson to continue representing it on the Supreme Council. So he remained the most powerful IRB official in Dublin and after regaining his self-assurance, Hobson was determined to frustrate Clarke and MacDermott's ambitions. In fact the struggle had just begun. Far from delivering a knock-out blow, Tom had landed himself in a war of attrition. And though Clarke had sworn never to set eyes on Hobson again, MacDermott was not so lucky since he still encountered Hobson's brooding presence regularly at Volunteer headquarters. Even Tom did not feel powerful enough to force Hobson out from his post as Secretary of the Volunteers. One Supreme Council member recalled that 'Clarke was insistent that the Volunteers should be made the nucleus of a fighting force no matter who controlled them, and he was more inclined to let Hobson have his way for the time being'.[106]

The events of June 1914 had shredded Clarke's nerves. He told Devoy that they had left him

feeling very much run down, over work and worriment is leaving its mark on me and I am feeling it within myself. But I must peg away. Flynn [i.e Sean MacDermott] is exactly in the same class and P. Cove [i.e P.S. O'Hegarty] looks even worse. Denny McCullough has been ordered away by the doctor, he is threatened with consumption. Magnificent workers are these young men.[107]

Tom also reproached himself for lowering his guard with Hobson: 'He and I had been more intimate than any other two men in this town so you can judge of the feeling against him in other directions when you find me speak as I do. It has been a terrible stab to me'. These strains further weakened Tom's already damaged constitution: 'Old age appears to be creeping on me. Most of the time I feel "moidered" and can't cope with all the work that is crying out to be attended on my doorstep'. Soon Clarke resembled a man in his late seventies; one glance in the mirror was enough to confirm he really was in a race against time.

Yet on 28 June 1914 things suddenly began going Tom's way. In the Bosnian town of Sarajevo, Serbian nationalists assassinated Archduke Franz Ferdinand, heir to the Austro-Hungarian throne, a murder that gave Vienna the pretext to crush its enemy, Serbia. A great international crisis was now in the making, as MacDermott realised next day when a friend read him the newspaper headlines:

> 'Give me that' said Seán excitedly. As he read the few lines his piercing eyes seemed to dart from their sockets. Holding the paper in his left hand, staring at me intently he smacked the paper with the upturned right hand (this was the usual method of emphasis for him) and addressed me 'Look out, Gearóid this is no joke for us. We're in for it now. Austria will move against those fellows (I didn't know who the fellows were), Russia will back those fellows up, Germany and Italy will back Austria, France will take on Germany. You'll have a European war. England will join and that will be our time to strike.[108]

But the full danger of war remained mostly hidden from the European public because of Vienna's leisurely diplomacy. After securing Berlin's unequivocal support on 6 July for drastic action, it waited until 23 July before presenting an ultimatum to Serbia, one designed to finish it as an independent state.

So during July 1914 Ireland continued to dominate British politics, obsessing cabinet, parliament, political parties, newspapers and the general public. As the Third Home Rule Bill entered its final stages, Asquith gambled on a last throw of the dice by summoning an all-party conference at Buckingham Palace. From 21 to 24 July, Asquith, Bonar Law, Redmond and Carson tried for a settlement, but the negotiations finally collapsed with the differences as wide as ever. By now many nationalists were alarmed at the UVF's military superiority. One Ulster Unionist leader warned that:

> If war did break out it would probably be a war of extermination. We have the Nationalists sandwiched between our forces and they have only a few old guns to rely on. They could not possibly have a chance. Our men are well armed and guns and ammunition are constantly being run into Ulster. We have the province in the hollow of our hands.[109]

For some months a plan had existed to arm the Irish Volunteers, though surprisingly it belonged not to the IRB or even the Provisional Committee but a group of Anglo-Irish Protestants sympathetic to Home Rule.[110] They included Casement, Alice Stopford Green (the widow of the famous historian, John Richard Green) and George Fitzhardinge Berkeley, an Oxford graduate and former British Army officer. Another was Erskine Childers. Raised in Co. Wicklow he had been educated at Cambridge, fought on the British side in the Boer War and written a classic espionage novel, *The Riddle of the Sands*. Despite their Irish roots, the conspirators' privileged background and London addresses would have aroused in Clarke the deepest antipathy and suspicion – had he known from the start about their involvement. On 8 May 1914, they decided to purchase arms on the Continent and run them into Ireland, even though there was only enough funding for 1500 rifles, let alone to charter a ship. Instead they decided to smuggle the weapons into Ireland in two yachts that would land at different Irish ports. In June 1914 Casement brought Hobson into the scheme by asking him to organise a Volunteer reception party that would unload weapons from Erskine Childers' yacht, the *Asgard*. Seeking a spectacular propaganda success that would boost Volunteer funds, Hobson opted for a daylight operation on Sunday 26 July when he planned that hundreds of Volunteers would converge on Howth, 8 miles north of Dublin. During July Hobson organised a series of uneventful Sunday Volunteer parades that bored watching police and deceived the British authorities about his real intentions. And to stop his plans leaking, Hobson revealed them only to a small inner circle that included MacNeill and Casement. Not even IRB members of the Provisional Committee like Pearse and Béaslaí were told. But Clarke and MacDermott did eventually learn about them, possibly from Cathal Brugha, Vice-Commandant of Dublin's Fourth Battalion and who belonged to the IRB's Teeling centre. Bulmer Hobson had ordered Brugha to have twenty IRB men in Howth on 26 July, ready to unload the *Asgard*'s rifles immediately.

A gunrunning that would arm the Irish Volunteers – an essential precondition for a rising – was a dream come true for Clarke and he was never going to tolerate Hobson excluding him and MacDermott from the operation. Their priorities were to land the weapons safely, distribute them to the people who would use them most effectively and ensure that the operation went as peacefully as possible Whereas at Larne in April the Ulster Volunteers had been ready to use force against police and soldiers in order to secure the *Clyde Valley*'s rifles and ammunition, Clarke and MacDermott knew that if troops from British army barracks in Dublin were used to confiscate weapons at Howth they could easily overwhelm the Irish Volunteers. And if a shoot-out occurred, another attempt at gunrunning would be virtually impossible. Tom therefore was determined to impose restraint on IRB members at Howth and rein in the hotheads. The most he was prepared to sanction was the use of wooden batons to deter police intervention and for a month before the *Asgard*'s arrival, 200 were manufactured in the cellar of Sean Tobin, Tom's Supreme Council colleague who lived in Hardwicke Street.[111] Since MacDermott's disability prevented him marching to Howth, he and Clarke intended acting as motorised scouts during the afternoon when they expected Volunteers would be returning to Dublin with the weapons. Travelling ahead in a taxi, Tom and Seán would look out for any police and army roadblocks.

At noon on 26 July, Hobson led 800 Dublin Volunteers and 100 Fianna into Howth just as the *Asgard* sailed into harbour. Within half an hour, 900 rifles had been unloaded and distributed among the Volunteers, though not the bullets since Hobson was nervous about putting these in the hands of raw recruits. Instead he had the cases of ammunition sent ahead separately in cars while the Volunteers left Howth immediately in pouring rain. Learning about these events, Assistant Commissioner David Harrel of the Dublin Metropolitan Police on his own initiative ordered out police units and two companies of the King's Own Scottish Borderers. Some travelled to Howth by tram along Amiens Street where Tom and Seán were having lunch, prompting them to leave hurriedly in a taxi. Soon afterwards at Raheny village, five and a half miles from Howth, they encountered the returning Volunteers. One of them noticed 'Tom Clarke, who stood and watched the armed men pass. It was a great day for him'. Clarke and MacDermott followed the column for a couple of miles and near Clontarf they encountered MacNeill who asked to travel with them in their taxi as they scouted the approaches to Dublin. Despite his capitulation to Redmond's ultimatum, Tom and Seán did not consider MacNeill *persona non grata*, just Hobson's dupe, and their plans required him to become their dupe. After the taxi drove unimpeded to Nelson's Pillar, MacNeill caught the train for Ulster where he had a speaking engagement. That MacNeill would even consider leaving Dublin for a meeting a hundred miles away just after many Volunteers had defied the Arms Proclamation but had not yet reached safety, must have convinced Clarke and MacDermott that this man could not be taken seriously.

After returning to Clontarf, Clarke and MacDermott twice filled their taxi with rifles hidden under a blanket and drove with them to Amiens Street. But on a third trip they encountered Harrel and a large force of police and soldiers blocking the main Howth road. And when the Volunteers arrived, there was a chaotic confrontation in which some policemen obeyed Harrel's order to seize rifles from the Volunteers. A few Volunteers fired handguns at the troops, though a tragedy was averted by the army commander's mistaken belief that the shots had come from a nearby crowd. In the confusion, Hobson ordered Volunteers to disperse across fields and make their way home, enabling Tom and Seán to collect more weapons and make a final taxi run to Clarke's Amiens Street house where a large arms cache now lay hidden. At Clontarf a dazed Harrel had ordered the soldiers back to the Royal Barracks and by early evening they were on Bachelor's Walk in the city centre being followed by 600 stone-throwing civilians. Finally, Major Haig ordered thirty soldiers to form a protective cordon and raised his sword to attract the crowd's attention, intending to warn it to disperse. But before he did so, Haig lowered his sword, a gesture that some troops believed was an order to fire. Decades later, however, the only surviving British officer from the incident, Major-General 'Tiger' Miles, gave another explanation, blaming 'the noise, confusion and great provocation after suffering many casualties from stones thrown by the mob. Persons in the mob were heard shouting "Fire", "why don't you fire" etc and in the babel this may have caused the first man to fire'.[112] Successive volleys wounded dozens and killed three people: Patrick Quinn, a 46-year-old coal porter, James Brennan, a 17-year-old messenger, and a 50-year-old housewife, Mary Duffy, who had a son and a nephew in the Royal Dublin Fusiliers. Nationalist Ireland exploded and accused Haig's men of deliberately massacring three innocent demonstrators, an outrage compounded by the fact that on the previous day the British Army had allowed over 4,000 armed Ulster Volunteers to march unhindered through Belfast city centre. Next day Tom travelled to Limerick openly carrying a Howth rifle. Madge Daly recalled him walking 'like a soldier from the train to our house in Barrington Street carrying the gun on his shoulder. I could see the police and G men at the station staring with astonishment, such a sight had not been seen for ages, but they did not know what to do'.[113] After Tom presented the rifle to Uncle John, the two men talked into Tuesday's early morning hours before Tom returned to Dublin for the Bachelor's Walk funerals. As he travelled back, Austria-Hungary declared war on Serbia.

Hobson got the credit for devising and directing the Howth operation and his organising ability must have grudgingly impressed even Clarke and MacDermott and taught them valuable lessons. By concentrating information in his own hands, Hobson ensured that he alone had the full picture while keeping ordinary Volunteers in the dark until the last moment. Moreover, his unexpected daring and sense of theatre had caught the popular imagination and achieved a great propaganda coup for the Volunteers. Perhaps surprisingly, Hobson had also demonstrated the cunning of a natural conspirator, using routine Volunteer parades to conceal his real intentions and completely deceive the British authorities. Finally Howth – and Larne – had apparently shown the ease with which arms vessels could evade the Royal Navy and cross the North Sea before rendezvousing like clockwork with Volunteers waiting on the Irish coast. But in time Tom would realise to his cost that he had misread this particular lesson.

On Wednesday 29 July, the Austro-Hungarian army bombarded the Serbian capital Belgrade and made a continental war almost inevitable. But Dubliners were thinking only about three coffins that were lying in St Mary's Pro-Cathedral close to O'Connell Street. During a Requiem Mass for the Bachelor's Walk victims, thousands of people stood outside, including shopkeepers like Clarke who had closed for the day. Afterwards mourners filed continuously past the bodies until late afternoon when the cortège finally began its two-and-a-half mile journey to the necropolis of Glasnevin Cemetery.[114] Headed by forty priests and a body of armed Volunteers, this was the capital's largest funeral procession in a generation. Consisting of relatives of the deceased, the Lord Mayor, councillors, politicians, trade unionists and members of cultural and sporting organisations, it took seventy minutes to pass any given point. Turning left into O'Connell Street, the marchers passed the General Post Office (GPO) with Volunteers clearing a path through dense crowds. There was a brief halt at the fatal scene on Bachelor's Walk where a newspaper reported 'the assembled thousands became overwhelmed with grief'.[115] Here too the procession passed film cameramen whose newsreels would soon affect cinema audiences throughout Ireland. Along Capel, Bolton and Dorset Streets, Irish flags flew from houses painted with the letters R.I.P., while spectators thronged the sidewalks, stood at windows and on balconies or crammed into the numerous cars, taxis and delivery vans stationed at road junctions. Generally the respectful silence was broken only by sobbing and solemn band music or the bell of St Joseph's church in Berkeley Road that tolled when the first Volunteers came into sight.

At 8 p.m., two and a half hours after leaving the Cathedral, the cortège finally entered a crowded Glasnevin where Provisional Committee members like MacNeill, The O'Rahilly and Éamonn Ceannt, greeted the hearses. An honour party of Volunteers then saluted priests accompanying the coffins into the mortuary chapel for a burial service. Afterwards, more Volunteers formed circles around the graves as the coffins were lowered in, but although a rifle party stood nearby, it did not fire a volley. At last in the gathering dusk the cemetery emptied of mourners and Volunteers set out on their return journey. A very different mood prevailed now as a large, raucous crowd followed them, whistling and singing 'A Nation Once Again', while thousands of spectators cheered and clapped. At the Volunteer offices in Great Brunswick Street (now Pearse Street), the riflemen were dismissed while other sections marched on to different destinations.

It was the Volunteers' Provisional Committee's more conservative members that organised the Bachelor's Walk funerals. But Dublin's greatest outpouring of grief since Parnell's death had provided Clarke and the IRB with the template for a nationalist 'state funeral'. Timing the burials for early evening meant the streets were filled with people just finished work and provincials coming to the city especially for this occasion. The planners had also created a microcosm of the nation by involving in the funeral men, women, children, workers, businessmen, farmers, priests, Volunteers, politicians and representatives from many popular organisations. And the trappings of a state funeral were everywhere – coffins lying in state, a guard of honour, the religious service in a great church, civic dignitaries, and uniformed men leading the cortège through a mourning multitude. But this had also been a vast political protest, not yet against the fact of British rule in Ireland but certainly its perceived cruelties and injustices. Embodying the mourners' anger and defiance were armed Volunteers carrying Howth rifles, their impressive discipline hinting at an army in the making. And the slogan 'Remember Bachelor's Walk' had already entered the political lexicon. To contemporaries it seemed unlikely that the Bachelor's Walk funerals could be surpassed as a spectacle, yet exactly a year later Clarke would set himself that very task.

One day after the funerals, Russia stood by its Serbian ally and ordered general mobilisation. Germany responded on 1 August by declaring war on Russia and two days later on France. When German armies then violated Belgian neutrality in order to attack France, Asquith's government declared war on 4 August 1914, embroiling England in the European conflict that Tom believed was necessary for an Irish rising to succeed. The climactic phase of Clarke's long revolutionary career had begun.

NOTES

1   Clarke Papers, Tom to Kathleen, 4 January 1908, NLI MS 49,351/1/6.
2   Clarke Papers, Tom to Kathleen, 6 January 1908, NLI MS 49,351/1/6.
3   Clarke Papers, Tom to Kathleen, 8 January 1908, NLI MS 49,351/1/6.
4   Clarke Papers, Tom to Kathleen, Undated February 1908, NLI MS 49,351/1/6.

5   Clarke Papers, Tom to Kathleen, 30 January 1908, NLI MS 49,351/1/6.

6   Clarke Papers, Tom to Kathleen, Undated January 1908, NLI MS 49,351/1/6.

7   Ibid.

8   Ibid.

9   Ibid.

10   Clarke Papers, Tom to Kathleen, 14 February 1908, NLI MS 49,351/1/6.

11   Clarke Papers, Tom to Kathleen, 14 April 1908, NLI MS 49,351/1/6.

12   Clarke Papers, Tom to Kathleen, April 1908, NLI MS 49,351/1/6.

13   Clarke Papers, Tom to Kathleen, April 1908, NLI MS 49,351/1/6.

14   Clarke Papers, Tom to Kathleen, April 1908, NLI MS 49,351/1/6.

15   Clarke Papers, Tom to Kathleen, 17 April 1908, NLI MS 49,351/1/6.

16   Clarke Papers, Tom to James Reidy, 3 January 1909, NLI MS 49,353.

17   Ibid.

18   P.S. O'Hegarty, 'Recollections of the IRB', NLI MS 36,210. Hereafter, O'Hegarty, 'Recollections of the IRB'.

19   Ibid.

20   Clarke Papers, Tom to James Reidy, 3 January 1909, NLI MS 49,353V. For Patrick McCartan's background, see P. McCartan, BMH WS 766.

21   P. McCartan in a letter of 31 March 1960 to Patrick Martin for a proposed life of Clarke, NLI MS 31,696.

22   Béaslaí, 'My Friend Tom Clarke', Béaslaí Papers, NLI MS 33,935(3). I am grateful to Liam Andres for translating this memoir from Irish into English.

23   Ibid.

24   Min Ryan (Mrs Richard Mulcahy), BMH WS 399.

25   Kathleen Clarke, *Revolutionary Woman*, pp. 40–1.

26   For Diarmuid Lynch's background, see the start he made to his autobiography, NLI MS 11,127.

27   For O'Hegarty, see BMH WS 26 and Keiron Curtis, *P S O'Hegarty 1879–1955* (London: Anthem, 2012).

28   P.S. O'Hegarty, 'Recollections of the IRB'.

29   Ibid.

30   Ibid.

31   Ibid.

32   Ibid.

33   Ibid.

34   Ibid.

35   Ibid.

36   P.S. O'Hegarty, 'Recollection of the IRB'.

37   Francis Jones, *History of the Sinn Féin Movement and the Irish Rebellion of 1916*, pp. 143–4.

38   Tom Clarke to John Daly, 28 June 1910, Clarke Papers, NLI MS 49,531/1/5.

39   O'Hegarty, 'Recollections of the IRB'.

40   Manuscript notes by Patrick McCartan on Louis Le Roux's biography of Thomas Clarke, NLI MS 44,683.

41   P.S. O'Hegarty, 'Recollections of the IRB'.

42   Manuscript notes by Patrick McCartan on Louis Le Roux's biography of Thomas Clarke, NLI MS 44,683.

43   Ibid. See also McCartan's account of the meeting in Pat McCartan, BMH WS 766.

44 Manuscript notes by Patrick McCartan on Louis Le Roux's biography of Thomas Clarke, NLI MS 44,683.

45 Ibid.

46 Clarke Papers, Tom to John Daly, June 1911, NLI MS 49,531/1/5.

47 Kathleen Clarke, *Revolutionary Woman*, p. 47.

48 Manuscript notes by Patrick McCartan on Louis Le Roux's biography of Thomas Clarke, NLI MS 44,683.

49 P. McCartan, a letter of 10 May 1960 to Patrick Martin for a proposed life of Clarke, NLI MS 31,696.

50 O'Hegarty, 'Recollections of the IRB'. See also P.S. O'Hegarty, BMH WS 26.

51 ibid.

52 Manuscript notes by Patrick McCartan on Louis Le Roux's biography of Thomas Clarke, NLI MS 44,683.

53 O'Hegarty, 'Recollections of the IRB'.

54 Ibid.

55 Manuscript notes by Patrick McCartan on Louis Le Roux's biography of Thomas Clarke, NLI MS 44,683.

56 Denis McCullough, BMH WS 915.

57 Piaras Béaslaí, 'My Friend Tom Clarke'. Béaslaí Papers, NLI MS 33,935(3).

58 Louis Le Roux, *Tom Clarke and the Irish Freedom Movement*, p. 110.

59 John Devoy, *Recollections of an Irish Rebel*, p. 392.

60 Clarke to James Reidy, 3 January 1909. Gerard MacAtasney, *Tom Clarke: Life, Liberty, Revolution*, p. 236.

61 Typescript draft of the Memoirs of Madge Daly. University of Limerick, Special Collections, Daly Papers, File 77. Hereafter, 'The Memoirs of Madge Daly'.

62 Kathleen Clarke, *Revolutionary Woman*, p. 41.

63 Ibid., p. 46.

64 O'Hegarty, 'Recollections of the IRB'.

65 *Cavan-Celt*, 24 May 1913.

66 *Irish News*, 7 November 1913.

67 Seán T. O'Kelly in his account of the foundation of the Irish Volunteers in F.X. Martin (ed.), *The Irish Volunteers 1913–1915*, p. 87.

68 Hobson, *A History of the Irish Volunteers*, p. 16.

69 Hobson, *Ireland: Yesterday and Tomorrow*, p. 43.

70 F.X. Martin, *The Irish Volunteers 1913–1915*, pp. 24–5. Béaslaí, *Irish Independent*, 6 January 1953.

71 Béaslaí, *Irish Independent*, 6 January 1953.

72 For MacNeill, see Michael Tierney, *Eoin MacNeill: Scholar and Man of Action, 1867–1945*.

73 Clarke to McGarrity, 8 December 1913, NLI MS 33,364.

74 Kathleen Clarke, *Revolutionary Woman*, p. 44.

75 Béaslaí, *Irish Independent*, 5 January 1953.

76 *Irish Freedom*, May and June 1914.

77 Devoy, *Recollections of an Irish Rebel*, p. 394.

78 Ibid., p. 395.

79 Ibid.

80 Clarke to John Daly, 29 April 1914, Daly Papers, University of Limerick.

81 Béaslaí, *Irish Independent*, 8 January 1953.

82 Clarke to Devoy, 23 June 1914, in Material for a proposed biography of Tom Clarke compiled by P.J. Madden, NLI MS 31,696.

83 Béaslaí, *Irish Independent*, 6 January 1953.

84 Casement to Devoy, 21 July 1914, *Recollections of an Irish Rebel*, pp. 410–11.

85 Béaslaí, *Irish Independent*, 8 January 1953.

86 Alfred O'Rahilly, *The Secret History of the Irish Volunteers*, p. 8.

87 Hobson, *Ireland: Yesterday and Tomorrow*, p. 50.

88 Clarke to Devoy, 23 June 1914, in Material for a proposed biography of Tom Clarke compiled by P.J. Madden, NLI MS 31,696.

89 Ibid.

90 The Memoirs of Eoin MacNeill, BMH Collected Documents no. 7.

91 Béaslaí, *Irish Independent*, 6 January 1953.

92 Ibid.

93 Seán McGarry, BMH WS 368.

94 'The Memoirs of Madge Daly'.

95 Ibid.

96 Clarke to Devoy, 23 June 1914, in Material for a proposed biography of Tom Clarke compiled by P.J. Madden, NLI MS 31,696.

97 Clarke to Devoy, 7 July 1914, NLI MS 17,609(9).

98 Ibid.

99 Piaras Béaslaí who was present at the meeting recorded the date and location in his diary. *Irish Independent*, 8 January 1953.

100 Hobson, *Ireland: Yesterday and Tomorrow*, pp. 52–3.

101 O'Hegarty, 'Recollections of the IRB'.

102 Hobson, *Ireland: Yesterday and Tomorrow*, p. 53.

103 Hobson, *Ireland: Yesterday and Tomorrow*, p. 53. In Material for a proposed biography of Tom Clarke compiled by P.J. Madden, NLI MS 31,696.

104 Clarke to Devoy, 23 June 1914, in Material for a proposed biography of Tom Clarke compiled by P.J. Madden, NLI MS 31,696.

105 Clarke to Devoy, 7 July 1914, NLI MS 17,609(9).

106 Richard Connolly, BMH WS 523.

107 Clarke to Devoy, 3 June 1914, William O'Brian and Desmond Ryan (eds.), *Devoy's Post Bag*, vol. 2, p. 448.

108 Lieutenant-General Gearóid O'Sullivan, 'Memoirs of the Wonderful Years', BMH, Collected Documents no. 90.

109 *Derry Journal*, 6 July 1914.

110 For the origins of the Howth gunrunning, see F.X. Martin, *The Howth Gun-Running 1914*.
For Hobson's organisation of the Howth route march, see BMH WS 55.

111 Seán T. O'Kelly, BMH WS 1765.

112 Volunteer Harry Nicholls, *Irish Times*, 29 July 1961.

113 In a letter written on 13 March 1955, Major-General E.J. (Tiger) Miles recalled the Bachelor's Walk affair. In 1914 he was a lieutenant in the King's Own Scottish Borderers. The letter is in the King's Own Scottish Borderers Museum, The Barracks, Berwick-on-Tweed.

114 'The Memoirs of Madge Daly'.

115 For the funerals of the Bachelor's Walk victims, see the accounts in the *Freeman's Journal* and the *Irish Independent*, 30 July 1914.

An early photograph of Tom Clarke.

Maria Clarke, Tom's favourite sibling.

An 1883 photograph of Clarke, taken in America just before he left on his bombing mission to England. Tom's clothes strongly suggest the English businessman whose guise he had adopted for the mission.

John Daly. He inspired Clarke's
revolutionary career.

John Denvoy, the American Clan
leader who became a major influence
on Clarke's life.

Jeremiah O'Donovan Rossa,
the prominent American Fenian who in
life and death greatly influenced Clarke.

Alexander Sullivan, the American
Clan leader who approved a
bombing campaign in England.

The police photograph of Clarke taken soon after his capture in 1883.

William Norman.

Bernard Gallagher.

Alfred Whitehead.

Henry Dalton.

John Curtin.

Thomas Gallagher.

THE ILLUSTRATED LONDON NEWS

REGISTERED AT THE GENERAL POST-OFFICE FOR TRANSMISSION ABROAD.

No. 2295.—VOL. LXXXII.   SATURDAY, APRIL 14, 1883.   WITH TWO SUPPLEMENTS   SIXPENCE. By Post, 6½d.

1. House and Shop occupied by Whitehead.
2. Detective-Sergeant Richard Price.
3. The Scullery, used as a Laboratory.
4. Kitchen behind the Shop.
5. Carboy containing 170 lb. of Nitro-Glycerine.
6. Vat containing explosive liquid discovered in the cellar.

THE FENIAN DYNAMITE PLOT IN ENGLAND: THE SECRET FACTORY OF NITRO-GLYCERINE IN LEDSAM-STREET, BIRMINGHAM.

A tabloid press depiction of the Gallagher Gang's bombing mission.

The front entrance of St Mary's
Prison, Chatham.

A youthful Kathleen Daly
who became Tom's wife.

Clarke's first shop in Dublin at 55 Amiens Street.

Clarke standing in front of his second and larger shop in Parnell Street that became the centre of his political operation.

Bulmer Hobson, a close friend of Clarke who became his bitter enemy.

Eoin MacNeill, President of the Irish Volunteers.

IRISH REBELLION, MAY 1916

P. H. PEARSE.
Commandant-General of the Army of the Irish Republic),
Executed May 3rd, 1916.
One of the signatories of the "Irish Republic Proclamation."

Patrick Pearse, the schoolmaster who became President of the Irish Republic during Easter Week.

James Connolly, the socialist revolutionary who committed his Citizen Army to the Easter Rising.

The body of O'Donovan Rossa lying in Dublin City Hall with an honour guard of Irish Volunteers. The statue is that of the great nationalist leader Daniel O'Connell.

Clarke, seated, with O'Donovan Rossa's widow Molly and daughter Margaret. Fr O'Flanagan is standing.

Patrick Pearse is standing beside Fr O'Flanagan. The fourth person to the right of Pearse in side profile has been identified as Tom Clarke.

John Daly, Tom Clarke and
Seán MacDermott in 1915.

WOODTOWN PARK,
RATHFARNHAM,
CO. DUBLIN.

22 apl 1916

Volunteers completely
deceived. All orders for
tomorrow Sunday are
entirely cancelled.
Eoin MacNeill

MacNeill's countermand order
which plunged Clarke's plans for
the Rising into crisis.

The ruins of the GPO and surrounding area after the Rising. This aerial shot was taken by a photographer positioned on top of Nelson's Pillar in O'Connell Street.

General Maxwell who suppressed the Rising and approved Clarke's execution.

The widowed Kathleen Clarke and her three children. The eldest son John Daly is standing between Kathleen and Thomas Junior. The youngest son Emmet is seated.

5

On the Road to Revolution, Part One: August 1914–September 1915

In August 1914 most Europeans shared Kaiser Wilhelm's confidence that after a few decisive battles the soldiers would return home before the leaves fall from the trees. Instead the conflict quickly became a total war of attrition, one that was to shatter mighty empires, shred great armies, topple governments and allow obscure revolutionaries from Moscow to Dublin to make real their hitherto fanciful dreams.

In Ireland the war initially produced a surging pro-British sentiment and emotional scenes as almost 40,000 troops embarked immediately for the continent. Cheering crowds sang 'God Save the King', bands played patriotic tunes and Union Jacks flew from public buildings and private houses, turning the capital red, white and blue. Dubliners even forgave the King's Own Scottish Borderers for Bachelor's Walk by giving them a stirring send-off as they marched to the docks. While loyalists could be relied on for a fervent display, on this occasion there seemed no doubt that most Dubliners were with the soldiers. When Piaras Béaslaí returned to the city from the west in late August, it seemed to him as if collective amnesia had descended upon its population: 'Following the shooting down of Dublin citizens by British soldiers only four weeks before, the change was almost bewildering'.[1] Kathleen Clarke was similarly confused:

One morning I put my head out of the window in a top room to see them passing, feeling sad that so many of them were Irish, going as I thought to be slaughtered for England. A soldier on top of a gun-wagon looked up and saw me, and blew a kiss. I nearly fell out of the window with rage. If I had had a brush or any other weapon I would have thrown it at him. The only weapon I had was my tongue. He could not hear what it said, so I stuck it out at him, and then was shocked at the vulgarity I had been guilty of.[2]

She was also taken aback by scenes of 'mass hysteria' in the city centre where crowds queued outside recruiting offices and multitudes wearing Union Jack badges and emblems blew Union Jack coloured sirens. Encouraged by Tom, Kathleen made hundreds of orange, white and green ribbon badges that flew off the shelves to a hardcore republican clientele. But many more women raised funds for the war effort, knitted socks and made bandages for Irish and British soldiers.

Overwhelmingly, nationalists blamed Germany for the war and believed that its victory would finish off Home Rule forever and probably result in Ireland's assimilation into a greater Reich. They also had a historical affinity with Britain's ally France and felt sympathy for Catholic Belgium where the German army was reported to be committing unspeakable atrocities. Speaking in the House of Commons on 3 August, Redmond captured the popular mood by declaring that the British government could safely leave Ireland's defence to the Irish and Ulster Volunteers. He probably hoped such loyalty would convince British public opinion that the Home Rule Bill – which became law six weeks later – should be rapidly implemented once the war ended. Although Redmond's action annoyed some Irish Volunteers and Pearse attributed it to 'either madness or treachery',[3] he had the strong support of MacNeill, the Catholic Church and almost every newspaper.

Republicans also welcomed the war but, of course, for very different reasons. According to Seán T. O'Kelly, they regarded it as 'the opportunity for which they had hoped and prayed for so long'.[4] Clarke indeed saw it as a once-in-a-lifetime opportunity, one that he was determined not to squander. MacDermott also vowed that 'if this thing passes without a fight I don't want to live. And Tom feels the same'.[5] Losing no time, Clarke and MacDermott sponsored and carried a motion at the Supreme Council's August meeting committing the IRB to an insurrection before the war's end; otherwise, Tom warned Council members, they were 'damned for posterity'.[6] This flushed out two dissenters, the Scottish representative Mulholland and Seamus Deakin, the Council President. From that moment onwards, Clarke regarded them as marked men whom he was determined to drive out not just from the Supreme Council but from the IRB altogether. P.S. O'Hegarty regarded Mulholland as a 'simple, genuine lifelong Fenian'[7] whose sole ambition was to keep the republican flame alive and pass it on to his sons. A former ally of Allan and O'Hanlon, he had somehow survived Clarke's clear-out of the old regime, but his time was now up. Soon afterwards Tom sent Seán T. O'Kelly to Glasgow, where he located Mulholland in the iron foundry where he worked, secured his resignation from both the Supreme Council and the IRB, and made him swear an oath of secrecy never to divulge anything about the Council's deliberations. His expulsion was all done painlessly and without protest. Mulholland was old and not up for a fight, especially as he had seen how futile the old gang's resistance had been. Probably he was glad just to be out of it. Taking his fall with good grace, Mulholland shook O'Kelly's hand as they parted.[8] But it had been an extraordinarily ruthless and presumptuous act on Clarke's part, one that had not been sanctioned by the Supreme Council's President, Deakin – Tom's next target – and which violated the IRB's own constitution. Such considerations never bothered Clarke, whose only guiding principle was revolutionary necessity. Mulholland stood in the way of a rising and he had to go. Deakin, a Protestant who managed a chemist shop in O'Connell Street, had been worried for years about the possibility of a rebellion causing widespread death among civilians and great destruction to property. When the IRB's Teeling circle had debated a rising, Deakin warned presciently of British artillery devastating Dublin in response to street fighting and rebels occupying public buildings.[9] Having been present at the first meetings that established the Provisional Committee of the Irish Volunteers, he had then dropped out for 'business reasons'. But unlike Mulholland, Deakin, the Council President and a Dubliner who represented Leinster, could not just be strong-armed out of the IRB. Instead, Tom subtly played on his fears and got him to walk away voluntarily. Soon after war started, a Post Office contact gave Clarke an updated list of suspects whose correspondence the British government wanted carefully monitored. On it were most members of the Supreme Council including Deakin – a fact that Tom immediately drew to his attention. Soon afterwards Deakin was gone not only from the IRB but from Sinn Féin and the Irish Volunteers.[10] His disappearance mystified most people including Denis McCullough, who claimed that Deakin 'simply cleared out, as far as I know, without apology or explanation'.[11] MacDermott simply blamed his defection on 'cold feet'.[12] For Clarke it was good riddance to two men, Mulholland and Deakin, who threatened his revolutionary ambitions; in his army there was no room for shirkers or conscientious objectors and no tolerance of passive resistance or mutiny.

From early on Clarke initiated military preparations for a rising. At Volunteer headquarters, an advisory committee of senior but unnamed officers began considering the implications of conflict between the Volunteers and the British Army. This committee's status was somewhat ambiguous. Although some members were in the IRB and reported directly to Clarke, others believed that the Provisional Committee had commissioned them to form defensive plans for a fight in the Dublin area in the event that the British introduced conscription or arrested Volunteer leaders. Diarmuid Lynch recalled Clarke's

dissatisfaction in November 1914 with aspects of the committee's report and
he warned Tom about the risks of relying on such an unwieldy group:

> To my mind the drafting of military plans for an insurrection was neces-
> sarily of a secret nature and should accordingly be entrusted to a much
> smaller committee; that the latter should in the course of their delibera-
> tions have the closest contact with the IRB Executive. I urged that the
> 'Advisory Committee' should be dissolved; it was allowed to lapse.[13]

Despite this tentative progress, Clarke found himself swimming against
a pro-British tidal wave that between 4 August 1914 and February 1915
carried over 50,000 Irish men into the British Army. Acknowledging that
his followers were 'only a handful',[14] Tom began reaching out to other
progressive nationalist and labour organisations like the Irish Volunteers, Sinn
Féin, the Citizen Army, and the Irish Transport and General Workers Union
(ITGWU). Coincidentally, James Connolly, the 36-year-old leader of both
the Citizen Army and the ITGWU, was doing the same. As a revolutionary
socialist, he had welcomed war as a wonderful opportunity to overthrow
British capitalism in Ireland, declaring in August 1914 that 'I will not miss this
chance'.[15] However, Connolly's prickly personality alienated many people
and he knew surprisingly few of the power players in Irish revolutionary
politics. His more affable assistant, William O'Brien, advised him 'that nothing
could be done without the cooperation of such men as Tom Clarke and Sean
MacDermott. He asked me if I could put him in touch with the right people,
and I undertook to do so'.[16] After O'Brien's friend Éamonn Ceannt inter-
ceded, Clarke arranged a conference for 9 September in the Gaelic League's
library at 25 Parnell Square, a discreet venue that was also Seán T. O'Kelly's
office. O'Kelly himself was there along with Joseph Plunkett, Patrick Pearse,
Major John McBride, Arthur Griffith, Thomas MacDonagh, Éamonn Ceannt,
Seán McGarry, Sean Tobin of the IRB's Supreme Council, Connolly and
O'Brien. In his opening speech as chairman, Clarke demanded a nationalist
crusade against the British war effort and a programme of action for achieving
Irish independence. Connolly argued emphatically for rebellion and securing
German military support. Everyone agreed to resist any British attempt to
enforce conscription or disarm the Irish Volunteers and to co-operate with
the Germans if they landed in Ireland – provided they only wanted to expel
the British and recognised Irish independence. But if the war was clearly
ending without any of these scenarios emerging, the participants would
organise an insurrection and claim a place at a subsequent peace conference.

Finally the meeting agreed to establish two committees, one that would contact Germany and another to campaign against the British war effort.[17] Nothing came of the first idea and the second proved short-lived. Although Connolly formed an Irish Neutrality League on 5 October with himself as president, it never really got off the ground, organising only a few lectures before British military restrictions closed it down. But significantly the conference had introduced Connolly to Clarke, who immediately recognised another natural leader.

Despite his Citizen Army having only 200 members, this uncompromising revolutionary also radiated a deadly seriousness and sense of mission. Born to a manure carter and a domestic servant in Edinburgh's Irish immigrant community, Connolly, like Tom, had clawed his way out of economic hardship and social deprivation. Having received little formal education, he had started working in a bakery at the age of 10 and later served for seven years in the British Army. Connolly then deserted and settled in Dublin where he steeped himself in the writings of Marx and Engels and became a revolutionary socialist activist. In 1903 he left for America ('the greatest mistake of my life'[18]), but seven years later returned to Ireland. From August 1914 a banner at Liberty Hall – the ITGWU's headquarters and Connolly's power base close to the city centre – proclaimed 'We Serve Neither King Nor Kaiser'. But like Clarke, he was really neutral for Germany. Sharing Tom's belief in a yellow peril, Connolly warned about a Russian army 'largely recruited from amongst millions of barbarians who have not yet felt the first softening of civilisation'.[19] Denouncing England for supposedly wanting to destroy its greatest industrial, commercial and naval rival, Connolly revelled in early German early victories that, he argued, strengthened both Germany's working class and revolutionary forces right across Europe.

Against all-pervasive pro-war propaganda and a press almost entirely closed to dissent, Clarke's only weapon was the monthly *Irish Freedom* after his attempt to establish a daily newspaper came to nothing. Indeed, the few opposition voices were soon fighting for survival. The Defence of the Realm Act had armed the political and military authorities with sweeping powers to censor and suppress newspapers and journals they deemed pacifist, injurious of national morale or helpful to the enemy. Soon they began harassing publications supposedly funded by 'German gold'. *Irish Freedom* was a prime target after its September 1914 headline proclaimed that 'Germany is not Ireland's enemy'. Instead the war was blamed on 'English jackals' out to destroy an industrial and naval rival. Furthermore, despite urging neutrality, *Irish Freedom* speculated on the benefits of a British defeat, discouraged recruiting and hinted at action in the near future to restore Irish freedom. By late November 1914, Dublin Castle had had enough. First it suppressed *Irish Freedom* and then *Irish Worker*, a militant trade union paper. Shortly afterwards *Sinn Féin* and *Éire-Ireland* folded voluntarily.[20]

Regulation of the press was just one facet of the state's greatly expanded power over political, social and economic life as the United Kingdom geared up for total war. Dauntingly for Clarke, this growth also vastly increased the disparity between British resources and those of the IRB and Irish Volunteers. With a battery of new controls, Dublin Castle could now intern citizens at will and confiscate their property and wealth. As a ticket-of-leave man, Tom was already vulnerable; one false move could return him to prison and ruin everything. Being IRB treasurer, he was also responsible for protecting IRB funds from seizure by British raiding parties. This war chest consisted mostly of gold coins that Clan na Gael had sent to the IRB for purchasing arms and Tom had secreted these in Uncle John's house in Limerick. But this building was now under police surveillance and so in August 1914, Tom built a safer hiding place underneath a brick arch in the cellar. He explained to Madge Daly 'that before the fight was over, in all possibility our house and the houses of all prominent republicans would be razed to the ground and if such happened the gold would be safe and could eventually be recovered'.[21]

Above all Clarke was concerned that the Irish Volunteers were being changed out of all recognition and escaping from the IRB's control. Redmond's conciliatory House of Commons speech had mistakenly convinced many Southern Unionists that the Volunteers now shared their pro-British sympathies and, according to Hobson, they 'flocked into the movement with a rush that was almost embarrassing. For a time we had as many members of the House of Lords as the Ulster Volunteers'.[22] Tom reviled this old Ascendancy class whose titles, military tradition and political outlook reminded him of a bygone age of privilege, one that differentiated them utterly from the first wave of Volunteers. Some newcomers presented their companies with Union Jacks, while others acquired influential positions on the headquarter's military staff and tried turning the Volunteers into a recruiting agency for the British Army. Incongruously, their influx had resulted in men prepared to sacrifice their lives for the British Empire training alongside comrades ready to die fighting against it. This ideological incoherence was anathema to Clarke and in the not-so-long run could only end in the Volunteers' fragmentation and possibly disintegration. Soon the sword that Tom envisaged wielding against England might slip from his hands.

Redmond also vexed Clarke by acting as if he were the real leader of the Volunteers, seemingly treating them more and more as uniformed auxiliaries of the Home Rule movement. But more immediately, Tom was concerned at Redmond's increasing influence over the Provisional Committee. The Home Rule nominees were led by John D. Nugent, a 45-year-old company director and a brilliant machine politician who regarded politics as war by other means and dissent as mutiny that must be crushed. He was also secretary of the Ancient Order of Hibernians and employed its strong-armed bruisers to assault Redmond's opponents. Now Nugent intended forcing the Provisional Committee into line as well by demanding its absolute loyalty to Redmond, a strategy that made peaceful co-existence on the Provisional Committee impossible even had Clarke and the IRB had wanted it. Nugent's objective was to drive out every opponent and doubter by employing against them his well-honed techniques of procedural haggling, verbal abuse and physical intimidation. Nobody was immune from attack, not even MacNeill or Hobson, who complained about Provisional Committee meetings being turned into a partisan battleground. It was a power struggle that could only end in victory or defeat. But while Clarke knew Nugent's intentions, there was little he could do to combat him. Redmond's nominees had a majority on the Committee and they operated as a disciplined unit, eliciting Hobson's reluctant admiration for its 'solidly machined vote',[23] one that overrode an IRB opposition which was already divided between the supporters of Clarke and Hobson.

During August and September 1914, IRB members on the Provisional Committee were joined in their opposition to Redmond's pro-British policy by some of the Volunteers' Dublin battalions and Laurence de Lacy, editor of the *Irish Volunteer* journal. But this coalition made little headway and Clarke faced the prospect of his IRB contingent walking away from the Provisional Committee rather than put up with being constantly harangued and vilified by Nugent's supporters. Longing to escape his tormentors, Pearse had almost given up in early August 1914 when he lamented his total ineffectiveness:

> I can never carry a single point. I am now scarcely allowed to speak. The moment I stand up, there are cried of 'put the question' etc.; after the last meeting I had half determined to resign, but have decided to stick on a little longer in the hope of being useful at a later stage.[24]

Pearse was especially frustrated by MacNeill's continuing support of Redmond and blamed him for 'bowing to the will of the Redmondites every time. He never makes a fight except when they assail his personal honour, when he bridles up at once. He is in a very delicate position, and he is weak, hopelessly weak. I knew that all along'.[25]

At the City Hall on Thursday 10 September 1914, these mounting tensions finally exploded at a full Provisional Committee meeting attended by over fifty people. An IRB member, Seamus O'Connor, recalled it as a 'very stormy'[26] affair. Although MacNeill was in the chair, John D. Nugent dominated proceedings and he was in sparkling form. Seemingly determined to drive out Redmond's enemies, his bloc vote first defeated resolutions from Pearse and Ceannt denouncing recruiting and conscription. Nugent's men then passed a motion repudiating the *Irish Volunteer* and withdrawing its official recognition before accusing both The O'Rahilly and Ceannt of embezzling Volunteer funds. Nugent then rounded on Pearse, calling him 'a lying contemptible cur'; Pearse retaliated by punching Nugent in the face. A brawl then erupted in which one Nugent supporter rabbit-punched Pearse from behind. Another – a Father O'Hare no less – waved a small automatic pistol at Ceannt and challenged him to draw his revolver. Ceannt simply smiled and urged O'Hare to keep quiet. Redmond's nominees might have been constitutional nationalists, but they could fight dirty as well. It was difficult to imagine this Provisional Committee ever meeting again and it never did, but not because of any decisive intervention by Clarke who seemed on the defensive and helpless. His adherents on the Provisional Committee had just had enough and according to O'Connor 'could no longer be identified with people like Nugent, Redmond and Devlin whose object was to betray the country'.[27]

Three days later the radicals assembled at the Gaelic League headquarters in Parnell Square. Although MacNeill could not attend, he had made it clear that he would support a break with Redmond. The meeting decided to expel Redmond's nominees from the Provisional Committee but not to go public until a further meeting at which MacNeill could approve a manifesto. But while this action was decisive, it was also a confession of weakness, because in the absence of some compelling issue of principle, it would be hard to justify to the Irish people splitting the Irish Volunteers. For Clarke this was the lowest point. At the last moment he was rescued by the most unlikely person – John Redmond himself. On 20 September 1914 at Woodenbridge, Co. Wicklow, Redmond urged an assembly of Irish Volunteers to serve 'not only in Ireland itself, but wherever the firing line extends, in defence of right, of freedom and religion in this war'. He might have acted out of gratitude for the Home Rule Bill having passed into law, but perhaps also because of the British Army's desperate need for troops in France where the Allied armies had their backs to the wall and Paris was in danger of falling. Although Redmond's closest colleagues, the press and most nationalists backed his new policy, a minority were disgusted, believing that in recommending Volunteers to don khaki he had finally crossed the line. Ironically, it was MacNeill and Hobson, both so instrumental in bringing Redmond's nominees on to the Provisional Committee, who spearheaded their ejection – a service that of course failed to win Tom's gratitude or, in Hobson's case, forgiveness A man not without vanity, MacNeill now realised his complete insignificance in Redmond's eyes and that if he had a future at all in the Volunteers, it was as a powerless figurehead. But he also believed that Redmond's dramatic policy shift violated the Volunteers' original aims and in language not usually associated with professors, MacNeill declared: 'I do not accept it as the destiny of Ireland, my mother country, to play the harlot to an alien power, and I do not envy the son of Ireland who takes upon himself the office of procurer'.[28] Hobson too thought Redmond's Woodenbridge speech made it inevitable that 'the time for a break had come',[29] but unlike in June, the Volunteers' high morale and more integrated organisation meant they could survive a split.

MacNeill had a justified reputation for procrastination, but occasionally in the midst of crisis he could surprise everyone by taking speedy and decisive action. A day after Redmond's Woodenbridge speech, he summoned about twenty members of the original Provisional Committee to a secret emergency meeting at the Gaelic League headquarters in Parnell Square. MacNeill arrived with a lengthy manifesto that he had composed and which amounted to both a declaration of independence from Redmond and war on him. Signed by everyone present, it strongly denounced Redmond, expelled his nominees and temporarily reconstituted the original Provisional Committee until a Volunteer convention on 25 November 1914 (the first anniversary of their inaugural meeting). Béaslaí recalled MacNeill remarking, 'Thank God. It will be a relief to be rid of those ruffians. His point of view had changed materially during the last few weeks'.[30] Soon afterwards, Clarke received a copy of the manifesto and he knew that after a mercifully brief detour down a blind alley, his revolutionary project was back on track.

The manifesto was not made public immediately but held back for dramatic impact to coincide with a great recruiting meeting in the Mansion House on 25 September which Redmond had invited Asquith to address. Connolly – ever the radical – wanted to prevent this by having Irish Volunteers and the Citizen Army occupy the building a day in advance. By floating this proposal, he intended testing participants in the 9 September conference, men whom Connolly doubted had 'sufficient dash and desperation to deal with the matter'.[31] Actually Clarke and MacDermott were also bound to challenge such a symbolic event as a nationalist-supported recruiting meeting and furthermore Connolly's plan was a very public way of breaking Redmond.

In Clarke's Parnell Street shop during the week before the Asquith meeting, Seán T. O'Kelly mentioned knowing most of the officials at City Hall and Tom instructed him to have someone cut the lighting system in and around the Mansion House just before the rally began. O'Kelly did get one man to agree, but he encountered serious technical difficulties, and also special detectives were swarming around the building.[32] However, Tom and Seán risked being bounced into something far more dangerous than just a protest demonstration because Connolly's ambitions went far beyond a propaganda coup. Like many left-wing revolutionaries, including Lenin, he regarded capitalist society as a tinderbox and envisaged one spark igniting a great conflagration. In September 1914 Connolly proclaimed that 'revolutions do not start with rifles; start first and get your rifles after'.[33] Naturally then he was excited by the possibility of British soldiers storming the Mansion House to prevent Asquith and Redmond's humili-ation – a bloody confrontation that would perhaps precipitate an immediate revolution. But equally it might give the British authorities an excuse to crush the Volunteers rather than allow an impression that extremists now controlled Ireland. If the Castle could not afford to lose face, neither could Clarke and MacDermott in the eyes of Connolly, a man with an unbridled contempt for those he considered craven and weak. Tom and Seán were compelled to go along with him whatever reservations they had about Connolly acting as if his destiny was at hand and declaring himself 'ready for any call'.[34]

MacDermott hid any misgivings about events possibly spinning out of control when he met leading Volunteer officers on 23 September. Many reacted negatively to Connolly's plan. Thomas Ashe, an uncompro-mising republican who lost his life three years later on hunger strike, told MacDermott: 'I am ready to die for Ireland tomorrow cheerfully, but this won't be dying for Ireland'.[35] Piaras Béaslaí recalled thinking that the whole enterprise was a 'fatal mistake':

'This will mean bloodshed', I said, 'and in that case the thing to do is go out in open insurrection'. 'We are not yet in a position to do that', said Sean, 'but something must be done'. I found it useless to argue with him. His only reply was that he had thought it out and his mind was made up; that he would go out if nobody else went, and die if necessary.[36]

But like Ashe, Béaslaí's loyalty to MacDermott and the IRB kept him in, and on the night of Thursday 24 September, he brought a group of Volunteers to a large hall in Parnell Square. Although MacDermott had hoped for 200 men only about 80 turned up, some cheerful but others grim and tense as officers distributed rifles and live ammunition. Raring to go, Connolly was in his element:'His face radiated energy, self-confidence, determination and a kind of grim satisfaction'.[37] After the Volunteers linked up at Stephen's Green with forty Citizen Army members coming from Liberty Hall, Connolly intended leading them in a descent on the Mansion House. Once in possession of the building he would be the last man to meekly surrender it again. But just before Connolly set out, a sudden message sent the leaders into a lengthy huddle from which he eventually emerged, having been reluctantly persuaded to announce that the whole thing was off: British forces with Lewis machine guns had already occupied the Mansion House and there were reinforcements on call at Dublin Castle.

Afterwards MacDermott stolidly defended the operation, but privately he and Clarke knew it had been a close call, one that might have cost the lives of many Volunteer and IRB leaders. They did, however, learn an important lesson – that although Connolly was a dedicated revolutionary, his impatience and thirst for action whatever the odds made him almost as dangerous to his allies as to his enemies. Allowing Connolly to make the running had brought them to the edge of disaster; it was a mistake they would not make again. Actually Tom finished 24 September on a high. Although MacNeill's manifesto would not be made public until next day, the formal breach with Redmond started that night when Volunteer officers across Dublin read it to assembled companies and warned them that anyone who attended the Mansion House meeting would be expelled. Simultaneously, anti-Redmondite Volunteers occupied the organisation's Kildare Street headquarters.

It could not have worked out better for Clarke. Only three months after Redmond's takeover, the Irish Volunteers had been prised from his grip, with MacNeill's side keeping the organisation's name, its Kildare Street headquarters and the *Irish Volunteer* journal. And although initially only 3,000 men stayed loyal and most members sided with Redmond's hastily created National Volunteers, a strong recruitment drive soon quadrupled membership, making the Volunteers especially strong in the key areas of Dublin, Cork and Limerick. Furthermore, the defection to Redmond of six moderates from the original Provisional Committee increased Tom's influence over the Volunteers. Clarke and MacDermott's next move was to consolidate their position by coaching IRB delegates attending an Irish Volunteer convention due to be held at the Abbey Theatre, Dublin on 25 October 1914. When it met, names were submitted for election to a new ruling Executive Committee until a proposal (that no doubt Clarke had pre-arranged) to re-appoint *en bloc* the old Provisional Committee's surviving members was passed unanimously.

Far from being just another fix of the kind that Tom routinely engineered in the IRB, this motion insulated the Volunteers from the infection of moderation and transformed them from a broadly based national movement into the armed wing of separatism. Now every member – whether in the IRB or not – was prepared in certain circumstances to fight England.

Satisfyingly for Clarke, IRB candidates (including MacDermott, Pearse, Ceannt, Joseph Plunkett and Thomas MacDonagh) also won eight of the twelve seats on a new inner Central Executive. And when on 5 December 1914, the Central Executive appointed a new headquarters general staff to overhaul the Volunteers' military organisation, the split again worked to Clarke's advantage. Losing many experienced soldiers to both Redmond and the British Army necessitated the promotion of intelligent, enthusiastic amateurs with leadership ability and often a passionate interest in military history and strategy. Accordingly, the Central Executive selected the six Headquarters Staff from within its own ranks. MacNeill – already President – became Chief of Staff, Hobson Quartermaster General and The O'Rahilly Director of Arms. Another trio owed their allegiance to Clarke: Pearse, the new Director of Organisation, Plunkett, Director of Military Operations and MacDonagh, Director of Training. So from the top the IRB now penetrated deep into the Dublin Volunteer organisation and throughout provincial Ireland. MacDonagh became Dublin Brigadier and commanded one of the capital's four battalions, as did Pearse, Plunkett and Clarke's brother-in-law, Ned Daly. In the west, commandants Austin Stack, Michael Colivet and Thomas MacCurtain facilitated IRB control of the Volunteers in Kerry, Limerick and Cork. Moreover, the new military prominence of Pearse, Plunkett and Ceannt enabled Clarke to discard the advisory committee of Volunteer officers and make them responsible for planning an insurrection. Although still without any formal status, the trio began drafting their ideas during the winter of 1914–15.[38]

As well as making political progress during the first year of the war, Clarke prospered personally. In October 1914 he sold the Amiens Street shop and moved his family to Richmond Avenue in the middle-class inner suburb of Fairview. There he rented the street's most desirable residence, a detached double-fronted early nineteenth-century house that was spacious and comfortable with rooms to spare and a garden where Tom could relax and take breakfast. Richmond Avenue was decidedly a step up the social ladder to middle-class respectability, visible proof that his hard work and frugality had paid off. Now a man of property, Clarke could walk or take the tram nearby and travel straight down through Ballybough Road and Summerhill to his shop in Parnell Street in the city centre a little over a mile from his home. Of course, the more he achieved emotional and material security, the more Tom had to lose if his political career ended in failure, but not for an instant did this consideration deter him from his chosen path. Ultimately, as Kathleen recognised and accepted, Ireland was the thing that mattered most in her husband's life.

The Richmond Avenue house also accommodated Kathleen's only brother, 24-year-old Ned Daly. He had been born in Limerick five months after his father's premature death in 1890, and along with his widowed mother and eight sisters, had come under the care and protection of his uncle John Daly after he was released from Portland Prison in 1896. Upon leaving school, Ned worked as a clerk in a timber yard, but his interest in music, singing and opera alienated the stridently masculine Uncle John who thought him rather effeminate. Ned for his part increasingly resented the discipline that the older man imposed on all his Daly charges; in Uncle John's household it really was his way or the highway. Ned took the road to Dublin where he worked as a clerk in a wholesale chemists.[39]

Tom had known Ned since his first visit to Limerick when he encountered the young schoolboy. However, now he treated Ned as the adult that he had become because, whatever Tom's authoritarian political style, he was, domestically, a very different person to the autocratic Uncle John. Kathleen declared that 'in his home he was the personification of gentleness, joyousness and good temper. I saw him out of temper only a few times in the nearly fifteen years we were together. He adored his children and was never happier than when playing with them'.[40] Tom and Ned got along famously. In many ways they were very alike: serious, withdrawn and taciturn with both following appropriately in the tradition of a family steeped in republicanism as Ned shared Tom's commitment to Irish independence. In a way Tom was also the respected father figure that Ned had never really had in his life and unlike John Daly, Tom realised perceptively that Ned had talent that could be very useful to the separatist movement. Ned really longed to be a soldier; his sister Madge recalled that 'Ned was a born soldier. He studied this subject with the greatest gusto – his bedroom was filled with all kinds of military books'.[41] After joining the Irish Volunteers, Ned rose quickly to become Commandant of the First Battalion and officially Tom's superior officer. Undoubtedly his connections helped Ned's rise since he came from republican royalty and his brother-in-law Clarke had the influence to facilitate his ambition, but Ned had earned promotion not because of nepotism but through his intelligence and efficiency. One of his officers thought that 'he looked every inch a soldier'[42] and during the Rising Ned was to fully justify Tom's faith in his military ability.

Historically, Irish rebels had relied on Spanish and French military assistance, but in 1914 Clarke and the IRB turned instead to Germany. They were acting on the age-old principle that England's foe was Ireland's friend, but also from a belief that the Germans were the real victims of unprovoked aggression. Tom had long thought that the Triple Entente had a strategy of strangling Germany diplomatically, economically and militarily, one that made war inevitable well before actual hostilities commenced. Bulmer Hobson's articles in *Irish Freedom* had also predicted war and advocated Ireland siding with Germany because 'as the ally of the victor we should share in the victor's advantage and our share would be our political independence'.[43] Hoping to attract Berlin's interest, Clarke and the Supreme Council sent Hobson to America in January 1914 with an early draft of Casement's document 'Ireland, Germany and the Next War'. This proposed a German-Irish alliance and joint action against the British Empire, and Hobson presented a copy to the German Ambassador, Count von Bernstorff.[44]

Once war started, any further communications with Germany were dangerous for Clarke and the IRB, risking not just accusations of betraying both 'gallant little Belgium' and many Irish soldiers in the British Army, but imprisonment and even death for treason. Outweighing these considerations in Tom's mind was the prospect of Berlin recognising Irish independence, sending arms and ammunition to the Volunteers and, best of all, dispatching a large expeditionary force to Ireland. So in August 1914 Devoy and a Clan delegation met von Bernstorff at New York's German Club where they disclosed the IRB's decision to rise before the conflict ended and appealed for both arms and German officers to lead the Volunteers during a rebellion.[45] Using wireless, von Bernstorff reported the encounter to Berlin, while Devoy kept Tom informed by courier. Communicating information secretly between America, Ireland and Germany had been made extremely difficult by British intelligence, postal censorship and the Royal Navy's blockade of Germany. Furthermore, on 5 August 1914, a British ship in the North Sea had severed the transatlantic cables between Germany and the United States, forcing the German embassy in Washington to rely on wireless messages. To add to the difficulties, travellers to Germany had to enter from a neutral country, a condition that almost invariably meant a circuitous journey. Even so, Clarke wanted personal representations made to the German government. For this mission Devoy selected John Kenny, the man who three decades earlier had sworn Tom into the Clan. Kenny would have no authority to negotiate and no detailed plans for a rising yet existed for him to pass on; his trip was more about establishing trust and convincing Berlin of the IRB's and the Clan's seriousness and their ability to damage the British war effort.

Supposedly travelling to Switzerland for the benefit of his health, Kenny bore credentials from von Bernstorff to present to the German government with documents from Devoy and Casement that amplified the proposals made to von Bernstorff.[46] On 21 August 1914, Kenny's ship left New York and reached Naples on 13 September. As a precaution against his mission going wrong later, Kenny stopped in Rome where he was granted a lengthy meeting with the German ambassador, Ludwig von Flutow. They discussed Irish history and von Flutow questioned Kenny perceptively about the political situation in Ireland and promised to forward an account of their talk to Berlin along with Kenny's documents. However, Kenny was uncertain whether his pleasant reception reflected genuine German interest or simply the ambassador's natural courtesy. In reality, the German General Staff was focussed almost entirely on the land war in France and the Eastern Front, and any ideas it had about undermining the British Empire were centred on India and Egypt, not Ireland. Von Flutow provided Kenny with an Imperial pass. For a week he observed Germany's great industrial plants, seemingly endless troop movements and the population's high morale. In Berlin he presented his case to Prince von Bulow, a former Chancellor who suggested the possibility of him meeting the Kaiser. But Kenny believed he had fulfilled his mission and decided to return home via neutral Holland.

After just missing a transatlantic liner out of the Dutch port of Rotterdam, Kenny sailed to Folkstone and then travelled on to Dublin. He regarded Clarke as 'the "hub" of the secret movement in Ireland' and intended briefing him on his recent mission. Tom had just returned from a short stay in Glandore, west Cork, at the Irish home of Judge Cohalan, a Clan leader and ally of Devoy. Fragile health now required him to recuperate regularly after spells of intense activity such as that in August and September which had caused him to tell John Daly, 'I need a rest very badly. I feel almost done up'.[47] But Kenny saw a Clarke who had been reinvigorated by the political impact of Redmond's Woodenbridge speech, which he claimed had shocked many nationalists. Redmond had left them 'struck all of a heap' by failing to demand immediate Home Rule in return for supporting the war effort. Tom now felt that he had regained the political initiative and he assured Kenny that 'our people have the Irish Volunteer Committee well in hand and will at once take drastic action with the Parliamentary men on it'.[48] For his part Kenny gave an upbeat assessment of the military situation. Although Germany's Schlieffen Plan for a knock-out blow against France had recently ended in failure at the Battle of the Marne, he predicted that its new strategy would ultimately triumph. Kenny said this was modelled on the methods of Rome's Scipio Africanus during the Second

Punic War: his army had penetrated deep into enemy territory, won successive battles and ground Carthage into submission. Kenny's analysis gladdened Clarke because stalemate gave him what he wanted most from Germany in September 1914 – time. Whereas most Europeans dreaded the prospect of a long conflict, Tom feared a short one. A war of attrition meant time to mature his plans for a rising, time to overcome the scepticism of Germany's political leaders, time for its General Staff to realise Ireland's strategic importance and time to edge the IRB into the victor's camp.

Kenny returned to America, but Devoy sent him back at the end of November to deliver Clan money to Clarke, the IRB's treasurer, and compile a report on political conditions in Ireland. He found that once again Tom had been ill. Recovering in Limerick, Clarke eventually returned 'pale and worn' in order to confer with MacDermott, Pearse and Kenny. The three IRB leaders predicted that the British government would soon arrest IRB and Volunteer leaders as a prelude to conscription, and arranged for Kenny to bring Devoy a list of replacements should this occur. Within days, though, their fears subsided because they believed the British now realised the likelihood of a violent reaction. But generally Clarke and his colleagues exuded confidence; the war had opened up great possibilities for them, whereas for Redmond it would mean the beginning of the end. Lord Kitchener, the Secretary of State for War, had seriously damaged the Home Rule leader by refusing to form National Volunteer recruits into an Irish Brigade, with their own officers, emblems and badges, while simultaneously establishing a 36th Division for the Ulster Volunteers. Such apparent British ingratitude helped precipitate a rapid decline in the National Volunteer organisation. Tom claimed many disillusioned members would defect immediately to the Irish Volunteers if an 'extraordinary event' offered them action. More generally he said pro-war enthusiasm had waned significantly as casualties soared and a more sceptical public questioned government propaganda; Clarke reported that many people in Limerick now regretted swallowing stories about German atrocities in Belgium. Since the British government was muzzling opposition newspapers, he wanted Devoy to get the Germans to send a Zeppelin or aeroplane over Ireland dropping anti-war leaflets. Even better, Tom declared, would be a German expeditionary force of at least 25,000 well-equipped soldiers.

Kenny could see Clarke, MacDermott and Pearse's preoccupation with building up the Irish Volunteers' stockpile of weapons for a rising. Tom estimated that nationalists had only 10,000 rifles but that with a few thousand more the Volunteers could seize Dublin. Rifles – and automatic pistols – were his weapons of choice rather than machine guns which expended too much ammunition and were too bulky to smuggle easily into Ireland. To procure them Clarke was attempting to establish contact with English gun dealers who had supplied the Boers during the South African War. He contemplated chartering a ship to run the arms into Achill Island or the Blasket Islands and getting local inhabitants to then transfer them to the mainland. Other ideas involved secreting arms in ships with cargoes of wheat or oil barrels that regularly docked in Dublin and training men in making explosives. Kenny said the Germans intended using grenades extensively in the war and that any competent Volunteer could manufacture them from readily available materials. In a subsequent conversation with Kenny, Clarke in an expansive mood evaluated many prominent individuals. He even described Hobson as likeable and amiable but added rather ambiguously that 'if Hobson's record had not been so good he would be summarily "fired" and that as it was he "was merely tolerated"'.[49]

However, it was Tom's drive for complete ascendancy over the Irish Volunteers that brought him into renewed conflict with Bulmer Hobson, his would-be nemesis. Far from leaving political life and even Ireland itself, as Clarke had hoped, Hobson had scores to settle and a vision of his own to fulfil. In addition, being Honorary Secretary and Quartermaster General made Hobson effectively deputy Volunteer leader and MacNeill needed him even more after Casement's departure for America and Moore's defection to Redmond. And since MacNeill enjoyed the kudos of being President more than time-consuming administration, Hobson carried the load instead with his days at headquarters now lasting from early morning until midnight. Hobson's enhanced authority meant he could shape the Volunteers' policy and stamp his political and military philosophy on them. Both MacNeill and the Central Executive endorsed Hobson's strategy as official Volunteer policy, and after becoming editor of the *Irish Volunteer* in December 1914, Hobson also used it to inculcate the rank and file with his ideas. In articles and training notes he argued that despite lacking sufficient military resources to defeat the British Army in open battle, the Volunteers could instead gradually dismantle the British system of government in Ireland. After passive resistance first paralysed the civilian administration, Hobson envisaged armed struggle beginning when the British introduced conscription, a measure that would swing popular opinion overwhelmingly behind the Volunteers and sustain them in a campaign of guerrilla warfare. In this phase flying columns would capture, buy and steal arms, exhausting the British authorities and finally draining them of the will to continue occupying Ireland.

At headquarters, Hobson also built up a talented inner circle that included J.J. ('Ginger') O'Connell, a 27-year-old graduate of University College

Dublin who had spent two years in the American army before returning to Ireland in early 1914. Another was 21-year-old Eimar O'Duffy, a former British Army cadet and budding playwright who, unlike O'Connell, was also in the IRB. Both men regularly contributed columns to *The Irish Volunteer*, using their military aptitude and specialised knowledge in support of Hobson. O'Duffy also worked in his office, while Hobson secured O'Connell's promotion to the general staff as Director of Inspection. Hobson also had a trio of young protégés, Padraig Ó Riain, Eamonn Martin and Liam Mellows, former Fianna officers and Provisional Committee members who had stuck by him during the political convulsions of 1914. Hobson now repaid their loyalty. Mellows, for instance, was appointed Provisional Committee secretary, a position he retained until the October Volunteer Convention when Hobson became Honorary Secretary and appointed Mellows as the organisation's first organising instructor. In this capacity he acted as Hobson's eyes and ears in the provinces and disseminated his vision of the Volunteers' future.

Hobson's gradualist vision impelled him to resist Clarke's insurrectionary ambitions though clearly personal animosity motivated him as well as principle. Tom's rejection of him had deeply wounded Hobson, whose subsequent conduct showed that hurt and bitterness flowed both ways. Moreover, Hobson knew Tom's conspiratorial methods, and the identity of his supporters on both the Central Executive and the headquarters general staff. In the undeclared war that soon existed at Volunteer headquarters, Hobson constantly sought to gain evidence that he could use against Clarke's loyalists. In the light of Hobson's renewed determination, Clarke and MacDermott avoided confrontation in favour of a silent coup; while their supporters publicly proclaimed undeviating loyalty to official Volunteer policy, they would secretly bypass it and Hobson as well. Occupying powerful posts at headquarters and in the provinces, they could manipulate Volunteer members and resources and transform the organisation into an IRB front. And this infiltration penetrated deeper than Hobson could ever have imagined – straight into his own inner circle where Liam Mellows was not quite what he seemed. Despite admiring Hobson's intellect, Mellows' down-to-earth personality and desire for action drew him more to Clarke. Tom had originally sworn Mellows into the IRB. While helping to distribute copies of *Irish Freedom* from Tom's shop, Mellows discovered that, like himself, the older man was from a mixed marriage and the son of a British Army sergeant. Mellows also fell under MacDermott's spell and Seán became his political hero. Clarke now got Mellows to perform an exquisite deception and betrayal in which Mellow pretended to be Hobson's loyal confidant while secretly spying for

Tom. Only much later did Hobson discover the extent of Clarke's subterranean plotting, but in June 1914, when Mellows voted against Hobson's recommendation to accept Redmond's ultimatum, he should have realised that Mellows' loyalty was not unconditional.[50]

On 16 May 1915 Clarke temporarily lost his right-hand man when MacDermott was arrested for an anti-recruiting speech in Tuam, Co. Galway. Transferred to Dublin and confined at Arbour Hill Military Detention Barracks, he was finally sentenced to four months in Mountjoy Prison. But Tom got Kathleen to visit him to establish a system by which coded messages could be smuggled in and out, while Clarke also visited MacDermott in jail. Actually an enforced sabbatical probably did Seán and the IRB good by preventing him burning out long before the Easter Rising; prodigiously long working hours and his many responsibilities were seriously straining MacDermott's already frail constitution and highly strung temperament.

During MacDermott's absence, Clarke intensified the planning for a rebellion that Ceannt, Plunkett and Pearse had been informally engaged in for months. By early March 1915, the trio had made sufficient progress for Clarke and MacDermott to brief Seán T. O'Kelly on the plans for a secret mission that he would make to America.[51] Meeting in a room above Tom's Parnell Street shop, Clarke and MacDermott revealed that they had decided on a rising, its date as yet unfixed. Volunteers would seize Dublin Castle, the GPO in O'Connell Street, the City Hall, Jacob's biscuit factory, the Four Courts, Boland's Mill, Beggar's Bush Barracks, the North and South Dublin Unions and the North City Flour Mills on the Royal Canal. The capital's railway termini would also be occupied and, if resources allowed, Kingstown (Dún Laoghaire) harbour to prevent the British Army bringing in reinforcements from England. Furthermore, Tom and Seán said plans were being worked on for the rest of the country. Memorising the details, O'Kelly left on 18 March for New York where he outlined them to the Clan leaders, John Devoy and Judge Cohalan. Six weeks later he returned with £2,000 in banknotes from the Clan to purchase arms, half going to MacNeill and the Irish Volunteers and the rest to Clarke, the IRB's treasurer.

At the end of May 1915, Diarmuid Lynch – MacDermott's acting replacement on the three-man IRB Executive – proposed upgrading Ceannt, Plunkett and Pearse into a formal military committee.[52] He did so on the basis that the three men had studied military tactics and were the best to formulate plans for an insurrection. Unsurprisingly his motion – undoubtedly Tom's idea – was carried because the Presidency of the Supreme Council had been vacant since Deakin's defection and Clarke was the only other

person in the room. Although he later told the Supreme Council about the
Military Committee's existence, Tom shrouded its activities in secrecy, while
the Committee's small size and completely trustworthy membership gave
him total control over it. Clearly his long dominant position in the IRB was
now unassailable, and by fast-tracking Ceannt, Plunkett and Pearse he had
created a group of loyal Young Turks with far more power and knowledge
than their nominal superiors on the Supreme Council.

At over 6ft tall, handsome, spare and erect, 33-year-old Éamonn Ceannt's
imposing presence had him frequently mistaken for a policeman – his late
father's occupation. Ceannt's life-long passions were Roman Catholicism,
Irish history, culture, music and – through the Gaelic League – the Irish
language. In search of an escape from his intellectually stultifying job with
Dublin Corporation's finance department, he became politically active and
MacDermott had sworn him into the IRB in December 1912. Joining the
Irish Volunteers' Provisional Committee at the start, he impressed a colleague
as 'a man of no surrender', stubbornly attached to principles from which
'he was almost morbidly afraid of a departure'. Ceannt always refused to
'compromise on even the smallest point and then if alone he would dispute
his point to the very end'.[53] As a radical militarist he had voted against
Redmond's ultimatum in June 1914 and later shot at British troops during
the Howth gunrunning. Ceannt's courage, command of detail and direct
manner got him promoted first to Commandant of the Fourth Battalion
and then in August 1915 as Director of Communications on the Volunteers'
Headquarters Staff. Clarke liked Ceannt's assiduousness, organising ability
and fierce determination, as well as his manifest belief that the British could
only be talked to from the barrel of a gun. In fact, Ceannt reminded people of
Tom and had the same unbending will and ability to keep a secret; like Clarke,
the taciturn Ceannt was a doer not a talker, a man of action not ideas.

Joseph Plunkett was the 27-year-old son of Count George Noble Plunkett,
a papal knight whose wife and seven children lived comfortably on his estate
in the Dublin suburb of Kimmage. Bookish and intelligent, Joseph acquired
from his Jesuit teachers a love of Roman Catholicism, philosophy and poetry.
Thin, pale and short-sighted, Plunkett's development was plagued by ill health
that required repeated surgery to remove tubercular glands from his neck
and frequent spells in hospitals and nursing homes. Attending the National
University of Ireland, he studied Irish and was tutored privately by Thomas
MacDonagh, a teacher at Patrick Pearse's school, St Enda's. Despite a nine-year
age difference, their mutual love of poetry made them best friends. When
MacDonagh became a lecturer in English literature at University College

Dublin, Plunkett followed him there as a student. At the end of 1913 his lifelong interest in war and military strategy attracted him to the Irish Volunteers and he was elected to the Provisional Committee. Despite his budding interest in revolutionary politics and increasingly militant utterances, Plunkett had been a follower of Redmond and voted to accept his ultimatum in June 1914 as the only way of ensuring the Volunteers' survival. However, unlike Hobson, Plunkett was not in the IRB and so escaped Clarke and MacDermott's censure. Indeed Plunkett soon regretted this action, subsequently joined the IRB, and after Redmond's Woodenbridge speech voted to expel his nominees.

Having concentrated on reviving the Irish language through the Gaelic League, 36-year-old Patrick Pearse had come late to revolutionary republicanism. As editor of the League's journal *An Claidheamh Soluis*, after 1903 he was on its politically conservative wing, scorning its militant members as wreckers. Pearse also derided the IRB as 'a lot of old Fenians who had run to seed or were doting and used to talk in public houses. He had at the same time a tolerant respect for them, but he never regarded them as a serious threat to British imperialism'.[54] To help preserve a distinct Irish identity, Pearse established St Enda's, a boarding school that thrived until 1908, when he over-reached himself by shifting to new premises on the outskirts of Rathfarnham. Situated in a large house with splendid gardens, it was a money pit out of which he could not climb, dragged down as he was by his administrative inefficiency and a somewhat impractical turn of mind. Nor could this shy and socially awkward man, who eschewed tobacco and alcohol, unwind easily or engage in small talk. This has prompted historian Ruth Dudley Edwards to suggest that in his desire to escape from difficult personal circumstances, 'a craving for action came to dominate Pearse's thinking'[55] and propelled him on to the public stage in search of a historically important role. His speech in March 1911 at the Emmet Commemoration had elicited Clarke's rather backhanded compliment that 'I never thought there was such stuff in Pearse'. For a time he still distanced himself from revolutionary separatism. On 12 March 1912 in O'Connell Street, Pearse even shared a platform with Redmond at a mass rally supporting the Third Home Rule Bill, believing that it was the best available stepping stone to independence. But he spoke in Irish and the significance of what Pearse said might have been missed, especially his warning that a British government betrayal would leave the Irish people 'no choice but to answer them henceforward with the strong hand and the sword's edge. Let the Gall understand that if we are cheated once more there will be red war in Ireland'.

Pearse's disillusion with constitutional nationalism increased as Ulster Unionist opposition to the Home Rule Bill intensified, and it became complete when the Irish Volunteers emerged in November 1913. In bellicose language he declared that 'before this generation has passed away the Volunteers will draw the sword of Ireland. There is no truth but the old truth and no way but the old way. I do not know how nationhood is achieved except by armed men'. Many IRB members were sceptical about Pearse's political transformation and Hobson's Teeling circle twice blackballed him from membership, ironically on the second occasion at the urging of Ceannt.[56] Eventually, in February 1914, Clarke and the Supreme Council had Hobson initiate Pearse into the Brotherhood as a member at large.

Although both men sat on the Volunteers' Headquarters Staff, Clarke's promotion of Pearse and Plunkett to high rank in the IRB was superficially puzzling. Relatively new to the Brotherhood, they apparently lacked the soldierly hard-headed, unromantic and practical qualities that the organisation usually sought in recruits. But Tom divined that these intelligent men, through lengthy intellectual struggle, had transformed themselves into fervent separatists, a process requiring great strength of character. And once they had worked through their doubts and committed themselves completely to armed separatism, Pearse and Plunkett displayed a willingness – unusual in a headmaster and the son of a count – to publicly stand outside the mainstream and passionately proclaim the beliefs of a small minority. Thereafter, Clarke knew intuitively that Pearse and Plunkett would stay the course to the very end. Piaras Béaslaí thought Pearse was 'better at inspiring people with speeches full of high objectives than at the practical activity of soldiering, more of a poet and an orator than an officer of the Volunteers, better at dreams and great visions'.[57] But Tom understood the power of Pearse's oratory to move an audience and also saw that his dignified and handsome appearance – his strong jaw, grey eyes and dark hair – made Pearse look like a leader. Furthermore, Clarke realised that one day soon the IRB would finally emerge from the shadows and stand in judgement before not only the Irish people but history itself. To avoid being classed as the underbelly of society, the organisation needed eloquent poets and playwrights like Pearse and Plunkett in its ranks. These middle-class intellectuals fluent in both Irish and English would affirm the IRB's claim to represent the whole nation, with Pearse especially providing a compelling face of the revolution.

Pearse and Plunkett were devout Catholics who exuded intense religious fervour and infused their writings with religious symbolism and the idea of redemption. Their cast of mind could envisage and welcome death as a political crucifixion that would lead to the resurrection of Ireland as an independent nation. However, though both were literary men, this was to be no revolution of the intellectuals but one in which men of proletarian origin who disdained theorising would control the intellectuals; a former foundry-man would direct a headmaster and a former barman would oversee a cosmopolitan scholar. Clarke and MacDermott were the IRB's driving forces and Pearse and Plunkett owed their rise to them; indeed without Tom's patronage Pearse would never have been recruited in the first place. And Tom had not spent decades striving for one great purpose only to throw his life away on a grand but ultimately futile gesture. Tom's goal was military victory, not heroic failure and posthumous vindication. He almost certainly intended his last years to be fulfilled through playing a significant role in an independent Ireland and helping shape its future.

However different, Clarke's inner circle all were all intelligent men, ruthless and driven. They were also bold, imaginative and daring, prepared to risk everything on realising a dream that almost everyone else considered unattainable. As Devoy wrote later:

> The idea of starting a revolution in Ireland after the outbreak of the world War with but a few thousand pounds in the hands of the IRB and volunteers was regarded by even the most sanguine of our countrymen as quixotic but revolutions don't go by the rules of logic and reasoning. If they did there would never be a revolution in any country in the world.[58]

By early 1915 planning for a rising was sufficiently advanced for IRB leaders to follow up on the previous autumn's request for a German arms shipment to Ireland. This time Tom decided to approach Berlin directly, probably believing that a leading conspirator needed to convince the German government that the Irish really were serious. Since shortly after the beginning of the war Sir Roger Casement had represented Irish separatism in Germany and in November 1914 had even secured a declaration endorsing Irish independence. But Casement had become increasingly ineffective. The German General Staff had ruled out a naval invasion of Ireland and Casement's grand project of an Irish Brigade drawn from captured Irish soldiers in the British Army had recruited a derisory fifty-six men. Tom had never liked or fully trusted Casement whose minimal progress and threats to give up and return to America convinced him that a new emissary was needed in Berlin to kick-start negotiations. For this secret mission Clarke and MacDermott chose Plunkett. As a high-ranking Volunteer officer, the son of a count and an educated man who spoke French fluently and German rather less so, he might elicit a sympathetic hearing from the German government.

Moreover, Plunkett had the perfect excuse for an extended absence from Ireland. Sir Arthur Chance, a prominent Dublin doctor, had recommended that Plunkett recuperate on the French Riviera and had persuaded the British authorities to allow him to leave the country.[59]

Slipping away on St Patrick's Day, 17 March 1915, Plunkett travelled incognito through England, France, Spain and Italy. Having grown a beard and moustache, he collected a false American passport in the name of John Peters and by Easter he was in Switzerland. Through the German embassy he contacted Casement who secured him accreditation and on 19 April Plunkett departed from Berne on a twenty-three-hour rail journey to Berlin. During the next two and a half months in Germany, he visited the Irish Brigade headquarters, wrote propaganda pamphlets and spent three weeks being treated in a Spandau sanatorium. But his primary purpose was to secure German help, so Plunkett also met German officials and submitted a thirty-two-page memorandum drafted by Casement and himself. Entitled 'The Ireland Report', it revealed the scale of Clarke and his fellow conspirators' ambitions for an Irish rebellion.[60] In the report Plunkett argued that a joint German-Irish military campaign could in a three-pronged but integrated military operation easily defeat a British garrison of 37,000 badly equipped troops. Irish Volunteers would begin by destroying railway bridges, canals and viaducts, and seizing Dublin where they would arrest British officials and military officers, station guards at banks and British commercial interests, and possibly appoint a military governor. Simultaneously, a German expeditionary force of 12,000 men would land in the west of Ireland with 40,000 rifles for the western Volunteers who would have already risen in rebellion. With a nationwide revolt in progress, Plunkett anticipated a joint German-Irish force marching from the west towards Dublin, overwhelming British resistance on the way. He then envisaged a final great battle when the rebel column would create a pincer movement that would trap between it and the Volunteers in Dublin large numbers of British soldiers attempting to recapture the capital. The IRB leaders clearly intended that after achieving military victory they would constitute themselves as the new rulers of an independent Irish republic. In return for German assistance, Plunkett dangled the promise that an independent Irish government would allow U-boats to operate from naval bases in Ireland and sever England's Atlantic lifeline. This was an especially tempting offer as Germany had just initiated its first campaign of unrestricted U-boat warfare against Allied shipping. In effect, Clarke and his colleagues were offering to align a free Ireland with the Central Powers against the Allies.

Despite its comprehensive detail, military analysis and citing of historical precedents, 'The Ireland Report' failed to win over the German General Staff.

It knew nothing about Plunkett, was losing confidence in his friend Casement, and above all believed the British Navy would destroy an amphibious German expedition to Ireland. Plunkett left Germany on 5 July 1915 without assurances even of an arms shipment. However, his mission had not failed completely. Behind Casement's back he had secretly conducted parallel negotiations with the General Staff and Foreign Office and concluded they would help the IRB leaders provided they proved their plans were serious – especially by setting a definite date for a rising. It made sense for Berlin to keep Plunkett in play since an arms shipment might disrupt the enemy war effort by igniting a rebellion that would divert British soldiers from France to Ireland. This hope emboldened Clarke and his fellow conspirators to press ahead more urgently. Soon after Plunkett had returned home, Pearse authorised the scouting of the west coast of Ireland for harbours where a German arms shipment might land.[61]

As well as seeking foreign allies, Tom consolidated his position on the home front by extinguishing all remaining opposition on the Supreme Council to his revolutionary policy. His primary target was P.S. O'Hegarty who favoured keeping the Volunteers intact until after the war and only rising then if a Peace Conference was sitting and every Volunteer participated willingly. Tom feared that O'Hegarty might influence others to waver; he had sat on the Supreme Council longer than Clarke and considered himself his senior, indeed the Council's most important individual. But the outbreak of war had helped Tom when the War Office – which knew about O'Hegarty's extremist politics – had him summarily transferred from his postmaster's job in Queenstown to Shrewsbury in England. Leaving on 8 August 1914, O'Hegarty stayed overnight in Dublin and breakfasted with Clarke who promised that the Supreme Council would take no significant decisions without first consulting him. O'Hegarty complained later that Tom's assurance 'was never kept in a single instance'.[62] Another transfer to Welshpool in Montgomeryshire, north Wales – where he was confined for the rest of the war under police supervision – further reinforced O'Hegarty's physical isolation. But in May 1915 MacDermott visited O'Hegarty and revealed that Pearse, Plunkett and Ceannt were planning for a rising in September, supposedly after an imminent German breakthrough on the Western Front led to simultaneous invasions of England and Ireland. O'Hegarty also claims MacDermott told him disingenuously that Clarke and he intended only a Dublin insurrection and that without sufficient arms the Volunteers had no prospect of success. They could only hope that if the British did not use artillery, the rebels could hold the capital for a week, but after that nothing mattered. MacDermott described the rebellion's purpose as 'a forlorn hope to awaken the people', necessary because 'the national morale of Ireland was so low that there no other way to arrest it than by the shock of a Rising'.[63]

Clearly MacDermott was holding important information back from O'Hegarty, especially about the scale of his and Tom's ambitions. O'Hegarty already knew him to be 'a master of the art of telling as little of the facts as he wanted to'.[64] MacDermott did not trust O'Hegarty completely and probably wanted to establish definitively whether he could be persuaded to support the revolutionary project. Instead O'Hegarty declared himself totally opposed, especially as he believed the Germans would never come to Ireland while the British fleet was unbeaten. He insisted that MacDermott report his disapproval to the Supreme Council, but Seán informed only Clarke on his return to Dublin. Tom's immediate reaction was simple; O'Hegarty had to go. Unlike Hobson's banishment, he disappeared quietly later in May during regular elections to the Supreme Council when Tom had him quietly dropped. Subsequently, as O'Hegarty bitterly recalled, Tom and Seán 'naturally co-opted only people who were in favour of a Rising and I had definitely asked to be recorded as against it'.[65] O'Hegarty – an IRB veteran – was replaced by Pearse, a member for just over a year, an astonishingly rapid promotion that demonstrated Clarke's authority. Tom's control became complete when a loyalist, Alec McCabe, replaced the imprisoned MacDermott as Connaught representative. Seán – whose many duties had finally compelled him to vacate the post – had actually been arrested in Tuam just before he supervised the election of his successor. So Clarke dispatched Diarmuid Lynch to arrange McCabe's victory, while MacDermott, who had initiated McCabe into the IRB, was immediately co-opted back on to the Supreme Council.[66]

O'Hegarty took his ruthless exclusion personally, complaining that afterwards he 'was left in blank ignorance of what was happening'.[67] But Clarke saw things differently; to him it was purely business. Once again he had shown his capacity for judging a person purely in terms of whether they were for or against the revolution. If he was not on Tom's side, then nothing else mattered, not past friendships, shared history, sentimental attachments or political partnerships. Unburdened by emotional constraints, Clarke could clinically dispose of even long-standing associates, comforted no doubt by a belief that history demanded he harden his heart and think only of Ireland. Tom had long ago learned to bury his emotions deep.

By mid-1915 Clarke was insistent that his followers also steel themselves for great tests that lay ahead, considering as he did that Irish separatism was now psychologically at war with England and that the final countdown to battle had begun. Tom was especially perturbed by British arrests of republicans for disrupting recruiting meetings and making anti-war speeches; these, he suspected, were intended to cow opponents before the introduction of conscription. In fact, the British government's Irish policy had remained constant since August 1914: don't mention anything but the war. The Chief Secretary's priority was to keep Ireland quiet and allow Asquith's cabinet to concentrate on defeating Germany. So Birrell appeased militant nationalism and avoided confronting the Irish Volunteers and Citizen Army. Far from intending to intimidate them, Birrell hoped that the arrest of prominent activists would turn down the volume by removing the most vocal trouble-makers at a time when recruiting and pro-war sentiment were on the wane. The British General Officer Commanding (GOC), Major-General Friend, also began excluding 'agitators' from sensitive parts of Ireland, confining others to designated areas, and even ordering some of them out of the country alto-gether. In early July 1915 he gave four prominent Irish Volunteer organisers a fortnight to leave Ireland: Liam Mellows, Ernest Blythe and Herbert Pim (two Ulster Protestant converts to the IRB), and Denis McCullough, a Supreme Council member and deputy commandant of the Belfast Volunteers. Volunteer headquarters summoned McCullough and Pim to a meeting that rejected Ceannt's proposal to have picked Volunteers surround both men and dare the British to come and get them.[68] Instead, MacNeill instructed McCullough to go on an American propaganda tour. But McCullough was lukewarm about the idea and went immediately to get Clarke's advice. Having never obeyed the terms of a prison amnesty requiring him to attend a police station regularly, Tom instinctively rejected co-operating with the British Army, police and legal system. Like soldiers at the front, he expected his followers to hold their line at all costs and defy Friend's banishment orders, otherwise, he warned McCullough, the enemy would deport even more opposition leaders 'and so put an end of all our hopes. If you obey that order and leave the country, for any purpose whatever that friendship is at an end. I will count you a traitor to the cause and to all your comrades'.[69] Along with his fellow Ulstermen Pim and Blythe, McCullough returned north to address protest meetings until they were arrested after two weeks. In August 1915 McCullough and Pim appeared at Belfast Magistrates' Court for a well-publicised trial, one that Clarke planned to turn into a propaganda victory for the IRB. By depicting the defendants as innocent victims of a heartless British government, he would inflame the political situation and incite Irish nationalists to rally behind them. Tom also hoped Irish Volunteers would conclude that Friend's deportation orders were the harbinger of an imminent British onslaught – one they would have to resist.

From a distance Clarke choreographed the Belfast trials through his emissaries, Seán T. O'Kelly and two trusted IRB solicitors, Seamus O'Connor and Charles Wyse Power.[70] Although official displeasure had now made most lawyers wary of accepting such politically sensitive briefs, the three men managed to get Henry Hanna KC as Senior Defence Counsel. Despite being a dyed-in-the-wool Unionist, he was a maverick who thought every accused person deserved a defence. Hanna also reluctantly endorsed Tom's strategy of making the trial a *cause célèbre* that would gain widespread publicity in Ireland and abroad. In court he began with sophisticated legal arguments querying the legality of Friend's orders, but when these got nowhere, Hanna suddenly transformed himself into a fervent nationalist, vehemently denouncing centuries of British repression in Ireland. Holding up McCullough and Pim as its latest victims, Hanna earned every penny of his fee with a bravura performance that had spectators stamping their feet, cheering and clapping while he periodically asked his minders, 'How am I doing, am I doing all right?'. Unfortunately, the only person left unmoved by Hanna's rhetoric was the magistrate who ordered a packed courtroom cleared, a decision that provoked a brawl between police and the defendants' supporters. He then sentenced Pim and McCullough to three and four months' imprisonment, respectively. But Clarke got all the headlines he wanted and more; McCullough himself called the proceedings 'a field day for the newspapers'.[71]

A prominent IRB member who breezed into Clarke's Parnell Street shop experienced Clarke's anger at anyone complying with a deportation order. A long-time friend, the visitor should have realised that Tom knew everything about the movement – including his recent order to leave Ireland. A witness to the incident recalled:

'Hello, Tom', he said. Without any preliminary, Tom said: 'I hear that you are thinking of going to America Jack. Is that true?' 'Well, you see, Tom', said Jack rather lamely, 'my business is not in the best of shape. If I am arrested, it will be bad. So I thought it would be better if I went to America for a little while'. 'All right', said Tom, 'goodbye Jack'. He turned his back on Jack who looked sheepishly at me and left the shop. Tom never spoke to him again.[72]

However, Tom urged on Diarmuid Lynch a course of action that would actually have ensured his deportation from Ireland. Contrary to most American citizens, Lynch was ordered in June 1915 to register as a 'Friendly Alien' and report to a police station daily when travelling throughout Ireland.

Ever the opportunist, Clarke immediately realised the possibility of the Clan whipping up anti-British propaganda in America over Lynch's deportation and recommended him not to register. But Lynch was set on staying in Ireland to participate in the coming rising and he ignored the advice. His commitment to the fight saved him from Clarke's wrath.[73]

During MacDermott's imprisonment, Clarke assumed responsibility for IRB policy towards the Gaelic League. Dissatisfied with the Gaelic League's performance, he was determined to change its leadership, constitution and programme. By 1915 the IRB had established a strong presence in the League; many members such as MacDermott – himself a fluent Irish speaker – had joined and some like Ceannt and Béaslaí also sat on its central council. But this numerical strength had not brought any commensurate influence. Seán's League policy had been cautious, fearing as he did that if separatists openly manipulated its affairs, they would get blamed for any subsequent split. However many ordinary IRB members wanted action and complained about the League not pronouncing on major political issues. Dublin's Keating branch of the Gaelic League – effectively an IRB front – contained many prominent dissidents who had lost patience, among them Cathal Brugha, Richard Mulcahy and Piaras Béaslaí. After Béaslaí penned a major newspaper article accusing the League of having lost its way, on 20 June 1915 Clarke summoned him to a meeting about the simmering discontent.[74]

Despite not speaking Irish, Tom had long supported the Gaelic League and – much more than MacDermott – envisaged it joining the IRB's campaign for independence. First he would have to overcome its President, Douglas Hyde. This 55-year-old academic had founded the League in 1893 to preserve the language and more generally promote Irish music, literature and culture, but he always insisted on it remaining non-political and non-sectarian. The League attracted many Protestant members and Hyde himself was the son of a Church of Ireland rector. By 1915 there were over 550 branches and its travelling teachers organised Irish classes, lectures and concerts. But the dissidents chaffed at Hyde's insistence on the League staying above politics, a stance they believed was motivated by fear of Protestants otherwise defecting. Béaslaí thought Hyde preferred retaining a single Unionist to recruiting a hundred 'extreme' nationalists and that the price of unity above all else was paralysis. Clarke shared Béaslaí's disenchantment. Although not religiously sectarian, he was innately suspicious of any pro-British element and equated Gaelic League Protestants with those retired army officers who for a while had flooded into the Irish Volunteers. In Tom's eyes, both were obstacles to severing the connection with England.

Clarke also regarded Hyde's inner circle as a reactionary clique that was more concerned about keeping office than building a vibrant national organisation. By 1915 Hyde had been re-elected President twenty-two times in succession and despite flagging energy, he seemed reluctant to let go of his creation. Almost certainly the Gaelic League leaders reminded Clarke of the sclerotic old gang that he had cleared out of the Supreme Council, their removal a necessary pre-condition of the IRB's renaissance. And once again Tom sided with the Young Turks in demanding radical change in the Gaelic League. Transformed, it would join a broad national coalition for freedom, providing unarmed soldiers to wage cultural war on West Britonism or even actual fighters for the IRB, in the same way that the GAA had become a recruiting ground for separatism.

At the June 20 meeting, Clarke denounced the Gaelic League as 'rotten' and he was determined to bring about a showdown. After drafting an amendment to the non-political section of its constitution – one committing the League to a Gaelic-speaking independent Irish nation free of foreign influences – Tom selected Béaslaí to propose it at the next annual Ard Fheis in Dundalk. Keen on avoiding a public split, he was prepared to retain Hyde as a powerless figurehead by offering a declaration binding the League to non-sectarianism. When the two-day Ard Fheis opened on 1 August 1915, IRB delegates went for effective control and nominated a large slate of candidates for election to the central council. Many were chosen, including Alec McCabe, Seán T. O'Kelly and the imprisoned MacDermott. Clarke's supporters then agreed to water down Béaslaí's resolution and accept a free rather than an independent Gaelic-speaking Ireland. But Hyde still considered that a political commitment to an Ireland free of British rule was devisive and he carried through his threat to resign. By now the dissidents were indifferent because they had an ideal successor in Eoin MacNeill who had founded the League with Hyde and was the hero of the hour after splitting from Redmond. Clarke was making a habit of penetrating organisations with the intention of retaining MacNeill only as a figurehead.

Subsequently, the League's general secretary resigned and two IRB members, Sean T. O'Kelly and Seán Ó Muirthúile, wanted to succeed him. In early October 1915, Clarke presided over a special meeting of IRB representatives on the League's central council when both candidates stated their case. Unsurprisingly, Tom's favoured his old friend O'Kelly and after the meeting endorsed him; the League duly elected him on 12 October.[75]

By mid-1915 Clarke's revolutionary project had made significant progress. A reinvigorated IRB and the increasingly confident Irish Volunteers provided him with a group of talented leaders and manpower, while the Military Committee's plans for a rising were evolving steadily. Furthermore, Ireland's political situation was shifting in his favour as pro-war enthusiasm waned during 1915 in the face of a seemingly endless conflict with casualties mounting inexorably and war wounded becoming a common sight in Dublin. Fear of conscription increased, especially after its partial introduction in Great Britain, while many nationalists regarded Sir Edward Carson's inclusion in the coalition government that Asquith formed with the Conservatives in May 1915 as rewarding his agitation against Home Rule. They also resented the War Office turning down Redmond's advice to create in the British army Irish brigades that would include officers drawn from his National Volunteers. All the time the IRB was manipulating anti-recruiting and anti-conscription campaigns in the press and at public meetings. As Redmond's National Volunteers lapsed into terminal decline, the Irish Volunteers came to the forefront of public consciousness, widening the organisation's popular base through its energy and an uncompromising hostility to the war effort. The Royal Irish Constabulary reported that 'a spirit of disloyalty and pro-Germanism, which had hitherto been confined to a small number, was spreading'.[76]

Clarke himself was seizing the political initiative by fanning nationalist unease about deportation orders and generally accusing the British government of aggression in Ireland. Capturing the Gaelic League had also reinforced his followers' belief that things were going their way. But many Irish people opposed the IRB, which was still only a politically active minority, or else had retreated into political apathy. Clarke needed to excite the popular imagination through some dramatic event that would make people's patience with the status quo finally snap. Suddenly on 29 June 1915, such an opportunity fell right into his lap when 83-year-old Jeremiah O'Donovan Rossa died at a Staten Island hospital in New York. During a lengthy final illness, his third wife had nursed O'Donovan Rossa at home almost to the end when she broke down under the physical strain of lifting him in and out of bed. Much later John Devoy – who had a deathbed reconciliation with his old friend turned enemy – wrote that 'in dying when he did and at the age he did Rossa performed his last and perhaps greatest service to the Fenian cause'.[77] Tom realised instantly that O'Donovan Rossa's passing 3,000 miles away had the potential to transform the political situation in Ireland. Knowing that in politics timing was everything, he cabled Devoy asking for the body to be sent home immediately, telling Kathleen that 'if Rossa had planned to die at the most opportune time for serving the country, he could not have done better'.[78] Tom intended staging a funeral that in scale and political significance would surpass any in the history of Dublin, as well as being an event of national significance he hoped would attract mourners from all over Ireland.

In doing so, Tom was motivated in part by his respect for a venerable old man who was the last of the original Fenian leaders to die. And he had also long admired O'Donovan Rossa's radical extremism – what Devoy called 'the unrelenting hostility to England and the implacable determination to get rid of it which were the chief characteristics of the Fenian movement'.[79] Moreover, that O'Donovan Rossa had survived imprisonment, exile and material and emotional suffering resonated strongly with himself; in many ways O'Donovan Rossa's life story was Tom's as well. However, he wanted the Irish people to empathise not just with O'Donovan Rossa but with the legion of Fenians who had suffered for their beliefs. Devoy said that 'the Fenians were self-sacrificing men. They had their own share of human frailties but their worst enemies do not deny that they immolated themselves on the altar of their country'.[80] And as Devoy's slightly barbed tribute recognised, nobody symbolised that quality better than O'Donovan Rossa himself:

> In the exercise of this predominant Fenian quality of self-sacrifice O'Donovan Rossa was the most typical Fenian of them all. He began to sacrifice himself, his family and his interests at the very inception of the movement and he continued it to his last conscious hour. Often the sacrifice was wholly unnecessary and, even unwise, but Rossa believed it was called for and never hesitated or counted the cost.[81]

Tom intended using the funeral to demonstrate that while O'Donovan Rossa's body had died, his ideals had not and that a new generation of Fenians stood ready to sacrifice themselves in order to complete O'Donovan Rossa's mission. Tom was consciously using the past in order to shape Ireland's future, for he wanted O'Donovan Rossa's funeral also be a drama, a pageant, a recruiting platform that would swell the ranks of separatism. It was also designed to be armed propaganda that would legitimise O'Donovan Rossa's political violence, and make constitutional nationalism seem just a temporary aberration in the centuries of resistance to British rule in Ireland.

In deciding that O'Donovan Rossa was to be buried in Ireland, Tom had put his prestige and authority on the line by committing the separatist movement's entire resources to organising a great funeral. But he believed that a resounding success might convince many people that a new political order was emerging in Ireland and this made him risk everything. Clarke was also gambling that his uncertain health would hold up because, as the producer and director of O'Donovan Rossa's funeral, he would spend weeks planning an event that was infinitely more complex than the annual pilgrimage that he had inaugurated to Wolfe Tone's grave at Bodenstown in Co. Kildare. For a man in his fifty-eighth year who had survived serious illness and was simultaneously organising an insurrection and running two shops, this was a workload that would tax Tom's physical and nervous stamina to the limit. Whether he knew it or not, he was in danger of joining O'Donovan Rossa in a grave at Glasnevin before his plans for a rising ever came to fruition.

Tom's vision for O'Donovan Rossa's interment resembled a military operation. As chairman of the main funeral committee, he supervised eleven subcommittees that dealt with matters like hotel accommodation, publicity, trains, badges, a souvenir booklet, the obsequies and Glasnevin cemetery. Every important Irish separatist was involved, including Arthur Griffith, James Connolly, Eoin MacNeill and even Bulmer Hobson, but Clarke relied most on another IRB member, 37-year-old Thomas MacDonagh. A lecturer in English at University College Dublin, MacDonagh was an academic colleague of MacNeill's, his Volunteer Chief of Staff, an ardent cultural nationalist and a poet. Although a rather introspective and temperamental young man given to melodramatic outbursts, MacDonagh was also a gifted administrator who had devised the scheme of organisation that the Irish Volunteers had adopted after their split from Redmond.[82] MacDonagh's organising talent brought him rapid promotion, first to the Volunteers' Headquarters Staff and then to the post of Dublin Brigadier. It also led Clarke to appoint him chief marshal of a funeral procession that would involve smoothly mobilising a full muster of Dublin Volunteers and a host of political, cultural and sporting organisations before marching them on time miles across Dublin to Glasnevin cemetery. During the planning, MacDonagh frequently visited Tom's shop to draw on his extensive knowledge of large American processions, impressing Clarke with his efficiency and command of detail. He also contributed a poem about O'Donovan Rossa to the souvenir programme which Tom had commissioned.

As final arbiter, Clarke made key decisions about the funeral arrangements. Knowing Glasnevin's symbolic importance as a place of pilgrimage where nationalists paid homage to fallen heroes, he wanted O'Donovan Rossa's grave located near the replica ancient Irish round tower standing over that of Daniel O'Connell and the large stone marking Parnell's final resting place. Using money from Tom, Seán T. O'Kelly purchased a plot right beside O'Donovan Rossa's old Fenian comrades John O'Leary and James Stephens and near the Manchester Martyrs cenotaph.[83] For the graveside oration Clarke had to choose between Patrick Pearse and Father O'Flanagan, a rebel priest from Co. Sligo whom his bishop had endeavoured in vain to silence. O'Flanagan was a socialist activist and Sinn Féiner who had garnered grass-roots popularity and national publicity through his campaigns against landlords and the Royal Irish Constabulary. He was also a fine popular orator and many funeral organisers backed him. But Tom went with Pearse. He knew him better, preferred someone wearing a Volunteer uniform instead of a clerical collar, and he had seen how Pearse's intensity moved an audience. Pearse was a choice that would have a lasting impact on Irish history.

After a High Mass in New York, O'Donovan Rossa's body was kept in a cemetery vault until 17 July 1915 when his widow Mary and daughter Eileen sailed with the coffin for Ireland. Tom had arranged a funeral for Sunday 1 August because the following day's bank holiday would facilitate people attending from all over Ireland. Although this left him relatively little time, Clarke already had a template in two previous Dublin funerals. These were the Fenian funeral of Terence Bellew McManus in 1861 and the Bachelor's Walk funerals that Tom had attended twelve months earlier. McManus, a leader of the Young Ireland rising of 1848, had died in American exile on 14 January 1861 – months before the Fenians realised that a re-burial in Ireland could win them new followers. And although he was largely forgotten in Ireland, McManus's funeral to Glasnevin in November 1861 struck a chord, attracting immense crowds to an event that became part of separatist folklore. The historian Louis Bisceglia regards it as

> the effective starting point for the organisation of the politics of sepa-
> ratism: the catalyst in the formation and expansion of Fenianism in
> Ireland and America. The funeral is seen as the occasion upon which
> militant opinion against British rule in Ireland was transformed into
> overt revolutionary activity.[84]

Tom also intended fusing aspects of the Bachelor's Walk funerals with O'Donovan Rossa's, especially the trappings of a state funeral like the coffin in the Pro-Cathedral, a High Mass, the procession with many politicians, civic dignitaries and priests, and a Volunteer honour party around the grave. And Tom wanted the streets thronged once again by Dubliners and provincials, men, women and children of every age, class and occupation, in effect a microcosm of the nation. Unlike the Bachelor's Walk victims, O'Donovan Rossa was an octogenarian who had died peacefully and so rather than anger and grief, Tom wanted a joyous celebration of his life and the cold defiance of England that was Clarke's own speciality. Dublin's four Volunteer battalions would march in uniform, illegally carrying rifles, while Pearse's graveside oration would be a clarion call to resistance since Tom's advice was to 'make it as hot as hell, throw discretion to the winds'.[85]

On 18 July Tom wrote that:

With one thing and another I am rushed as I have never been before and am sometimes 'moidered' as to which thing of the heap should receive attention first. Just now a good deal of extra work is coming my way and as things must be made a success I am not disposed to shirk anything.

But Tom was also confident that the funeral would draw vast crowds; railway companies would be putting on seventeen special trains from all across Ireland: 'At present from the reports we are receiving from different parts of the country the funeral promises to be the largest seen here since that of McManus'.[86] On Tuesday 27 July 1915, O'Donovan Rossa's remains arrived in Dublin and were taken immediately to St Mary's Pro-Cathedral in Marlborough Street. Unlike his predecessor Cardinal Cullen, who had strongly denounced McManus in 1861, Archbishop Walsh allowed O'Donovan Rossa's coffin to have a catafalque and a Volunteer guard of honour. Next day at 11 a.m. Mrs O'Donovan Rossa and Eileen joined the packed congregation at a Solemn Requiem High Mass. Then Volunteers under the command of Tom's brother-in-law, Ned Daly, escorted the hearse through crowded streets and over the Liffey to the City Hall. There O'Donovan Rossa's body was borne through its great portico and placed on another catafalque under the dome of the spacious rotunda within. For twelve hours on each of the next four days, thousands of mourners filed past his casket, gazing on O'Donovan Rossa's face through a glass cover. Situated between the two main entrances to Dublin Castle, the City Hall was right at the front door of British rule in Ireland and Clarke could not have picked a more significant place to launch this spectacle of defiance. He must have relished the sheer effrontery of it all.

Clarke was lucky with the weather because Sunday 1 August turned out a brilliantly sunny day. During the morning at Dublin's four main railway stations, trains disgorged thousands of excursionists who then joined local mourners at designated vantage points across the city. A divisive figure in life, O'Donovan Rossa had in death united every section of Irish nationalism as well as drawing sympathisers from Great Britain and America. Shortly after 2 p.m. Tom officially began the funeral by closing O'Donovan Rossa's coffin lid and draping it with a tricolour. Volunteers then carried the remains outside the City Hall and into a waiting hearse. Three-quarters of an hour later the cortège set off for Glasnevin followed by a 2-mile-long procession of

20,000 mourners. At the head was an honour guard of armed Irish Volunteers, a cavalry unit and the wreath-covered hearse. Then came many priests and a coach containing O'Donovan Rossa's widow and daughter. Behind marched politicians and councillors from all over Ireland, members of the Citizen Army, Redmond's National Volunteers, the Ancient Order of Hibernians, the Irish National Foresters, political societies, labour unions and sporting organisations, including the Gaelic Athletic Association, and thousands of armed Irish Volunteers. They were accompanied by many bands, while the inclusion of women and young children furthered the image of a nation literally on the march and a rising generation joining the fight early.

Instead of going directly to Glasnevin, the procession took a circuitous 5-mile route so that many more people could see the casket as it passed places of historical significance; even during the short distance from College Green to the Rotunda at the far end of O'Connell Street, an estimated 30,000 people watched in respectful silence. In contrast, the bands played national airs, so making the funeral a triumphal celebration of O'Donovan Rossa's life and principles, and kept moving at a steady pace a procession that needed sixty-five minutes to pass any given point. Upon reaching Glasnevin at 4.30 p.m., bands began playing 'The Dead March' as Volunteers escorted the hearse through the cemetery gates and then between two lines of Volunteers to the mortuary chapel. After a service in which absolution was pronounced and prayers said for the dead, priests led the coffin and mourners to the grave. When O'Donovan Rossa's remains were laid to rest, the grave was filled in and Father O'Flanagan recited prayers in Irish.

In the uniform of a Volunteer officer, Pearse then stepped forward to deliver the graveside oration that would interpret all that O'Donovan Rossa had stood for and the sufferings which had made him a political martyr. Having memorised his carefully honed words, Pearse achieved immediacy with his audience as first in Irish and then in English he spoke with great fluency and controlled passion. Into a five-minute *tour de force*, Pearse compressed the IRB's message to the Irish people that he was 'speaking on behalf of a new generation that had been re-baptised in the Fenian faith and that has accepted the responsibility of carrying out the Fenian programme'. This younger generation was in spiritual communion with O'Donovan Rossa and those of his comrades living and dead as well as Irishmen still suffering in prison. On their behalf Pearse declared 'we pledge to Ireland our love and we pledge to English rule in Ireland our hate'. And despite being in a place of peace, his message was one of war, unceasing war until English rule in Ireland ended because, although the enemy seemed overwhelmingly strong, 'the seeds sown by the young men of '65 and '67 are coming to their miraculous ripening today'. Soon they would greatly shock their foe:

They think they have pacified Ireland. They think that they have purchased half of us and intimidated the other half. They think that they have foreseen everything, think that they have provided against everything; but the fools, the fools, the fools! – they have left us our Fenian dead, and while Ireland holds these graves, Ireland unfree shall never be at peace.[87]

Pearse's oration was well calculated to electrify those who heard it and resonate far beyond the occasion that called for it. But Clarke had a final ace to play, a *coup de théâtre* he had kept secret until the end. As a band played 'The Last Post', an officer, Seamus Sullivan, summoned forward a party of Volunteers who fired three volleys over O'Donovan Rossa's grave. Less a farewell to an old Fenian warrior than a new generation's defiant battle cry against England, it was an event unique in the history of modern Ireland and in a sense the sounds reverberated throughout the entire country.

O'Donovan Rossa's funeral had indeed fulfilled Tom's great expectations. Vast crowds did come, some no doubt for a day out, others through curiosity or just to be seen, but many, without endorsing his methods, had also dreamt O'Donovan Rossa's dream of Ireland charting its own destiny. For a day Clarke had provided them with a glimpse of a country that could be imagined and the way things might be in a free land. On 1 August 1915 the armed representatives of British power virtually disappeared off Dublin streets and apparently ceded them to Irish separatism. Afraid of another Bachelor's Walk, Chief Secretary Birrell confined soldiers to barracks and the few Dublin Metropolitan policemen who appeared on the funeral's periphery contented themselves with making notes. Irish flags flew everywhere though mourners' eyes were fixed on the lone tricolour draped around O'Donovan Rossa's coffin. And his impressive funeral – the equal of that for a European monarch – was the achievement not of aristocratic courtiers but ordinary, if talented, Irishmen. In efficiently mobilising multitudes of people, they had also buried the old argument that Ireland in the hands of its own population would rapidly descend into anarchy. Newspapers noted the national unity on display as bickering parties and organisations united for a great occasion; even Redmond's almost moribund National Volunteers marched alongside the rival Irish Volunteers. Journalists particularly reported spectators' pride in 8,000 armed and uniformed Irish Volunteers who resembled a parade of regular troops. Beyond the good feelings and fond memories, mourners sensed that something tangible was gestating – what one paper called 'the nucleus of a national army'.[88]

By the evening of 1 August 1915, Clarke could savour a great triumph. Politically the most successful day of his life so far, it had validated Tom's judgement in his followers' eyes and enhanced his status as the leader of Irish separatism. While Pearse's memorable graveside oration was to have lasting effect, Tom was clearly the organiser behind O'Donovan Rossa's funeral. A day after the Solemn High Mass, one newspaper noted how 'at the request of Mrs O'Donovan Rossa, Mr Thomas Clarke, an old friend of the deceased, took charge of the arrangements in connection with the secular portion of yesterday's functions including the removal of the remains'. Many onlookers would no doubt have observed with some curiosity this stranger directing Ned Daly to transfer O'Donovan Rossa's body from the Pro-Cathedral to City Hall and later closing the coffin to start the funeral procession, but to those in the know it was their leader confidently exercising his power and authority.

When O'Donovan Rossa's funeral was finally over, weeks of exertion had clearly taken a great toll on Tom. But although he arrived exhausted in Limerick for a week's recuperation, Madge Daly found him still basking in the afterglow of his great achievements: 'He was wild with delight and believed that the effect would be splendid'.[89] Clarke was especially overjoyed at having pulled off a tremendous organising feat, one that bore more than a passing resemblance to a military operation. It can only have confirmed Tom's faith in his ability to bring off a rising.

NOTES

1   Piaras Beaslai, *Irish Independent*, 12 January 1953.
2   Kathleen Clarke, *Revolutionary Woman*, p. 53
3   Pearse to Devoy, 12 August 1914, NLI MS 31,696.
4   Sean T. O'Kelly, BMH WS 1765B.
5   P.S. O'Hegarty, 'Recollections of the IRB'.
6   Richard Connolly, BMH WS 523.
7   P.S. O'Hegarty, 'Recollections of the IRB'.
8   Sean T. O'Kelly, BMH WS 1765.
9   Piaras Beaslai, *Irish Independent*, 5 February 1953.
10 Sean T. O'Kelly, BMH WS 1765.
11 Denis McCullough Papers, NLI MS 31,653.
12 Piaras Beaslai, *Irish Independent*, 21 January 1953.
13 Diarmuid Lynch, BMH WS 4.
14 Clarke to John Kenny, *Gaelic American*, 3 May 1924.
15 Thomas Morrissey, *William O'Brien 1881-1968*, p. 91
16 William O'Brien, *Labour News*, May 1937.
17 Sean T. O'Kelly, BMH WS 1765.

18 Recounted by Cathal O'Shannon, December 1950, NLI MS 33,8718/H.
19 Quoted by Donald Nevin in *James Connolly: A Full Life*, pp. 521–2.
20 For this see Ben Novick, 'DORA, Suppression and Nationalist Propaganda in Ireland, 1914–1915', *New Hibernia Review*, Vol. 1, no. 4, Winter 1997, pp. 41–7.
21 Madge Daly, 'The Memoirs of Madge Daly'.
22 Bulmer Hobson, *The History of the Irish Volunteers*, p. 183.
23 Ibid., p. 169.
24 Pearse to Devoy, 12 August 1914, NLI MS 31,696.
25 Ibid.
26 Seamus O'Connor, Statement on National Activities in Dublin 1913–1916, BMH Collected Documents, no. 64. See also Piaras Beaslai's account of the City Hall meeting in the *Irish Independent*, 22 January 1953.
27 Ibid.
28 Quoted in Ben Novick, *Conceiving Revolution: Irish Nationalist Propaganda During the First World War*, p. 124.
29 Hobson, *Ireland, Yesterday and Tomorrow*, pp. 55–6.
30 Beaslai, *Irish Independent*, 12 January 1953.
31 Donal Nevin (ed.), *Between Comrades: James Connolly, Letters and Correspondence 1889–1916*, p. 521. Connolly to William O'Brien, 22 September 1914.
32 Sean T. O'Kelly, BMH WS 1765.
33 *Irish Worker*, 5 September 1914.
34 Donal Nevin (ed.), *Between Comrades: James Connolly, Letters and Correspondence 1889–1916*, p. 521. Connolly to William O'Brien, 22 September 1914.
35 Piaras Beaslai, *Irish Independent*, 12 January 1953.
36 Ibid.
37 Ibid.
38 Diarmuid Lynch, BMH WS 4.
39 For Ned Daly, see Helen Litton, *Edward Daly* (Dublin: O'Brien Press, 2013) .
40 Kathleen Clarke, *Revolutionary Woman*, p. 69.
41 Madge Daly, 'The Memoirs of Madge Daly'.
42 Patrick Stephenson, 'The Epic of the Mendicity', Allen Library, Dublin.
43 'When Germany fights England', *Irish Freedom*, October and November 1911.
44 Bulmer Hobson, BMH WS 87.
45 For this meeting, see Devoy, *Recollections of an Irish Rebel*, p. 403.
46 For Kenny's mission to Germany, see his two articles in the *Gaelic American*, 28 April and 3 May 1924.
47 Clarke to John Daly.
48 Kenny's account of his first visit to Ireland is in the *Gaelic American*, 3 May 1924.
49 In Kenny's account of his second visit to Ireland in the *Gaelic American*, 10 May 1924.
50 For Mellows, see Desmond Greaves, *Liam Mellows and the Irish Revolution*.
51 Sean T. O'Kelly, BMH WS 1765.
52 Diarmuid Lynch, BMH WS 4.
53 Colonel Maurice Moore, *History of the Irish Volunteers*, NLI ILB 94109.
54 Ibid.
55 Ruth Dudley Edwards, *Patrick Pearse*, pp. 153–4.
56 Piaras Beaslai, Beaslai Papers, NLI MS 33,944 (3).

57 Piaras Beaslai, 'My Friend Patrick Pearse', Beaslai Papers, NLI MS 33,935 (3).

58 John Devoy, *Recollections of an Irish Rebel*, p. 421.

59 Sean T. O'Kelly, BMH WS 1765.

60 For the Ireland report, see Michael Foy and Brian Barton, *The Easter Rising*, pp. 25–7.

61 Diarmuid Lynch, *The IRB and the 1916 Insurrection*, pp. 29–30.

62 P.S. O'Hegarty, BMH WS 27.

63 Ibid.

64 P.S. O'Hegarty, BMH WS 841.

65 P.S. O'Hegarty, 'Recollections of the IRB'.

66 Diarmuid Lynch, BMH WS 4.

67 P.S. O'Hegarty, 'Recollections of the IRB'.

68 Denis McCullough, BMH WS 915.

69 Ibid.

70 Sean T. O'Kelly, BMH WS 1765.

71 Denis McCullough, BMH WS 915.

72 Robert Brennan, BMH WS 779.

73 Liam Lynch, BMH WS 4.

74 Piaras Beaslai, *Irish Independent*, 15 May 1957.

75 Piaras Beaslai, *Irish Independent*, 13 January 1953. For the Gaelic League controversy, see also Sean T. O'Kelly, BMH WS 1765.

76 In a reported entitled 'The Sinn Fein or Irish Volunteers and the Rebellion' which was drawn up for the Chief Secretary. It is reproduced in Brendan Mac Gilla Choille, *Intelligence Notes 1913–1916* (Dublin: State Paper Office, 1966), p. 222.

77 *Gaelic American*, 31 July 1915.

78 Kathleen Clarke, *Revolutionary Woman*, p. 56.

79 Devoy, *Recollections of an Irish Rebel*, p. 319

80 Ibid., pp. 319–20.

81 Ibid., p. 320.

82 John Kenny, *Gaelic American*, 10 May 1924.

83 Sean T. O'Kelly, BMH WS 1765.

84 Louis Bisceglia, 'The Fenian Funeral of Terence Bellew McManus', in *Eire-Ireland*, vol. XIV, no. 3, 1979.

85 Kathleen Clarke, *Revolutionary Woman*, p. 56.

86 'The Memoirs of Madge Daly'.

87 For Pearse's speech at the O'Donovan Rossa funeral, see Sean T. O'Kelly, BMH WS 1765. For an interesting analysis of the symbolism of nationalist political burials at Glasnevin, see Nina Ranalli, 'The Dust of Some: Glasnevin Cemetery and the Politics of Burial'.

88 *Freeman's Journal*, 29 July 1915.

89 'The Memoirs of Madge Daly'.

6

On the Road to Revolution, Part Two: September 1915–April 1916

On 18 September 1915, Tom and Kathleen collected MacDermott on his release from prison and brought him to Richmond Avenue where they had breakfast in the garden and relaxed as birds sang on a gloriously sunny, peaceful morning. Enforced absence had actually refreshed the overworked MacDermott and made him eager to plunge back into politics. Soon he and Clarke involved themselves directly in the planning of a rising when they joined Pearse, Plunkett and Ceannt on what became known as the Military Council. Over the next four months the pace accelerated at meetings held discreetly in places such as Clontarf Town Hall – whose librarian was Clarke's friend – and Ceannt's house in south Dublin, but, piquantly, most often in the back of Tom's old premises at 77 Amiens Street. He had sold this to an old friend, Mrs Houlihan, who had converted it into a basket-maker's shop. As one of the Military Council's first steps, it sent Diarmuid Lynch to the west of Ireland where he identified Fenit harbour in Tralee Bay as a possible landing place for a German arms shipment.[1] During the last three months of 1915, it also ordered battalion commandants in Dublin to reconnoitre locations that might become rebel garrisons. These included Boland's Mills, public buildings such as the Four Courts on the Liffey quays, and Ireland's largest poorhouse, the South Dublin Union. Battalion commandants were also instructed to prepare their men psychologically and militarily for urban warfare through night classes on street-fighting techniques such as constructing barricades, cutting passages through buildings, loopholing walls, sandbagging windows and firing from rooftops.

In early December 1915 Clarke and McDermott tightened their hold on the IRB when the Supreme Council elected a new President to succeed the vanished Deakin. Just before voting, Denis McCullough — who had recently been released from Belfast prison — told MacDermott that he intended nominating Pearse. But Seán and Tom had a different script and MacDermott, disingenuously, tried putting McCullough off. As McCullough wrote later:

> He asked me 'for God's sake' to do nothing of the kind, as 'we don't know Pearse well enough, and couldn't control him' — an important factor then. He told me that they — I presumed Tom Clarke and himself, in whom I had absolute trust — would propose a name in due course.[2]

And when nominations came up, Tom immediately proposed and Sean seconded none other than McCullough himself. McCullough protested that he didn't want the responsibility and lived in Belfast when an effective President really should reside in Dublin. It never dawned on McCullough that in Clarke and MacDermott's eyes these factors made him an ideal President. Since McCullough was re-building his business in Belfast after imprisonment and also had family commitments, he could only rarely travel to Dublin for meetings of the three-man IRB Executive, but naturally his empty chair would suit the other two members — Tom and Seán — just fine. Clarke of course could have had the Presidency for himself, but staying in the shadows was now too deeply ingrained in his character and anyway he had always preferred the reality of power to its trappings. Furthermore, as would soon become clear, Tom had another — surprising — reason for selecting McCullough.

At Christmas 1915 Tom and Seán enjoyed a brief respite from war planning when they, Kathleen, the three Clarke boys and Ned Daly travelled to the Dalys' house in Limerick. Both men badly needed a break; Eamon Dore had observed them 'worn out and tired'.[3] Although the adults relaxed and enjoyed themselves playing cards and talking long into the night, Madge Daly recalled that it was a bittersweet time:

> We all felt that many changes would occur before the next Christmas. We knew instinctively that we should never be all together again, that in the coming effort many would fall but this seemed to add to our enjoyment in each other's society and certainly made the ties of love and friendship stronger.[4]

Kathleen shared her sister's sentiment: 'We had a feeling it might be the last Christmas we would spend together'.[5] And it was not just the prospect of some of them falling in the coming fight that hung over the celebrations.

Everyone knew Uncle John was fading fast. Weakened by imprisonment and long afflicted with syphilis, his body was now gripped by motor neurone disease, an incurable illness that was progressively wasting his muscles, causing paralysis, difficulty in swallowing and a slurring of speech that made him hard to understand. The symptoms had first appeared around 1909 and two years later after Uncle John had taken 'a turn', Tom asked his doctor for a candid opinion. Since motor neurone disease had not yet even been identified as an illness, Dr Broderick reassured him that Uncle John had every chance of living to a ripe old age. In fact, a sufferer's life expectancy is five years and by 1915 Daly's race was almost run. Having first met Uncle John in his magnificent prime, Tom found his rapid decline painful to watch; in July he said to Madge: 'Oh God! If Uncle John were only able to be with us these times. Many and many a time do I regret that he is knocked out'.[6] By Christmas this once vibrant autocrat whose word had been law in the Daly household was completely dependent on Madge. Uncle John's pitiable decline probably strengthened Tom's determination to strike while his own precarious health still held.

Madge remembered that 'a few days after when were seeing Sean off at the station one of my sisters asked him if he would be down for Easter. He gave me a look and said – perhaps, if possible'.[7] Cagey as ever, MacDermott did not reveal that just before Christmas the Military Council had fixed the Rising for Easter 1916. Originally it had chosen Good Friday, 21 April, but changed the date to Easter Sunday after realising that mobilising large numbers of Volunteers – many of them civil servants – on a Friday might alert the British authorities to something more than routine practice manoeuvres being intended. Nor did Clarke and MacDermott tell the Supreme Council when it met for the last time before the Rising at Clontarf Town Hall on Sunday 16 January 1916. Encouraged by the super-vigilant Tom, everyone agreed to resist any British raid on the premises and placed their revolvers on the table – except for Pearse who sheepishly confessed that he had forgotten his weapon.[8] MacDermott then proposed a motion blandly reaffirming the decision of August 1914 to rise 'at the earliest possible date'. Of ten or eleven members present, only Pat McCartan hesitated about making such a firm commitment irrespective of the domestic or international situations. McCullough was in the chair and recalled how McCartan

pointed out that we were taking a great responsibility in committing the country to war, without having, at least, a considerable section of the population behind us. I had to quieten the protests of at least two of those present and enthusiastically in favour of a fight, by pointing out that McCartan's contention was a very just and reasonable one in accordance with the I.R.B. Constitution and must be considered calmly. Against that I stated that we had been organising and planning for years for the purpose of a protest in arms when an opportunity occurred and if ever such an opportunity was to arrive, I didn't think any better time would present itself in our day.[9]

This satisfied McCartan and MacDermott's motion passed unanimously, though the Military Council's arrangements for a rising still needed the Supreme Council's final approval.[10]

The international situation was hardly conducive to the IRB striking 'at the earliest possible moment'. During 1915 Germany's prospects of imminent victory had gradually receded as Britain's armed forces, economy and society adapted to total war and Britain became its most formidable enemy. Kitchener's new armies had swelled Allied strength on the Western Front for a series of offensives against German lines, while at sea American protests had forced a halt in September 1915 to Germany's six-month campaign of unrestricted U-boat warfare against merchant shipping around the British Isles. And on the Eastern Front, battle lines had stabilised for the winter after German soldiers occupied Warsaw in September 1915. Furthermore, months after Plunkett had returned from his German mission, there was no sign of Berlin helping the IRB materially. Instead, the German army and naval authorities vetoed military assistance to Irish revolutionaries and when in October 1915 Devoy asked for 'a small quantity of arms' to be sent to Ireland, the German Admiralty pigeonholed his request.

Yet in January 1916 Clarke was even more determined to bring about an Irish rising in the near future. He was motivated partly by a fear of Germany's armed forces suddenly collapsing or else Berlin agreeing to a peace conference at which Irish nationalists would be unrepresented. Tom also worried that perpetual inaction was demoralising the Volunteers, that they were tiring of drills, route marches and manoeuvres that seemingly were going nowhere. Moreover, Tom suspected that the opportunity for military action in Ireland was receding fast. In the war's early stages, the British government had been extraordinarily tolerant of Volunteers arming and drilling, but the rising tide of arrests and deportations during 1915 convinced Tom that its patience was running out. Just as in 1798 and 1865, the British might suddenly arrest opposition leaders, leaving the Volunteers, IRB and Citizen Army leaderless and disorganised. Connolly had actually spoiled Tom's Christmas because Seán T. O'Kelly and Diarmuid

Lynch had arrived in Limerick with a warning that Connolly's agitation was dragging everyone to the brink of disaster. Eamon Dore recalled that:

> The Citizen Army 'night manoeuvres' round the Castle nearly set off, and I think did alarm the British authorities but it certainly upset Tom and Seán, because I heard the latter say 'Connolly is becoming impossible'. They wanted a showdown before he, by his impetuosity, destroyed their years of planning.[11]

Concern about Connolly forced Tom to cut short his Christmas holidays and return to Dublin with Ned Daly on St Stephen's Day. By January 1916 Tom feared that Connolly's provocative language and activities would give Dublin Castle an excuse to crush all its enemies in Ireland. Having abandoned his hopes of a socialist international revolution, Connolly was intensifying his military preparations for a national uprising against British rule in Ireland, acquiring weapons, holding route marches and conducting mock attacks on government buildings. Demanding immediate action, Connolly threatened that if nobody else took the lead, he would strike alone with his 200 followers. Unaware of the Military Council's existence, he was denouncing Irish Volunteer leaders as spineless and had begun appealing over their heads to ordinary members, hoping that if the Citizen Army did rise they would drag the Volunteer Executive and Headquarters Staff into the struggle. Clarke was on edge. He regarded Connolly's behaviour as reckless and feared it would ruin the Military Council's own plans.

At January's Supreme Council meeting, Tom had warned against Connolly dragging them into a premature rising, but even the ultra-cautious McCartan felt that if Connolly acted they could not stand aside, otherwise the British would follow up their inevitable victory over the Citizen Army by suppressing all remaining opposition in Ireland. Diarmuid Lynch witnessed the IRB leaders' trepidation at Connolly's 'sheer madness':

> It was chiefly the mercy of Providence that blinded the British authorities and kept them [in the first place] from pouncing on Connolly and his I.C.A. of 200 men – who could been nabbed outside the precincts of Liberty Hall in the early months of 1916. Had they [the British] attacked the I.C.A., the Irish Volunteers were bound to become involved in some haphazard fashion. Incidentally, the leaders of the IRB as well as those of the Irish Volunteers [as such] might have been caught off their guard and arrested by the British. One shudders to think of the possible result![12]

As well as Connolly, Eoin MacNeill and Bulmer Hobson also weighed heavily on Clarke's mind in early 1916. All three men had the ability to complicate and even derail the IRB's rising. So during January Tom and the Military Council acted to neutralise or navigate their way past these potential troublemakers. MacNeill concerned Clarke least, sharing as he did his inner circle's scorn and contempt for the Volunteer President. Once, when he was reviewing Limerick Volunteers, MacNeill had stayed with the Dalys and made a poor impression on them. Madge recalled that:

> My uncle had a long talk with him. He said to me afterwards that he feared that MacNeill was a misfit in the position he held in the Irish Volunteers, that he lacked the essentials of a revolutionary and wished he could be induced to resign before the Rising. He spoke of it to Seán and Tom, they agreed, but hoped when the critical time came to be able to control him and get him to resign.[13]

Pearse was also sceptical, describing MacNeill as 'weak, hopelessly weak' and even friends thought him indecisive and lethargic. Although MacNeill had a gift for capturing the spirit of the times by enunciating big ideas like the Gaelic League and the Irish Volunteers, he shrank from the daily grind of building up his creations. He avoided many Executive meetings of the Irish Volunteers and left the daily administration to Hobson. And as a leader of men MacNeill entirely lacked Clarke's drive and appetite for politics. But though Tom would have welcomed him walking away from Volunteer headquarters, MacNeill just could not let go of his creation and his position as Volunteer Chief of Staff. He had succumbed to the aphrodisiac of power, the thrill not just of writing history but actually making it. However, Tom had miscalculated by greatly underrating MacNeill, an intelligent man who held himself in high esteem, commanded the Volunteer rank and file's loyalty and – as events would prove – was not inclined to be shunted into political oblivion.

Tom discounted MacNeill partly because he seemed completely under the influence of Hobson, someone the conspirators considered a much more dangerous man. Ever watchful for radical manipulation of the Volunteers, he had forced Clarke's supporters to constantly engage in subterfuge to hide their subterranean activities. While he hated Hobson, Tom also feared him – and with good reason. If Hobson could ever prove that a conspiracy existed at Volunteer headquarters, he could get MacNeill to purge the organisation. To prevent this happening, Clarke decided to risk a bold gamble. It did not involve a conciliatory gesture to Hobson or a grand rapprochement with him. The split between Clarke and Hobson was irreparable, their ideological and personal differences as deep as ever, and too much vitriol had flowed under the bridge. Instead Tom thought Hobson might be cajoled into line by using against him his IRB membership, his still important posts in the movement and the IRB's insistence on loyalty and obedience to higher authority. If anyone could get through to Hobson it was surely his oldest political friend, and newly elected Supreme Council President, Denis McCullough. Unlike Clarke and MacDermott, McCullough had stayed on civilised terms with Hobson and resisted calls to expel him from the IRB.

Many years later Hobson claimed that in early 1916 an irregular source had told him about a rebellion happening in the near future. His assertion has evoked considerable scepticism from historians, but it was actually true. McCullough recalled that on Monday 17 January 1916

> with the consent of the S.C., if not directly on their instructions, I waited over in Dublin, on the Monday after the decision by the S.C., to have an Armed Rising, before the war ended, to advise Hobson (who had been a member of the S.C., and was still Chairman of the Dublin Centres Board of the Organisation) that this decision had been taken and warned him to adjust his attitude and actions accordingly. He seems to have completely ignored this warning then and later.[14]

Tom had miscalculated that Hobson would have to listen to a direct warning from the IRB's highest authority, especially since continued defiance of the Supreme Council and its President was tantamount to mutiny. But Hobson could trump them with an IRB constitution that forbade a rebellion without the Irish people's support. And he kept going his own way, heightening Clarke and MacDermott's already considerable fury. Furthermore, although Hobson was bound by the IRB's oath of secrecy, they could never be certain that he might not use the information to sabotage their plans. One day there would be reckoning with Hobson, but for the moment Tom would have to wait.

Clarke, though, could not delay dealing with Connolly. Indeed Connolly's agitation had also impelled MacNeill and Hobson to confront him at Volunteer headquarters on Sunday 16 January 1916, a meeting that Pearse also attended just hours before he was due at the IRB's Supreme Council. All three men were appalled by Connolly's candid admission that he hoped to drag the Irish Volunteers into a rising, and afterwards Pearse would have warned his fellow conspirators that they had to act quickly before Connolly spiralled right out of control. Nevertheless, Clarke had to decide between using the stick or the carrot. Whatever his fury at Connolly's provocative tactics, he knew that employing the Volunteers to crush him and the Citizen Army risked the very British repression he wanted to avoid in the first place. Reaching out to Connolly would have to be done more imaginatively and generously than in Hobson's case and would have to stand a chance of being reciprocated. Fortunately for Clarke, he knew this might happen, because Connolly had already approached him. The intermediary was Eamon O'Dwyer, an IRB county centre from Tipperary and an Irish Volunteer organiser who was friendly with both Tom and Connolly's trade union assistant, William O'Brien.[15] In late 1915 O'Brien introduced him to Connolly, who told O'Dwyer that even if Volunteer leaders intended rising, he feared they might leave it too late; the time to act was while England was at war. But the conflict would not last forever and Connolly 'said that he was determined to strike and before long unless he had some assurance that the Irish would strike soon'.[16] O'Dwyer suggested Connolly might learn more about a possible rising from Clarke, MacDermott and Pearse, and got his permission to brief Clarke in his Parnell Street shop. Tom was intrigued by O'Dwyer's report and backed the idea of meeting Connolly. By mid-January 1916, it was time to test the seriousness of Connolly's feelers.

At about 4 p.m. on the afternoon of Wednesday 19 January, Ned Daly, Eamon Dore and Frank Daly, a First Battalion officer, arrived by car at Liberty Hall.[17] While Dore and Frank Daly waited outside, Ned Daly entered the building and was allowed to see Connolly, whom he invited to meet high-ranking IRB members. Since Ned was Clarke's brother-in-law and Commandant of the First Battalion, Connolly knew he was acting on orders from the top. That Ned had not threatened Connolly is clear from Frank Daly's recollection that within a few minutes Ned came out chatting in a friendly manner with a smiling Connolly and that 'there was never any question of producing weapons'.[18] After Connolly shook hands with Frank Daly, the four men left in the car. Although Connolly had gone willingly, it might have been different had he spurned Ned's invitation. Dore said that 'Clarke and MacDermott were fed up with Connolly at this time and they were going to talk to him whether he was agreeable or not and would have forced him to listen whether he was agreeable or not',[19] but almost certainly not on this occasion as Ned Daly alone could hardly have forced Connolly out of Liberty Hall. Driving along the South Circular Road, the party reached Dolphin's Barn and the house of John Cassidy, an IRB member who managed the local brickworks. Pearse and almost certainly

Plunkett and Ceannt were waiting for Connolly. Tom never put in an appearance – he was in his Parnell Street shop – and MacDermott spent all day in the city centre.[20] But undoubtedly both men had agreed with their Military Council colleagues the approach to take with Connolly. He was now told everything including the Military Council's existence, the IRB's planning for an Easter rising, the secret infiltration of the Irish Volunteers and the efforts to secure German military aid. Instead of mutual hostility, the Volunteers and Citizen Army should work together and then rise together. With a seat on the Military Council, Connolly would be able to shape that insurrection.

Then Connolly disappeared for three days. Cassidy's house was too small to accommodate a group of men and so almost certainly he spent the second and third day elsewhere considering the IRB's proposals. Connolly said later that he had gone through hell while walking 40 miles – most likely on roads somewhere in the countryside around Dublin. When he returned to Liberty Hall, Connolly had decided to accept the Military Council's offer. Despite his agonising, it was an offer he really could not refuse, a sweet deal that gave him everything he could have dreamt of. In return he just had to wait another four months for a rising that would stand a far better chance of succeeding than any he could instigate by himself. In order to share the IRB's military secrets, Connolly was required to join the organisation. He was sworn in as a member-at-large who did not have to attend circle meetings.

The alliance with Connolly was Clarke's master stroke, an inspired and audacious gamble that ended the danger that Connolly's inflammatory rhetoric posed to the IRB. It also gave the IRB something it lacked – a military face to the revolution. Unlike Clarke, MacDermott, Pearse, the dying Plunkett and Ceannt, Connolly had the personality, credibility and desire to lead a rebel army. He had been a soldier, was passionately interested in war, and had lectured and published articles on military history. In addition, Connolly already commanded an army that he had created from nothing. He also looked the part. Authoritative with a habitually fierce expression, Connolly radiated integrity and seriousness. And he demanded from his followers sobriety, obedience and ideological commitment, brutally reprimanding anyone who fell short of his high standards. And although the Irish Volunteers numerically dwarfed the tiny Citizen Army, in almost every other respect Connolly's organisation was superior. Its members were dedicated to the single goal of revolution, trained for urban warfare, and had a unity of purpose and discipline that contrasted strongly with the faction fighting that disfigured the Irish Volunteers.

After committing themselves and their organisations to fighting in the same rising, Clarke and Connolly got along very well. Whatever his feelings about Connolly's exasperating behaviour, Tom had never lost his respect for someone who, like him, had dedicated his life to the cause of revolution. And in other ways both men were very similar: taciturn and serious, doers not talkers, men who had known poverty and hardship but had risen entirely through their own ability and effort. Natural leaders, they had had instilled in their members the efficiency, organisation and strength of will that a revolution required – qualities that Clarke and Connolly possessed in full measure. Once Clarke and Connolly became allies, the Military Council had to explain why Connolly had suddenly abandoned his public calls for an immediate revolution; they did this by concocting a cover story which Tom got Pearse to deliver at the next Volunteer Executive meeting. It was not an easy story to sell. A highly sceptical Sean Fitzgibbon recalled that:

> Pearse, obviously in great stress of emotion, and speaking very tensely, said that he and MacDermott had induced Connolly to take no action without the aid of the Volunteers. I asked Pearse if he had given any promise or had pledged the Volunteers. Pearse said 'No'. His right knee kept quivering as he spoke. He kept raising his right foot slightly, tapping the ground with it, like a horse pawing as he answered my questions. He was lying, for at that time the date of the Rising had been decided upon.[21]

Nor did Hobson buy the story, but as yet he still lacked the smoking gun that would expose the conspiracy in which he now knew Clarke, MacDermott, Pearse and the others were engaged.

At the end of January 1916, Clarke's buoyant mood suffered a setback literally at the hands of a trusted follower. Late at night Kathleen was summoned to Seán McGarry's house on Ballybough Road where she found Tom wounded and awaiting a doctor.[22] He and McGarry had been on their way home when McGarry showed off to a member of Cumann na mBan (the Irish Volunteer's women's auxiliary organisation) by doing cowboy tricks with his pistol. Pointing it at Tom, McGarry brushed aside his protests and insisted that the gun was not loaded. But when he saw the weapon pointed at his heart, Tom moved out of the way just before McGarry's finger slipped on the trigger, a shot rang out and a bullet lodged in Tom's right elbow joint. Kathleen brought her husband home and put him to bed, but Tom was in agony from pain and shock and he walked the floor all night, feeling very cold despite the heat from a big coal fire. Next morning a doctor at the Mater Hospital located and removed the bullet, but not before Clarke upset the Sister of Mercy nurses by refusing the sacraments before his operation.[23] Although the wound healed, he endured acute pain for weeks and because the sinews had contracted, Tom never recovered full use of his right arm. Fortunately, he was ambidextrous and learned to shoot with his left hand for the rising. Kathleen was furious at McGarry's irresponsibility and would have been glad to see the back of him, but Tom ignored all her pleas: 'He had a strange love for Seán McGarry and though suffering from McGarry's carelessness he had all sorts of excuses for him and hated to hear me damning him as I often did'.[24] Clarke gave him a fool's pardon because of McGarry's loyalty to him. Despite having almost killed him, Tom knew that in an instant McGarry would lay down his life for him and that counted. Afterwards Tom recuperated in Limerick, but was back in Dublin for St Patrick's Day.

On 7 February Clarke's transatlantic courier, Tommy O'Connor, reached New York by ocean liner carrying a cipher message from the Military Council to John Devoy who was to reveal the contents only to the Clan's Revolutionary Directorate and the German ambassador. It said the rising was definitely set for Sunday 23 April, but that Clarke and his colleagues now shared Devoy's opinion that 'the sending of a military expedition from Germany to Ireland was an absolute impossibility'.[25] They had also written off any hope of getting even an arms shipment before 23 April; the most Clarke and his fellow conspirators expected now was that after the rising began, Germany would send all possible military help to the rebels. Instead Tom and his fellow conspirators asked Devoy and the Clan to send a shipload of arms from America that would reach Limerick Pier between 20 and 23 April. When Devoy immediately convened the Revolutionary Directorate and read the dispatch, 'all were startled by the contents. They had no idea that the men in Ireland would decide to fight until the military and naval situation was more favourable than it was then'.[26] Moreover, the Clan was now without the funds to purchase a shipload of arms, having just arranged to send its last $25,000 to Clarke, the IRB's treasurer. This brought to $100,000 the money Tom had received from America within a year, the largest sum ever made available to start an Irish insurrection. Even if Devoy had been able to raise the money, he knew that the vigilance of the pro-British Wilson administration would have sabotaged any arms shipment from the USA to Ireland.

Devoy and the Revolutionary Directorate still hesitated to recommend that the rising should be postponed. Delay had brought disaster in Fenian times and besides, the Military Council was not asking for their advice but announcing a decision. So Devoy decided on one last appeal to the Germans. Through the German embassy he sent the Military Council's message about an imminent rising to Berlin along with his own request for a German arms shipment to Ireland. Devoy's timing was perfect because by early 1916 Berlin had become more receptive to the aspirations of Irish revolutionaries. The Chief of the General Staff, Falkenhayn, now believed that England was Germany's most dangerous enemy and would soon have seventy army divisions ready. To knock its 'best sword out of her hands', he intended launching a great battle at the historic fortress of Verdun that would destroy the French army. Simultaneously, the German navy would resume unrestricted submarine warfare in the waters around the British Isles. It was Devoy's good fortune that his request arrived just as the German army was ready to begin battle at Verdun on 21 February 1916. Concerned as he now was about the strength of the British Army, Falkenhayn considered that it was worth sending some military assistance to an Irish rebellion that might divert British troops to Ireland and the British government's attention away from the Western Front. On 4 March a wireless message to the German embassy in Washington informed the ambassador that it would be possible to send two or three small fishing craft to Fenit pier in Tralee Bay on 20 April carrying ten machine guns, 20,000 rifles, ammunition and explosives in the form of bombs and grenades.[27] Devoy sent the offer to Clarke in Dublin, where the Military Council accepted it and got Devoy to ask the Germans to send further military supplies later, including artillery and some officers. When another German message stated that the arms would arrive in a single merchant vessel, Devoy notified Tom immediately of the new arrangements.

A new German offensive on the Western Front and the certainty of military help from Berlin thrilled Tom. A visitor to the *Irish Freedom* offices in D'Olier Street noticed him, MacDermott and others following the Verdun battle with intense interest, absolutely convinced of a 'coming German victory': 'Nearly all the people there were strongly pro-German. They used very frequently to have maps following the movements at Verdun and various places'.[28]

With Connolly now involved, his military expertise helped the Military Council refine its plans for a rising. By early February 1916 these were well advanced. The centrepiece remained Dublin, where Irish Volunteers would seize and garrison a ring of inner-city locations, declare an Irish Republic and set up a provisional government. This was intended to inspire the rest of the country to join in, transforming the insurrection into a truly national affair. In the west where the Volunteers were relatively strong, a German vessel – which the Germans had not yet finally approved – would dock at Fenit. The Military Council now preferred Fenit to Limerick, having discovered that the latter's garrison had about a thousand soldiers. Pearse had also sent secret oral instructions to Volunteer commandants in the south and west setting out the areas their men would occupy when the rising began.[29] For months Volunteers had also been training in handling explosives and bomb-throwing and attending classes on street-fighting, a style of fighting that drew heavily on Connolly's extensive knowledge of urban warfare in European cities. Clarke and the Military Council were also impressed by the effectiveness of submarine warfare and hoped that German U-boats would attack British troopships bringing reinforcements to Ireland during the rising. The Military Council's big idea was that if the British garrison in Dublin could be isolated, then Volunteers in north Co. Dublin and the surrounding counties would exert pressure on it before they were joined by Volunteer columns coming from the west. In this scenario, then, the Volunteers' inner-city cordon was designed to lure the British into a trap. Finally, British troops would be squeezed between the rebel strongholds in the city centre and the large numbers of provincial Volunteers pushing forward to relieve the inner cordon. In that event, Clarke and his colleagues envisaged the rising ending in the capitulation of the British Army and political leadership.

Bringing those plans to fruition between January and April 1916 was bound to severely test Clarke and the Military Council's conspiratorial skills. As preparations intensified and information was passed on to Volunteer officers throughout Ireland, there would be a heightened risk of the British and moderates in the Volunteers finally discovering what was going on. The Military Council countered this danger by skilfully fooling the British, exploiting their anxiety to keep Ireland peaceful by encouraging the belief that the revolutionary threat had been greatly exaggerated. Connolly had the Citizen Army adopt a strategy of 'wolf, wolf, wolf' that involved endless exercises in the vicinity of Dublin Castle and Wellington Barracks which were even advertised in advance on a blackboard outside Liberty Hall.[30] This strategy eventually succeeded; through repetition of what seemed harmless play-acting, the British authorities became bored and lost interest. Pearse also lulled the Irish administration into a false sense of security. He toned down public displays of extremism by the Irish Volunteers with a prohibition on carrying the tricolour and the use instead of a flag with a plain gold harp on a green background that was identified with conservative nationalism.

Keeping Ireland quiet meant Birrell and Under-Secretary Nathan avoiding
political crises and refraining from open confrontation with the Volunteers,
though even in the modest ambition of containment they constantly
discovered the limits of their apparently sweeping emergency powers.
At a conference in Dublin Castle on 17 March 1916, for instance, Nathan,
the British General Officer Commanding Major-General Sir Lovick Friend,
the British chief intelligence officer in Ireland Ivon Price, the Irish attorney-
general and police representatives examined proposals to frustrate the
Volunteers. As they worked their way through a list of options, political expe-
diency or legal complexity led them to reject interning Volunteer instructors,
jailing Clarke for breaching his parole conditions and even banning Volunteer
and Citizen Army night manoeuvres.[31] Under-Secretary Nathan also backed
away from suppressing the Volunteers because of the likelihood of serious
violence. Complacently he argued that 'though the Irish Volunteer element
has been active of late, especially in Dublin, I do not believe that its leaders
mean insurrection or that the Volunteers have sufficient arms to make it
formidable if the leaders do mean it. The bulk of the people are not disaf-
fected'.[32] By 13 April Nathan was even more optimistic, informing Birrell
that 'things are getting better for the moment'. Only a few officials dissented.
The Royal Irish Constabulary's Inspector-General, Sir Neville Chamberlain,
repeatedly described Volunteer leaders as a pro-German 'pack of rebels' who
should be arrested and whose incendiary speeches meant that the Volunteers
were 'being organised with a view to insurrection'.[33] But getting proof of a
conspiracy was a different matter. Chamberlain's detectives had managed to
plant inside the Volunteers two spies code-named 'Granite' and 'Chalk' who
provided some useful if inconclusive evidence about the organisation's intentions. However, British information on Clarke and the Military Council was
virtually non-existent, partly because financial stringency and bureaucratic
complacency had weakened the legendary British intelligence system in
Ireland even before many officers left for military service. Clarke himself had
also played his part with the heightened security measures he had imposed
on the IRB which ensured, uniquely, that for the first and last time in history,
British intelligence never penetrated the inner leadership of an Irish revolutionary movement.

Clarke and the Military Council also outmanoeuvred Volunteer moderates.
Although Hobson knew that MacDermott, Pearse, Plunkett and Ceannt
were plotting a rising, he just could not secure conclusive evidence against
men whom he said operated like 'a secret society within a secret society'.[34]
Clear-sighted, mendacious and ruthless, they never left a political fingerprint

for Hobson – or anyone else – to convict them. And whereas Clarke had instilled in the Military Council discipline and unity of purpose, MacNeill's ramshackle and divided Executive reduced Hobson to despair. A former colleague recalled MacNeill conducting Provisional Committee meetings like a never-ending seminar:

> Discussions were most diffuse. Hardly anybody had experience of public affairs and how business was organised or regulated. A number of members were reasonably silent but others insisted on giving their opinions on every point and at length, some few not once but a dozen times; one or two were of so determined a disposition that when outvoted the matter in dispute was brought up again and again under different forms. MacNeill feared to limit the discussion because of the discordant elements represented.[35]

Drift at Volunteer headquarters in early 1916 suited the Military Council very well because it distracted MacNeill, though Clarke had always hoped that MacNeill would eventually resign as Volunteer President and disappear entirely. Ultimately it had become clear this was not going to happen and so instead in the second week of April 1916, Tom established a conduit to MacNeill by appointing Thomas MacDonagh to the Military Council.[36] This made no sense militarily, since planning for the rising was complete, but as the Volunteers' Dublin Brigadier and MacNeill's academic colleague at University College Dublin, MacDonagh could act as intermediary between him and the Military Council. Tom no doubt hoped that as the rising approached, MacDonagh would also counterbalance the influence that Hobson exercised over MacNeill.

During April Clarke and the Military Council made a change to the arrangements for receiving the German arms shipment, one they believed was simply a matter of fine-tuning. In fact, it significantly affected the rising's prospects of success. Originally it was intended that the vessel would dock at Fenit sometime between 20 and 23 April 1916, but late in the day the Military Council decided that possibly three days of Volunteer activity around Fenit might alert the British authorities. So on 14 April 1916 a messenger brought Devoy a dispatch from the Military Council stating that the German ship should not arrive at Fenit until 23 April, just as the rising was timed to begin.[37] Next day Devoy got the German embassy to transmit this message to Berlin. But the arms ship was already at sea, having set sail on 9 April. As she was not equipped with a wireless, she could not be contacted. And even if she could have been, the Military Council's request was completely unrealistic and revealed Tom and his colleagues' ignorance of naval warfare in believing that a ship could navigate hundreds of miles through a war zone, evade a British blockade and reach the west coast of Ireland at exactly the time demanded by them.

In preparation for the rising, Clarke deliberately helped stimulate a state of psychological warfare that mentally conditioned Volunteers for the coming fight. By accusing the British government of aggression and provocation, he encouraged Volunteer Executive moderates and radicals to unite against British harassment. And the government policy of arrests, constant police surveillance, closure of militant newspapers, imprisonment and deportation of Volunteer organisers, and pressure on employers not to recruit extremists were also unsettling the population generally. Clarke's propaganda aimed to create a sense that Irish nationalism as a whole was under attack, that British government policy in Ireland was ultimately about disarming and suppressing the Irish Volunteers before a military regime crushed all opposition. Then a chance event occurred that seemingly vindicated Clarke's analysis. On 20 March 1916 at Tullamore in King's County, there was a violent confrontation between pro- and anti-war nationalists when supporters of 'separation women' (wives of men enlisted in the British Army) invaded the town's Volunteer hall. A Volunteer fired over their heads and when the police arrived and threatened to search the premises for arms, he wounded a sergeant before escaping in the ensuing melee. Thirteen Volunteers were subsequently arrested and charged with attempted murder, though they were eventually released on a legal technicality.[38] Although the affair had not been deliberately engineered, the events and their timing were wonderfully convenient for the Military Council. Volunteer Executive moderates were outraged and closed ranks with the radicals, declaring that further government raids would be met by 'resistance and bloodshed'. MacNeill also warned that Volunteers would 'defend our arms with our lives'.[39] In this situation the radicals were able to explain away any activities that looked suspiciously like preparations for a rebellion as purely precautionary and defensive measures, designed to protect the organisation from attack.

The final problem that the Military Council had in getting the rising started was how to bring thousands of armed Volunteers on to the streets without provoking an immediate powerful response from the British army and police. This it overcame with exquisite guile. For some years the Irish Volunteers had been conducting large parades in Dublin on St Patrick's Day and at Easter, and so those scheduled for Easter 1916 could be presented as routine manoeuvres. As Director of Organisation, Pearse announced them publicly and well in advance on 8 April 1916, having had them approved by MacNeill and the entire Volunteer Executive. And their stated purpose, 'to test mobilisation with equipment' was reassuringly anodyne. Furthermore, as another masterly piece of camouflage, each battalion commander was ordered to submit to Pearse before 1 May a detailed report on the manoeuvres carried out by his unit.[40] This implied a peaceful training exercise that the Headquarters Staff would review subsequently at leisure.

The great Irish historian F.X. Martin has described brilliantly the Military Council's belief that despite representing a tiny minority of the Irish people, it had the right to override everyone else:

> The Easter Rising was a coup d'état against the British Government, it ran flat counter to the wishes of Redmond and the majority of Irish Nationalists, it was a mutiny against MacNeill and the constitution of the Irish Volunteers, and it usurped the powers of the I.R.B. itself. But Pearse, Clarke and their followers believed they were the eternal minority who had the duty of preserving Ireland's identity. They were what Jacques Maritain calls 'the prophetic shock-minority' who had to rouse a people from national slumber. And as Maritain observes, 'People as a rule prefer to sleep. Awakenings are always bitter'.[41]

Clarke never doubted that the rising was morally justified and he was surrounded by – or had surrounded himself with – men who shared his attitude. Denis McCullough declared:

> Frankly, I believe neither my colleagues or myself was greatly troubled about questions like 'moral insurrection'. To us the issue was a simple and straightforward one, vis to break England's grip on Ireland and to get rid of her occupation of all our territory. We were prepared to use every just means – men, movements or materials – that came to hand to achieve our purpose. We pledged our lives and those of our members to that purpose.[42]

Although Clarke and the Military Council never doubted their right to deceive Volunteer Executive moderates, Tom knew that future generations would debate the morality of manipulating into battle ordinary Volunteers and IRB members who had not explicitly consented to a rising. But on security grounds alone, the conspirators could argue the impossibility of consulting hundreds if not thousands of men. Widening the circle of knowledge would have inevitably led to someone tipping off the British authorities, the kind of intelligence leak that had doomed previous Irish rebellions. Clarke also believed rightly that by 1916 just about every Irish Volunteer – including moderates like MacNeill and Hobson – was, in certain circumstances, prepared to fight British forces in Ireland. Indeed most members thought that conflict was inevitable. For him and the Military Council, the issue of rebellion had been reduced to a matter of timing rather than one of principle between 'extremists' and 'moderates'. Sometimes it was hard to differentiate between the two camps. Even a 'moderate' like The O'Rahilly could advocate – as he did in 1914 – seizing Dublin Castle, proclaiming Home Rule and inviting Redmond to become President of Ireland. Although he had refused to join the IRB, there was clearly no unbridgeable political chasm separating him from Clarke and his colleagues, and in fact The O'Rahilly was to join them on the first morning of the rising. The Military Council also went as far as it dared during early 1916 in conditioning ordinary Volunteers to the inevitability of revolution. In a series of cleverly ambiguous speeches to Volunteer companies, Pearse galvanised his audiences by openly backing separatism and talking about them 'being called into action', though he simultaneously lulled Dublin Castle by stressing that they should not assume that action was imminent. By constant repetition, Pearse gradually effected an almost unconscious transformation in the outlook of many Volunteers from a defensive into an offensive cast of mind.[43]

Nor as an anti-cleric was Clarke bothered about whether the rising would contravene the Roman Catholic Church's doctrine on a just war. However, most Volunteers were devout Catholics who might hesitate upon discovering themselves involved not in an Easter parade but a rebellion, especially if the Church hierarchy denounced it with the same ferocity as they did the Fenians in the previous century. This possibility raised the spectre of an immediate split in the rebel ranks, so the Military Council decided to go over the Irish hierarchy's head and seek approval for the rising from the Holy See itself. If successful this initiative would not only neutralise the Irish bishops, but inspire the Volunteer rank and file in the righteousness of their cause. They had reason to hope, because the Archbishop of Dublin's secretary who was a friend of Pearse and Seán T. O'Kelly, had probably told them about Pope Benedict XV's sympathy for Irish nationalism. As an intermediary with the Vatican, the Military Council chose Plunkett's father, a papal count who would be assured of an audience with Benedict. After being sworn into the IRB, Count Plunkett travelled to Italy and on 8 April he met the Pope

privately for two hours. Plunkett presented Benedict with a letter revealing
that an Irish rebellion was imminent and justifying it on the grounds that
an oppressed Catholic nation had no choice but to rise because its imperial
rulers had driven them to the edge of famine. With England involved in a
great war and help to the rebels on its way from Germany, the insurrection
had a real chance of success. But the Pope had also been under pressure from
Asquith's government and no doubt feared the consequences if the rising
failed. Consequently, the furthest he appears to have gone was to give a
general blessing to the Volunteers as good Catholics but refused to endorse
the rising itself.[44]

NOTES

1   Diarmuid Lynch, *The IRB and the 1916 Insurrection*, p. 29.
2   Denis McCullough, BMH WS 915.
3   Statement of Eamon Dore, Béaslaí Papers, NLI MS 33,935 (17).
4   'The Memoirs of Madge Daly'.
5   Tom Clarke to Madge Daly, 14 May 1912, Daly Papers, University of
     Limerick Archives, Box 1, Folder 7.
6   Ibid.
7   'The Memoirs of Madge Daly'.
8   Manuscript notes by Patrick McCartan on Louis Le Roux's biography of
     Thomas Clarke, NLI MS 44,683.
9   Denis McCullough, BMH WS 915.
10   So McCullough told P.S. O'Hegarty: Denis McCullough, BMH WS 915;
     O'Hegarty, 'Recollections of the IRB'.
11   Statement of Eamon Dore, Béaslaí Papers, NLI MS 33,935 (17).
12   Diarmuid Lynch, BMH WS 4.
13   'The Memoirs of Madge Daly'.
14   Denis McCullough in a letter of 25 July 1960, a copy of which is in my
     possession.
15   Eamon O'Dwyer, BMH WS 1403.
16   Ibid.
17   See the Statements of Eamon Dore and Frank Daly, Béaslaí Papers,
     NLI MS 33,935 (17). See also Dore BMH WS 392 and Frank Daly BMH
     WS 278.
18   Statement of Frank Daly, Béaslaí Papers, NLI MS 33,935 (17).
19   Statement of Eamon Dore, NLI MS 33,935 (17).
20   Béaslaí Papers, NLI MS 33,935 (17).
21   Sean Fitzgibbon, 'The Easter Rising from the Inside', Part 1, *Irish Times*,
     18 April 1949.
22   Kathleen Clarke, *Revolutionary Woman*, p. 65.
23   Statement by a member of the Community of Sisters of Mercy, Mater Hospital,

Dublin, BMH WS 46.

24 Kathleen Clarke, *Revolutionary Woman*, pp. 65–6.

25 Devoy, Germany Kept Faith with Ireland, NLI MS 17,609 (11).

26 Ibid.

27 Ibid.

28 Right Rev. Mgr Peter Browne, BMH WS 739.

29 D. Lynch, BMH WS 4.

30 Helena Moloney, transcript of interviews for a 1966 BBC programme on the Easter Rising, NLI MS 15,015.

31 Nathan Papers, Bodleian Library, MS 472.

32 Ibid., MS 478.

33 Ibid., MS 466.

34 Ibid., Hobson, *Ireland Yesterday and Tomorrow*, p. 72.

35 Colonel Maurice Moore, *History of the Irish Volunteers*, NLI ILB 94109.

36 For MacDonagh's accession to the Military Council, see Foy and Barton, *The Easter Rising*, p. 50.

37 Devoy, Germany Kept Faith with Ireland, NLI MS 17,609 (11).

38 For the Tullamore affair and its consequences, see Foy and Barton, *The Easter Rising*, pp. 43–4.

39 Foy and Barton, *The Easter Rising*, p. 43.

40 Ibid., p. 45.

41 F.X. Martin, *Leaders and Men of the Easter Rising*, p. 251.

42 Denis McCullough Papers, NLI MS 31,653.

43 For this see Foy and Barton, *The Easter Rising*, pp. 42–3.

44 For this see Jerome aan de Wiel, *The Catholic Church in Ireland 1914–1918: War and Politics*, pp. 84–6.

7

Prelude:
Holy Week 1916

Just before Holy Week 1916, rumours about an imminent rising reached Denis McCullough in Belfast. As President of the IRB Supreme Council that had to finally ratify any insurrection, he was puzzled that Clarke and MacDermott had told him nothing officially. Determined to find out more about the Military Council's intentions, McCullough travelled to Dublin on Saturday 15 April 1916, having informed MacDermott in advance that they should meet at Tom's Richmond Avenue home. But Seán did not show up there and he ignored further messages from McCullough. Apparently perplexed, Tom played out the charade of waiting patiently for MacDermott to appear while he effortlessly deflected McCullough's guileless attempts to extract information:

> Tom told me, on his solemn word, that he knew nothing whatever about the arrangements or plans, that all he knew was that he was to report to Captain Ned Daly (his brother-in-law) on Easter Sunday morning and carry on under him. I am convinced that Tom was telling me the truth and that he had no detailed knowledge of the arrangements for the Rising. He knew that the Rising was timed for Easter Sunday morning but that was the total extent of his knowledge. He told me that Seán MacDermott had control of all matters connected with the Rising, together – I think he said – with Pearse and Connolly; and I must get any information I required from him.[1]

Incredibly, McCullough went to his grave decades later still believing Clarke's bogus assurances, proof positive of the gullibility that made him Tom and Seán's ideal Supreme Council President. They had wanted a useful idiot who

would keep out of their way and almost to the end he had not let them
down. But at this crucial juncture McCullough's lack of insight worked
against Clarke and MacDermott. Not realising that he was now surplus to
requirements, McCullough wasted their valuable time by plaintively insisting
on at least being told what was going on. So for almost that entire weekend,
MacDermott literally gave McCullough the run-around until Sunday
afternoon when he suddenly arrived at Tom's house. McCullough recalled
that 'he was evidently surprised and very much upset at finding me there'.
MacDermott admitted to him that he had got his first message but claimed
he was too busy. He refused to talk then and left saying he was going to meet
MacNeill. MacDermott fobbed him off with a half-promise to talk next day,
but McCullough was determined to settle matters before he left the capital.[2]

In fact McCullough encountered Seán again accidentally later on that Palm
Sunday night at an evening fundraising concert for the Irish Volunteers in
Parnell Square. There McCullough listened to a speech in which Hobson for
the first time went public – although in coded language – with his fears that
Clarke and the radicals were about to send Irish Volunteers into a rising. Many
of Tom's associates were in the packed audience and they regarded Hobson's
contribution as premeditated treachery. McCullough felt the same: 'To me
it sounded like bedlam. I feared that divided councils would be fatal to any
attempt at an armed Rising'. Afterwards as he left the hall, McCullough met
MacDermott limping in and told him about Hobson's intervention; Seán
uttered 'a good, round oath' and vowed to 'damned soon deal with that fellow'.[3]
The situation was all the more serious because many IRB members believed
wrongly that Hobson was still on the Supreme Council and that his remarks
indicated a split had occurred at the top of their organisation. Soon afterwards
Seán T. O'Kelly met Clarke and MacDermott who 'were very interested in the
words used by Hobson and were surprised that he had got such an opportunity
to address a gathering of that kind and to sow seeds of suspicion and dissen-
sion among the Volunteers and their supporters'.[4] They believed that by using
the information that they got McCullough to give him in January about an
imminent rising, Hobson had finally crossed the line into outright treason. Tom
and Seán now considered it an urgent matter to put Hobson out of action.

On the following Monday morning, 17 April, McCullough finally
cornered MacDermott at his city centre office in D'Olier Street, locked the
door and insisted on them having a discussion: 'Seán laughed and said all right,
he would tell me all I wanted to know, which was everything. He told me of
the plans for Dublin and of the coming of the German arms'.[5] McCullough
then surprised MacDermott by magnanimously saying that he would obey

Pearse and Connolly's orders during the rising but absurdly threatened him with an inquiry afterwards into his behaviour! Seán 'laughed and said that there wasn't much chance of that, if the Rising came off, so he wasn't worried about answering for his actions'.[6]

And far from telling McCullough 'everything', Seán concealed the fact that within twenty-four hours he and Tom planned to send him into political retirement. On Tuesday 18 April, the Military Council assembled in 21 Henry Street, the residence of Mrs Wyse Power, a member of Cumann na mBan and friend of Kathleen Clarke. There they approved the text of a Proclamation of an Irish Republic to be inaugurated on the first day of the Rising. They also established a Provisional Government – themselves – that would conduct the rising and administer Ireland in the aftermath of an anticipated victory. Out of respect for him personally and his long service to the republican cause, Clarke was apparently offered the presidency, but having spent a lifetime shunning the limelight, he declined. Instead the post went to Pearse, who had both the presence and oratorical ability to make a historic address. Pearse was also appointed Commandant-General of the Army of the Irish Republic, an amalgamation of the Volunteers and the Irish Citizen Army. Connolly was made vice-president and commandant-general of the army's Dublin division, in effect military commander of the rebel forces in the capital. Clarke bowed to his colleagues' insistence that his name alone should have pride of place on the Proclamation. Later, Tom told Pat McCartan that he had proposed Pearse as the first signatory, but Pearse had replied that Tom should take precedence because of his long service to the cause.[7] Kathleen recalled:

Tom then told me that when he was proposed as first signatory he had demurred, saying that he did not think that such an honour should be conferred on him, that he was seeking no honours. He was very surprised when Thomas MacDonagh rose and said that to his mind no other man was entitled to the honour. 'You Sir, by your example, your courage, your enthusiasm, have led us younger men to where we are today.' If Tom Clarke did not agree to accept it, MacDonagh would not put his name to the Proclamation. 'No man will precede you with my consent.' Being very much touched by what MacDonagh had said Tom agreed to sign.[8]

Finally, the Military Council approved the so-called 'Castle Document'. Apparently concocted by Plunkett, this was an exercise in disinformation that purported to reveal a British plan for the mass arrest of opponents, including the entire Irish Volunteer Executive.

Constitutionally the Military Council – in effect a subcommittee – should have reported its plans for a rising back to the Supreme Council for final approval and then been wound up. Instead Clarke and MacDermott not only kept it in being, they transformed that body into the government of an Irish republic that they anticipated soon coming into being. Extraordinarily, Tom and Seán left the Supreme Council completely in the dark, failing to inform it of the Military Council's plans, withheld from it the date of the rising and ignored the Supreme Council's sole authority to give final sanction to a rebellion. Nor did they once convene an IRB Executive meeting between January and April 1916 to acquaint its third member – McCullough – with the Military Council's work. The Proclamation of an Irish Republic, a Provisional Government and Pearse's appointment (not McCullough's) as President and Commander-in-Chief was the apogee of Clarke's disdain for constitutionalism – even the constitution of the Irish Republican Brotherhood itself. Diarmuid Lynch conceded that the Military Council's decisions were 'tantamount to an act of military dictatorship', though he believed that they were 'in the circumstances understandable'.[9] In effect Tom and his colleagues were acting like a junta enacting a coup, one that overthrew the elected president and government, appointed themselves as their replacements, suspended the constitution and produced a Proclamation that in part resembled a new constitution. They had also empowered themselves to rule by decree. These were the boldest examples yet of Tom's lifelong conviction that constitutions were not worth the paper they were printed on. He had long sworn that nothing – and nobody – would stand in his way and he was as good as his word.

Kathleen claimed that on Tuesday night she asked Tom who would act as permanent President in the event of victory. She described him saying that complete victory would take a long time and that he feared he would be too old to do the job. The younger men would have to shoulder the burden, but they would need a wise head to guide them, a man of iron: 'He thought it would have to be someone with a touch of Cromwell in him for the first five years.' 'Would Pearse be suitable?' I asked. 'God Almighty no', he said, 'He is too Christ-like.'[10] Somewhat disconcertingly, Clarke considered that only John Devoy possessed the necessary knowledge and experience as well as the force of character and ruthlessness, a choice that said more about Clarke's admiration for his mentor than his political judgement. Envisaging the return of a 74-year-old autocrat after almost half a century's exile in America raises the disturbing possibility that Clarke envisaged Devoy's iron hand ruling an independent Ireland on similar lines to the Clan and IRB.

On Spy Wednesday, 19 April 1916, the Castle Document became public
knowledge when the Military Council passed it to Alderman Tom Kelly for
him to read out at a meeting of Dublin Corporation. The following day's
newspapers electrified the political atmosphere in Dublin and stimulated a
war fever at Volunteer headquarters where MacNeill issued orders warning
members to prepare to resist an enemy onslaught. It was a perfect smokescreen
to conceal the Military Council's intentions and activities during the final
countdown to a rising. That evening, while the Castle Document dominated
public attention, Volunteer and Citizen Army commandants finally learned
that the Rising would commence in Dublin at 6.30 p.m. on Easter Sunday
23 April and half an hour later in the provinces. But the Military Council
still did not inform the rank and file, conscious of how premature leaks had
crippled the Fenian Rising in 1867. Madge Daly was in Dublin at the time
and she and recalled that:

> Tom was in great spirits; he believed the youth of the country would
> flock to their standard; that the fight would develop into a guerrilla
> warfare all over the country; that England could not spare sufficient
> forces to put down a general rising for at that time the French were
> pressing the English to increase their forces in France and to take a larger
> part in the war. So they were told by friends returning from Europe.[11]

On Holy Thursday 20 April, Tom sent Kathleen to Limerick with dispatches
for Volunteer leaders in the west of Ireland. She also brought along their three
boys who were to stay with her mother for the duration of the rising. A third
son, Emmet, had been born in August 1909. Kathleen recalled that Tom 'did
not dare to say goodbye to his children. He feared it might break even his
rigid self-control'.[12] However after delivering the messages, Kathleen was to
return to Dublin on the night train because she had been assigned important
duties in the capital during the insurrection. Kathleen was to receive vital
dispatches that would be brought to the Clarkes' home in Richmond Avenue
and Tom had instructed Supreme Council members, Joseph Gleeson, Richard
Connolly and James Carrigan that if they missed out on the fighting they were
to contact Kathleen and keep the IRB organisation intact.[13] Furthermore, Seán
MacDermott had persuaded the Supreme Council to appoint Kathleen as the
custodian of its decisions and she was given a list of names to be contacted
in the event of a government swoop on the Council.[14] Her plan to return to
Dublin on Holy Thursday was upset when lengthy meetings of the Volunteer
leaders kept her overnight in Limerick. Pat McCartan who stayed overnight

with Tom in Richmond Avenue on Holy Thursday, recalled him saying 'there
were at least 5,000 Germans coming and he was all enthusiastic about how
thorough the Germans were and that they would do things in a big way, so that
I left him for the first train next morning as enthusiastic as himself'.[15]

On Holy Thursday evening, the Military Council's plans suddenly ran into
difficulty. During a Dublin Centres Board meeting, one delegate mentioned
that Pearse had instructed him to sabotage a railway line on Easter Sunday.
Very late in the day this gave Hobson the smoking gun that he had sought
for so long.[16] Abruptly terminating the meeting, he and Ginger O'Connell
alerted MacNeill and drove with him to St Enda's. There, at 1.30 a.m. they
confronted Pearse, only for him to nonchalantly dismiss their angry protests
and warn MacNeill against interfering with the Sunday manoeuvres. MacNeill
later recalled telling Pearse that 'we had learned about these instructions and
I said "That means immediate action". He admitted that it did'.[17] The party
then returned to MacNeill's house, Woodtown Park, where he drafted orders
nullifying Pearse's secret military instructions. But before Hobson sent these
out, Pearse alerted MacDermott who arrived to see MacNeill at 8.00 a.m.
on Friday. MacNeill had just awakened when MacDermott was shown
into the room. That MacDermott came alone for a summit meeting with
the Volunteer Chief of Staff demonstrates that he had suddenly emerged as
the Military Council's chief conspirator, marginalising even Clarke himself.
With the Volunteer Executive and Headquarters Staff now split, an ordinary
member like Tom would have had no standing to negotiate with MacNeill.
And this was a crisis that also required MacDermott's ability to move around
Dublin as well as his negotiating skills and talent for silky dissimulation.
Furthermore, having for years been MacNeill's colleague on the Volunteer
Executive, Seán knew his man and how to play him.

MacDermott later told his Military Council colleagues that he had laid all
his cards out for MacNeill. But that was a lie by a man whom P.S. O'Hegarty
knew as 'a master of the art of telling as little of the facts as he wanted to'.[18]
Not respecting or trusting MacNeill, Seán certainly wasn't going to tell him
everything – or anything close. On the contrary, by playing up the Castle
Document and fears of an imminent British attack on poorly armed Volunteers,
MacDermott could spin Pearse's secret instructions as simply a desperate
attempt to organise resistance against coming enemy aggression. And while
conceding that Pearse of course should have cleared his orders with MacNeill
himself, MacDermott would have soothingly stressed the need to set aside
personal egos for the greater good of Volunteer unity. He could also downplay
Sunday's parades as simply being designed to distract the British government's

attention from an arms landing in the west of Ireland – just like the Howth route march and gunrunning in July 1914. If the arms landed peacefully, then either the Volunteers would be better able to resist British aggression – in a war in which Ireland would be regarded as a victim – or the better-armed Volunteers might even force the British to call off their intended onslaught. Alternatively, if the British interfered with the gunrunning, causing another Bachelor's Walk, they would unite nationalist Ireland and give the Volunteers a *casus belli*. From this perspective, MacNeill's focus would have been on the west of Ireland and not Dublin, and certainly this is the scenario that MacNeill claimed subsequently he had been led to believe would happen.[19]

Afterwards MacNeill and MacDermott breakfasted with Pearse and MacDonagh who had arrived separately at Woodtown Park. By now MacDermott had ascended to the pinnacle of the IRB; henceforth all lines of communication ran through him, ensuring that he alone among the rebel leaders fully understood what was going on. Only at noon on Friday – and from Diarmuid Lynch, not MacDermott – did Clarke and Connolly learn about MacNeill's proposed countermand orders: 'Both of them expressed themselves in very strong language'.[20] However, shortly afterwards MacDonagh was able to tell Lynch that all was well. After leaving Woodtown Park, MacDermott sent dispatches to Munster ordering Volunteer commandants to proceed with the Rising. MacNeill instructed Hobson to put his countermand orders on hold though without mentioning his meeting with MacDermott, Pearse and MacDonagh. Having re-programmed MacNeill, the Military Council had to keep the notoriously irresolute Chief of Staff away from Hobson. Hobson had ruined their plan to keep MacNeill in the dark right up to the start of the Rising and his intervention on Thursday night had almost derailed their plans. They could not allow him another opportunity to repeat that action. By now their hatred of Hobson was boundless. Clarke called him the 'Devil Incarnate', MacDonagh, an 'evil genius' and Connolly, 'the villain of the piece'. Ceannt however could see both sides: 'He is perfectly honest, he is not a traitor. But it would be better that he were then we could shoot him'.[21] Instead, Connolly arranged for Hobson to be summoned on Friday evening to a supposedly hastily arranged IRB meeting in Cabra Park where three armed IRB men from Hobson's own Teeling circle detained him. Provided he kept the location secret, Hobson was allowed to send a message to MacNeill telling of his arrest. But MacNeill did not break off his pact with MacDermott and Pearse, presumably believing that Volunteer unity was now more important than the fate of any individual.

When the Military Council convened on Friday afternoon for a final overview session, everything seemed back on track and the mood was one of excited anticipation. Soon afterwards Seamus O'Connor encountered Ceannt acting like a euphoric schoolboy, talking about how well he was eating and sleeping and how much he was looking forward to the fight: 'We are rising on Sunday and we are going to win. We are going to bring off something unprecedented in the way of revolutions. We are going to smash the bloody old empire'.[22] Later on Good Friday, Kathleen Clarke finally got out of Limerick on the night train, accompanied by her sister Laura who wanted to see their brother Ned before the Rising began. Because the train arrived in Dublin late, they did not reach Richmond Avenue until the early hours of Saturday morning, and upon opening the front door Kathleen and Laura saw Tom, Ned and some bodyguards pointing revolvers at them. MacNeill's wobble and a fear of the British learning something about the intended Rising had made Tom nervous about the possibility of a police or army raid.[23]

Although that danger had apparently passed, events later on Saturday and on Sunday 22 and 23 April once again brought the Military Council's plans to the brink of disaster. Things began unravelling first in Kerry, the destination of two German vessels. One was the *Aud*. Disguised as a Norwegian merchantman passing along the west coast of Ireland on its way to the Mediterranean, it was in reality an arms ship carrying rifles and ammunition for the rebels. By noon on Thursday 20 April, the *Aud* was 45 miles from Fenit where the crew began preparing to land weapons for what they thought was a party of waiting Irish Volunteers. But disastrously, while the *Aud* was at sea the Military Council had sought to delay its arrival at Fenit until the evening of Sunday 23 April in order to coincide with the start of the Rising. However, even had the Germans agreed with this request, they could not have transmitted a message to the *Aud* because it was not equipped with a wireless. But the Military Council simply assumed that Berlin had accepted the new arrangements and so there was no reception party of Kerry Volunteers waiting for the *Aud* as it approached Fenit on the night of Holy Thursday 20 April.

The *Aud* had also expected to rendezvous with another German vessel, a U-boat carrying Sir Roger Casement home to Ireland. Believing the Germans were using Ireland for their own selfish ends while providing the IRB with only minimal assistance, Casement managed to convince them that he needed to return home to prepare for the arms shipment's arrival. In fact, Casement's real intention was to stop a rising that he thought was doomed to failure. Just after noon on Good Friday 21 April, the submarine he was travelling in reached a prearranged point off the Kerry coast, but the *Aud* was

several miles away and out of sight. A few hours later, Casement and two Irish
Brigade officers clambered into a small boat and made their way ashore where
local police soon captured Casement. The *Aud* remained free but only for a
little while longer. Increasingly nervous about waiting for an Irish Volunteer
reception party to show up, its captain weighed anchor and headed into the
Atlantic where he intended attacking Allied merchant ships. But British naval
intelligence had broken German codes and were tracking the *Aud*. After two
British sloops eventually cornered it on Friday evening, they led the ship back
towards the Irish coast, but as it approached Queenstown in Co. Cork on
Saturday morning, the *Aud*'s captain scuttled his vessel within sight of harbour.

As reports of Casement's arrest spread, Kerry Volunteers dispatched a
messenger to Dublin. Reaching the capital at dawn on Saturday, he reported
to Liberty Hall where Connolly immediately summoned a Military Council
meeting. This decided to conceal the setback in Kerry from MacNeill,
a deception that was repeated on Saturday afternoon when the Military Council
also learned about the loss of the *Aud* – a calamity that would transform the
Rising from a planned national insurrection into a predominantly Dublin affair.
Despite this, when a Limerick emissary arrived at MacDermott's safe house
in Hardwicke Street near the northern end of O'Connell Street, he found
Seán exuding a surface bonhomie and insisting that there was no going back
now. With scant regard for the truth, MacDermott even claimed that more
German arms shipments were on their way.[24] Under immense strain and
fearful of everything falling apart, he was now prepared to lie to anyone and
everyone, even his Military Council colleagues, in order to prevent the Rising
being derailed at the very last moment. Everything – including the truth – was
subservient to MacDermott's credo that 'the only failure in Ireland is the failure
to act'.[25] Nevertheless, a few hours later, when another Limerick Volunteer
arrived and suggested postponing the Rising, MacDermott's composure disintegrated completely. Physically sick, he began shouting that delay was out of the
question: the Volunteers would fight even if they only had sticks and stones.[26]

On Saturday morning, 22 April, Military Council members went into
hiding at safe houses in order to avoid being arrested in any last-minute
swoop that the British government might launch. Tom was to stay in Gardiner
Place at Fleming's Hotel whose owners, Mr and Mrs O'Mahony, were
strong republican sympathisers. MacDermott moved to another house in
Hardwicke Street, the home of a friend, Mrs Kissane, who lived about 150yds
north of Parnell Square. Both men would be guarded by young Volunteers
who were under orders to resist to the death any British arrest parties,
a security measure that Clarke had introduced after detectives put him under

intensified surveillance. Only Connolly stayed put with the Citizen Army giving him all the protection he needed in Liberty Hall. Clarke left his home in Richmond Avenue accompanied by his wife and her sister Laura. Kathleen was to open and serve customers all day at the Parnell Street shop because its closure might have led the British authorities to suspect that something unusual was about to happen. The trio walked down Ballybough Road and Summerhill before parting at the corner of Parnell and Gardiner Streets. Kathleen recalled that 'though both of us feared it might be our final parting, we dared not say so. We dared not indulge in goodbyes. There was work to be done, and goodbyes would break us and leave us unfit for anything'.[27]

Unaware that their alliance with MacNeill had already crumbled, the Military Council hoped on this final night to recuperate from the hectic events of recent days. On Saturday afternoon MacNeill was visited by Sean Fitzgibbon, a member of the Volunteer Executive who had spent most of Holy Week in Kerry preparing for the *Aud*'s arrival. Upon learning about Casement's arrest and the sinking of the *Aud*, Fitzgibbon decided to return immediately to Dublin where he collected The O'Rahilly and drove to Woodtown Park. After telling MacNeill about the happenings in Kerry, Fitzgibbon then shocked him by revealing that Plunkett had fabricated the Castle Document. MacNeill now concluded that without the *Aud*'s weapons the Volunteers would suffer a catastrophic defeat in any conflict with the British. In order to avoid this, MacNeill decided to convene an eight o'clock meeting at the house of a friend, Seamus O'Kelly, and 'stop all this damned nonsense' by calling off Sunday's military parades. But first the trio drove to St Enda's where Pearse told MacNeill: 'We have used you and your name and influence for what it was worth. You can issue what orders you like now, our men won't obey you'.[28] MacNeill retorted angrily that he would follow his conscience but if Pearse wanted to talk further he could do so later at O'Kelly's residence on Rathgar Road. There MacNeill assembled Volunteer Executive loyalists such as The O'Rahilly and Fitzgibbon as well as friends like Arthur Griffith and Seán T. O'Kelly. Besides inviting Pearse, MacNeill had also sent word to MacDermott, McDonagh and Plunkett. Only MacDonagh showed up as an intermediary with MacNeill, the role for which his fellow conspirators had appointed him to the Military Council. But far from working his magic on the Volunteer President, MacDonagh reacted angrily upon learning that MacNeill had already dispatched countermanding orders to senior Volunteer officers throughout Ireland. Defiantly, MacDonagh warned MacNeill that the radicals would just ignore him and they had the loyalty of the Volunteer rank and file. He delivered an ultimatum: 'The fight is on and it is up to you to decide whether you are in it or not'.[29] MacDonagh then stormed out. Determined to go over the conspirators' heads, MacNeill cycled into Dublin city centre at about 1 a.m. and placed a message cancelling the Sunday parades in the *Sunday Independent* – the only Sunday paper then published in Dublin.

At about midnight on Saturday, MacDonagh and Plunkett arrived at MacDermott's safe house in Hardwicke Street and told him about MacNeill's countermand orders. Diarmuid Lynch was also present and observed that MacDermott was 'shocked beyond measure'.[30] Seán immediately dispatched messengers to collect the four absent Military Council members but only Pearse turned up. Lynch remembered being

> called into the conference and I shall never forget the location. MacDermott, whose health had been shattered years before in his work for Ireland and who was physically worn out by the strenuous months of anxiety through which he had just passed, writhed in anguish. All were shocked at the desperate situation which had suddenly been thrust upon them.[31]

We now know that the crisis meeting ended with the four Military Council members present voting on whether to commence the Rising as planned in eighteen hours. Lynch stated that two people – one of them Pearse – wanted to stick to the original timetable and so did Lynch himself.[32] Although without a vote, Lynch was allowed to take part as a Supreme Council member and Lynch argued strongly that it would be disastrous to change the plans at this late stage. Another two Military Council members urged delay so that the full Military Council could assess the implications of MacNeill's actions. How MacDermott, MacDonagh and Plunkett voted remains unknown, but had MacDermott sided with Pearse and Lynch, it is inconceivable that three Supreme Council members could not have carried Plunkett and MacDonagh with them or allowed the pair to block them. This is especially true given that MacDonagh had only joined the Military Council a few weeks earlier. In that case, MacDermott presumably argued and voted for delay and managed to split MacDonagh and Plunkett. Given MacDonagh's defiance of MacNeill in Rathgar Road, he probably backed Pearse while Plunkett sided with MacDermott. The resulting deadlock necessitated what MacDermott must have wanted – a full Military Council meeting later that Sunday morning. The outcome might have been different had Clarke, Connolly and Ceannt been present, something that makes their absence seem not entirely accidental. It was a thought that occurred to Kathleen Clarke when she turned up with an urgent message from Pat McCartan in Ulster. She told

MacDermott that Tom would be very angry when he learned that his fellow
conspirators were meeting without him. Kathleen considered going to Tom's
safe house in Gardiner Place, but, fearing that detectives might be following
her, she changed her mind and instead went straight home.[33]

During the early hours of Sunday morning, word of MacNeill's cancellation filtered back from the provinces to Liberty Hall. There Nora Connolly
saw tears running down her father's cheeks as he declared that 'the only
thing we can do is to pray for an earthquake to come and swallow us up
and our shame'.[34] Connolly then sent her and other messengers to round up
the rest of the Military Council and when Nora returned he had regained
control of his emotions. Now in uniform, Connolly was singing as he always
did when in good form and he told his daughter firmly that 'we have got
another saviour now. That saviour is the sword'.[35] When members of the
Military Council arrived at Liberty Hall, they encountered tumultuous
scenes. Connolly's bodyguard, Henry Walpole, volunteered to assassinate
MacNeill, while Countess Markievicz who blamed Hobson more, rampaged
around the building, waving her small automatic pistol and shouting 'I want
to shoot him'.[36] When Clarke learned about MacNeill's action he broke down
completely, denouncing it as 'the blackest and greatest treachery'.[37] At 9 a.m.
an angry and emotionally drained Military Council began a four-hour session
that methodically examined their options. Everyone agreed that abandonment
or even lengthy postponement of the rising was out of the question. Apart from
being committed to an insurrection, they all believed that either the British
would soon suppress the Volunteers or MacNeill would expel them from
the organisation. This narrowed the discussion down to whether MacNeill's
countermand could best be overcome by delaying the rising – and if so by
how long. Naturally, Clarke urged the others to simply ignore MacNeill and
stick to the original plan; Tom insisted that once the Rising began, Volunteers
would either assume MacNeill's cancellation was a hoax or that events had
overtaken it. Once again there was a vote and to Tom's astonishment he stood
alone; everyone else supported a short delay that would give Pearse time to
draw up new secret orders superseding MacNeill's countermand. Men whom
Clarke had groomed and promoted had now rejected his advice and even
MacDermott, Tom's greatest confidante, had deserted him. But it was even
worse. Two Military Council members who earlier that day had resisted delay
had now changed their minds, while Connolly and Ceannt had been persuaded
to support a pause. Only someone of great authority and eloquence and with
all the facts at his disposal could have achieved that shift and that person must
have been MacDermott. For three days Seán had been acting increasingly

independently and even his partnership with Clarke was now secondary to beginning a rising in the least disadvantageous circumstances. But Tom had seen little of MacDermott in recent days and only realised on Sunday morning that their interests now – for the first time – diverged. Watching Seán rally the Military Council against him must have shocked and hurt him as deeply as Hobson's 'betrayal' in June 1914. By the end of the conference Clarke had gone from being the Military Council's dominant member to someone who was not even first among equals, an amazingly rapid diminution in his power and authority and one that left Tom a shaken man.

Once the Military Council agreed to postpone the Rising until noon on Easter Monday 24 April, its priority was to preserve the element of surprise by keeping both the British and MacNeill in the dark for another twenty-four hours. The British had to remain in blissful ignorance about the real purpose of the Volunteer parades since otherwise their soldiers in Dublin could stop the rebels even reaching the GPO and other strategic locations. They also had to be convinced that MacNeill's cancellations of the parades had removed any likelihood of immediate trouble. The Military Council could quickly stand down the four Dublin battalions because their commandants, MacDonagh, Ceannt, de Valera and Ned Daly, were all in the IRB and two actually sat on the Military Council – though de Valera only fell into line reluctantly.[38] The greatest danger was that some provincial Volunteers would proceed as originally planned and reveal to the British that a rising had been intended. With only hours left, Pearse began creating a smokescreen by sending out messengers to provincial Volunteer commandants confirming MacNeill's cancellation order. But secretly Pearse began drafting fresh orders that would be distributed later stating that the rising would in fact proceed – just a day later than planned. To prevent this information leaking to the British, Dublin Volunteer captains would not receive their mobilisation orders until the early hours of Monday morning.[39]

After the Liberty Hall conference Clarke went home. Seán McGarry thought that 'for the first time since I knew him he seemed crushed. He was weary and seemed crestfallen. I accompanied him home that evening. He was very silent'.[40] Another bodyguard recalled Tom bitterly denouncing MacNeill and the confusion his countermand order had caused:

> He spoke with unusual emotion: 'We had got over so many difficulties', he added 'and all seemed working well. Our plans were laid in the most thorough and efficient manner. We had a great opportunity. Now in a way we could never have foreseen all is spoiled. I feel as if I would like to go away somewhere and cry'.[41]

Having shut up shop at noon in order to be at home in Richmond Avenue when the first shots of the Rising rang out, Katherine Clarke was astonished when in mid-afternoon Tom suddenly turned the street corner. He seemed 'like a broken man'. The husband who had left her on Friday 'full of hope and courage' now appeared 'old and bent, and his walk, which was usually very quick and military, was slow. He looked very ill, and seemed scarcely able to speak'.[42] Tom also looked very cold so Kathleen seated him by the sitting room fire and gave him an egg flip containing – unusually for Clarke – a good measure of whiskey. She also made Tom a meal but he had lost his appetite and did not eat anything until breakfast next morning. Eventually he opened up to Kathleen about what had gone wrong, vehemently denouncing MacNeill's supposed 'betrayal':

> Tom said, 'I could understand MacNeill … if he thought the Rising should be put off and came straight to us and told us how he felt about it, leaving the decision with us and withdrawing if our decision did not agree with his belief that the Rising should be abandoned. That would have been the honourable course. To send out countermanding orders secretly, giving us no hint of what he was doing was despicable and to my mind dishonourable'.[43]

Tom also claimed that the Military Council had only discovered what MacNeill was doing when MacDonagh 'by mere chance' had walked into O'Kelly's Rathgar Road house when MacNeill was issuing his countermand orders. But MacNeill – who might well have complained about being kept in the dark himself – had on Saturday evening gone straight to Pearse, who for the second time in three days treated him with derision. MacNeill had also invited the radical leaders to Rathgar Road, only for MacDermott and Pearse to spurn him. And Tom's assertion that MacDonagh had stumbled accidentally on MacNeill's meeting was ludicrous and raises questions about the extent and accuracy of the information that his fellow conspirators had given him earlier in the day at Liberty Hall.

Almost as if he was trying to convince himself that no great setback had occurred in the west, Tom assured Kathleen that the German arms shipment had really only been intended as a propaganda coup to boost Volunteer morale. Losing the *Aud* was of no great significance since there were plentiful stores of weapons in police and army barracks that were lightly defended by raw recruits and could be easily stormed by determined Volunteers. Clarke was now swinging between optimism and depression. When a Volunteer arrived with a message from Pat McCartan, he sent the reply that 'It is hopeless but we must go on',[44] a startling contrast to the exuberant confidence McCartan had witnessed only three days earlier. With almost two years of detailed planning in ruins, this was Tom's admission that the rising would now be a leap in the dark and that all the Military Council could hope for was that against all odds they could still land on their feet. Before retiring Tom and Kathleen agreed that if the police or army raided their home it was to be a fight to the finish with everyone firing at anyone who came through the door. Kathleen recalled that she 'had a pistol and knew how to use it, and if necessary meant to take a hand' in what would be 'a fight to the finish'. There was indeed a knock on the door but it turned out to be only an agitated old man: 'It took Tom a long time to quieten him down and persuade him to go home, but he finally went, still protesting. I slept in my husband's arms for the last time that night and slept soundly'.[45]

Presumably MacNeill also slept well. He had sent messengers across Dublin urging Volunteer battalion to obey his countermand orders and from Liberty Hall came Pearse's promise that MacDonagh had cancelled parades in the capital. The Military Council also arranged one final deception to convince MacNeill that his appeals had won them over. During the afternoon they sent MacDonagh to act one last time as their intermediary with MacNeill, his assignment being to perpetuate Pearse's fraudulent assurances. To pull off the sham, MacDonagh exchanged the truculence and defiance that he had displayed a day earlier for sweet emollience and respect. Sean Fitzgibbon was present and recalled how:

> He, MacNeill and I walked around the grounds and talked. He was most friendly and assured us that everything was off. He was quite optimistic and said that all that had been intended was to occupy certain buildings as barracks and that the British would then come to terms with us.[46]

Later, the returning provincial emissaries brought more good news including an exhausted O'Rahilly's report that all was quiet on the western Irish front. By Sunday evening 23 April, MacNeill believed he had checkmated the conspirators. But he had failed to grasp that unlike chess in real life, the game continues after checkmate,[47] that Clarke and his colleagues had invested too much in their dream to give up now. As MacDonagh's own brother acknowledged, the rising 'completely dominated their lives and no consideration such as family or strict adherence to any formal procedure could be allowed to interfere with their accepted destiny, to which they gladly dedicated their lives'.[48] At the Gaelic League offices in North Frederick Street, Pearse and MacDermott arrived at 8 p.m. with secret dispatches that couriers would take to local Volunteer commandants throughout the country. These read: 'We start

operations at noon today, Monday. Carry out your instructions. P.H. Pearse'.
Some messengers left Dublin that night, others not until Monday morning,
their travel expenses paid for out of £300 that Tom – the IRB's treasurer – had
sent to MacDermott shortly beforehand.[49]

Confident that capturing the *Aud* and Casement meant the danger had
passed, both Chief Secretary Birrell and General Friend, the Irish GOC,
departed for London, leaving Under-Secretary Nathan responsible for Irish
affairs. On Saturday evening Nathan met the Viceroy, Lord Wimborne, who
eventually persuaded him to order the arrest of Volunteer leaders – provided
Birrell approved.[50] But Nathan's telegram to this effect did not reach the
Chief Secretary until the following day and while he awaited Birrell's decision,
Nathan contented himself with compiling lists of those men to be arrested in
a government clampdown.

NOTES

1 Denis McCullough, BMH WS 915.
2 Ibid.
3 Ibid.
4 Seán T. O'Kelly, BMH WS.
5 Denis McCullough, BMH WS 915.
6 Ibid.
7 Manuscript notes by Patrick McCartan on Louis Le Roux's biography of
   Thomas Clarke, NLI MS 44,683.
8 Kathleen Clarke, *Revolutionary Woman*, p. 69.
9 Diarmuid Lynch, NLI MS 5173.
10 Kathleen Clarke in a manuscript draft of her autobiography located in the
   Clarke papers. This part was deleted from *Revolutionary Woman*.
11 'The Memoirs of Madge Daly'.
12 Kathleen Clarke in 'A Character Sketch of Tom Clarke' in the Clarke Papers,
   NLI MS 49,355/12.
13 Joseph Gleeson, BMH WS 367.
14 Emmet Clarke to Seán O'Mahony, O'Mahony Papers, NLI MS 44,041/7.
15 Pat McCartan, BMH WS 766.
16 Bulmer Hobson, NLI MS 13,171 and MS 13,174. Gregory Murphy in BMH
   WS 150 states that he attended a meeting of the Dublin Centres Board at
   41 Parnell Square during which one Centre, P.J. Farrell, asked Hobson if
   the instructions he had received to interfere with the railway were all right.
   Bulmer Hobson told him that nothing should be done without instructions
   from MacNeill.
17 Eoin MacNeill, BMH Collected Documents, no. 7.
18 P.S. O'Hegarty, BMH WS 841.
19 Seán T. O'Kelly has recorded that, 'It is fair to MacNeill to state at this point

that when I discussed this point on the Saturday night before the Rising with MacNeill, first at Rathfarnham in the presence of Arthur Griffith and later in the house of Dr Seamus O'Kelly at Rathgar Road, MacNeill definitely stated that he was never told an insurrection had been decided upon to take place at Easter. MacNeill's story to me was that Pearse told him a couple of weeks before Easter that a large consignment of arms would arrive from Germany and that this was to be landed on the Kerry coast on the Saturday, that the mobilisation and manoeuvres ordered Easter Sunday were intended to cover the bigger operation in Kerry. My recollection is that MacNeill did promise co-operation so far as a landing of arms was concerned and for this purpose did consent to the Easter manoeuvres'. Talk by Seán T. O'Kelly, NLI MS 27,702(7).

20 Diarmuid Lynch, BMH WS 4.
21 Seamus O'Connor, 'Statement on National Activities in Dublin 1913–1916', BMH Collected Documents, no. 64.
22 Ibid.
23 'The Memoirs of Madge Daly'.
24 Mannix Joyce, 'The Story of Limerick and Kerry in 1916', *Capuchin Annual* (1966).
25 William O'Brien, BMH WS 1766.
26 Mannix Joyce, 'The Story of Limerick and Kerry in 1916'.
27 Kathleen Clarke, *Revolutionary Woman*, p. 73.
28 'Memoirs of Eoin MacNeill', BMH Collected Documents no. 7.
29 Ibid.
30 Louis Le Roux, *Tom Clarke and the Irish Freedom Movement*, p. 204.
31 Diarmuid Lynch, in a lecture entitled 'The Story of Easter Week' that he gave to the Clan na Gael, New York, NLI MS 11,129(1).
32 Ibid.
33 Kathleen Clarke, *Revolutionary Woman*, p. 75
34 Norah Connolly O'Brien, BMH WS 286.
35 Ibid.
36 Seamus O'Sullivan, BMH WS 393.
37 Seán McGarry, BMH WS 368.
38 Michael Staines, BMH WS 284
39 Diarmuid Lynch, in a lecture entitled 'The Story of Easter Week' given to the Clan na Gael, New York, NLI MS 11,129(1).
40 Seán McGarry, BMH WS 368
41 Piaras Béaslaí, *Irish Independent*, 16 January 1953
42 Kathleen Clarke, *Revolutionary Woman*, p. 75.
43 Ibid.
44 P. McCartan, BMH WS 776.
45 Kathleen Clarke, *Revolutionary Woman*, p. 77.
46 Sean Fitzgibbon, 'The Easter Rising from the Inside', *Irish Times*, 19 April 1949.
47 Isaac Asimov's brilliant aphorism.
48 John MacDonagh, BMH WS 219.
49 Gregory Murphy, BMH WS 150.
50 On the following see a memo by Nathan in Nathan Papers MS 476. See also Leon Ó Broin, *Dublin Castle and the 1916 Rising*, pp. 83–4.

8

The Easter
Rising

From daylight on Easter Monday, the Citizen Army and Irish Volunteers began assembling outside Liberty Hall. Clarke himself left home after breakfast with his two bodyguards, having promised Kathleen that he would never surrender.[1] He had no illusions about the odds stacked against the rebels and told his wife that 'if we last out as long as Emmet did, we'll be doing well'.[2] For Tom it really was a question of victory or death.

Inside Liberty Hall he joined the entire Military Council apart from Ceannt who was preparing his Fourth Battalion to occupy the South Dublin Union. The mood was very different from their fraught meeting in the same building a day earlier when the rising had seemed on the brink of implosion. Having regained control of the situation, they now knew that this would be a special day. Eventually MacDonagh departed to lead the Third Battalion into Jacob's factory, but Tom, MacDermott, Pearse, Connolly and Plunkett stayed on. Collectively they would lead Volunteers into the General Post Office in O'Connell Street, which had been designated as the rebel headquarters. Overnight, Tom and the other leaders had no doubt been anxious to find out just how much MacNeill's countermand order would damage the turnout. To their disappointment, it soon became clear that many Volunteers had obeyed their Chief of Staff and either stayed at home or left Dublin for a day's holiday. A message from Ceannt that only 80 of his men had mobilised was followed by similar reports from other battalion areas. Outside Liberty Hall there were barely 150 men of the Headquarters Battalion that was going to seize the GPO. Unexpectedly, The O'Rahilly arrived to join them, his motor car laden with rifles. Having been tipped off late that the rebellion was going ahead, he could not resist playing a role in the forthcoming drama, declaring that 'it is madness, but it is glorious madness'.

The Easter Rising was planned to commence at noon. At 11.45 a.m., Captain Sean Connolly led a Citizen Army contingent away from Liberty Hall to occupy the City Hall and soon afterwards Michael Mallin and a contingent of the Citizen Army entered Stephen's Green. Across the city Irish Volunteer battalions occupied their designated garrisons. Ned Daly's First Battalion seized the Four Courts, MacDonagh's Third Battalion took Jacob's factory, de Valera's Third Battalion occupied Boland's Bakery, and Ceannt and his men marched through the South Dublin Union gates. Soon afterwards, James Connolly, as Dublin Commandant-General, led out the Headquarters Battalion. Pearse and Plunkett (swinging a sword cane) marched beside Connolly but in deference to age and ill health, Clarke and MacDermott had travelled ahead by motor car and were waiting at the Prince's Street corner of the GPO. Only one woman, Connolly's devoted political secretary Winifred Carney, was present and to avoid making the British authorities suspicious just a single cart carried ammunition and explosives. For the same reason the column avoided the direct routes until the last moment by marching along Eden Quay, turning into Lower Abbey Street and then wheeling right on to O'Connell Street. From there it moved northwards, passing the Metropole Hotel where British officers, standing on the pavement outside, grinned and chortled at the passing column. It being Easter, Dublin was in festive mood and its population relaxed and unsuspecting. Unlike many European capitals, the city was physically distant and strangely detached emotionally from the war. Conscription had not been imposed on Ireland and Dublin had not been subjected to the Zeppelin raids that were terrifying Londoners. At Easter 1916 it was very much 'business as usual', with Dublin a magnet for British soldiers from every part of the empire in search of rest and recreation as well as prosperous English couples on motoring tours.

When the Volunteer column reached the General Post Office at noon, Connolly shouted 'Wheel! – The GPO! – Charge!' Rushing inside the imposing classical building, Volunteers evicted customers and staff and captured a few British soldiers who were there on private business. One army officer was temporarily put in a telephone box, his hands tied with string. Plunkett offered him a cigarette and lit it for him in a touch of common humanity before impending events.[3] The three-storeyed GPO had been recently renovated. At the centre was the main sorting hall around which ran offices whose windows looked on to the street, while a door and glass partition separated this hall from the public office at the front. On the upper floors were a telegraphic office and a staff restaurant. The roof would provide Volunteer snipers with a commanding view of the surrounding area that

contained many shops, offices, restaurants, a cinema and the large Gresham
and Imperial hotels. Under Connolly's guidance, Volunteers began fortifying
the building, knocking out windows, barricading them with furniture and
posting guards. Clarke helped men who were smashing down the door
and glass partition separating the public hall from the main sorting office,
and although a wounded arm restricted his movement, he did fire one of the
first shots of the Rising by blowing a lock off the door. Screens were used to
create a hospital, a kit store stocked with boots, trousers, shirts and overcoats,
and also an armoury. Sorting tables became beds and a secluded corner was
set aside for a priest to hear confessions. Behind a counter facing the main
door was an area dubbed the 'front line trenches' where Connolly directed
military operations and he and Pearse conferred with Clarke, MacDermott
and Plunkett. Here too at night the five men slept on mattresses until proper
beds were provided.

Easter Monday was politically the happiest day of Clarke's life as events
long dreamt of suddenly became real. Within half an hour of the GPO's occupation, a tricolour was run up at the Henry Street corner and a green banner
with the inscription 'IRISH REPUBLIC' was hoisted on the Prince's Street
side. At 12.45 p.m. Clarke, the mastermind, handed the Proclamation of the
Irish Republic to Pearse for his allotted role, and stepping outside, Pearse the
orator began:

> Irishmen and Irishwomen: In the name of God and of the dead
> generations from which she receives her old tradition of nationhood,
> Ireland through us, summons her children to her flag and strikes for her
> freedom…

Only some bystanders heard him, but Connolly also spoke for Tom when he
shook Pearse's hand, saying 'Thank God, Pearse we have lived to see this day!'[4]

Volunteers then posted up hundreds of copies of the Proclamation around
the city centre or took them across the capital to other garrisons. Soon afterwards the GPO rebels also struck first blood when they opened fire on British
cavalry investigating supposed disturbances in O'Connell Street. They killed
three soldiers instantly and fatally wounded another. During the afternoon
dispatch carriers reported to the GPO that Volunteer and Citizen Army
battalions had occupied Stephen's Green, the City Hall, Jacob's factory and
Boland's Bakery. At the South Dublin Union, Ceannt with less than fifty men
had almost immediately commenced a battle with British soldiers that was
to rage throughout Easter Week. With the rebels controlling central Dublin,

the British administration in Ireland was in a state of paralysis, symbolised by the absence in London of the hapless Chief Secretary Augustine Birrell and Army GOC Major-General Sir Lovick Friend. This left only a disorientated Under-Secretary Sir Matthew Nathan in charge at Dublin Castle, which itself was virtually unguarded. At his disposal he had just 2,400 troops, scattered over nine barracks in Dublin and throughout the rest of Ireland; at noon on Easter Monday, only 400 of them were available for immediate duty in Dublin against about 1,000 rebels. And only about 200 unarmed policemen were on duty when the Rising began; all had been withdrawn by three o'clock in the afternoon.

Everyone who met Clarke on Easter Monday remembered his elation. Diarmuid Lynch recalled the two of them reading reports in the Royal Irish Constabulary's pigeonholes on the Irish Volunteers and Tom chuckling 'at the fact that all their spying was in vain, and that neither the police nor their superiors realised the imminence of the climax'.[5] For him this was a moment to savour, a dream that had long seemed impossible was now reality. Both Clarke and MacDermott were in their element. Physically and emotionally revived, they sat on the edge of the mails platform, beaming satisfaction and congratulating uniformed Volunteers. Seán McGarry observed the entire leadership's jubilation:

We had with us five members of the Provisional Government – Tom Clarke, his eyes sparkling with elation, MacDermott in joyous mood, Connolly happy as a schoolboy at a picnic, Plunkett who was very ill on Sunday seemed to have taken on new life and Pearse quiet as usual but in high humour.[6]

But there was serious work to be done. In a central hall crammed with the tools of war – boxes of ammunition, knapsacks, blankets and tents – Clarke also radiated intense seriousness of purpose. In a tiny room on the ground floor, Charles MacAuley of the Volunteer medical services saw 'Tom Clarke in civilian clothes with a bandolier across his shoulders and a rifle between his knees. He was silent and had a look of grim determination on his face. I was greatly impressed by him. It was as if he thought his day had come'.[7]

During Monday rebel reinforcements trickled into the General Post Office, some of them Volunteers who could not reach their own battalion's location but also others who had changed their mind after initially obeying MacNeill's countermand order. Women from the Cumann na mBan and the Citizen Army also arrived in the late afternoon and Connolly allocated them to the nursing and kitchen staff or appointed them dispatch carriers. Amidst the hectic activity, Clarke and MacDermott found time for magnanimity and authorised Seán T. O'Kelly to release Bulmer Hobson from detention. Tom had also had a letter for Kathleen that O'Kelly brought to Richmond Avenue where he discussed the day's events with Mrs Clarke. When O'Kelly returned to the GPO, Clarke and MacDermott listened attentively as he described his encounter with Hobson:

> They would have liked him to have agreed to come with me to the Post Office and expressed regret that he had not adopted my suggestion. I think, in their hearts both of them must have felt that it would have been a difficult thing for him to do after the way he had been treated.[8]

However, it is doubtful if Tom and Seán genuinely wanted reconciliation with Hobson; relations between both sides had soured too much. More probably they would have regarded his appearance as their victory and Hobson's admission of great error. And it is hard to see Clarke and MacDermott generously allocating Hobson a role in the rebellion commensurate with his ability and standing in the Volunteers as they had done with The O'Rahilly.

Despite being Volunteers, Tom and Seán were in civilian suits and neither fought nor even fired a shot in anger during Easter Week. Clarke was in charge of the armoury, supervising the overhauling of guns, making grenades and packing buckshot into shotgun cartridges. Like MacDermott, he also circulated throughout the GPO, boosting morale, listening to Volunteers' concerns and resolving problems. As a troubleshooter, Tom was very punctilious about observing military rank and political hierarchy, always deferring to both Connolly and Pearse. He gave Pearse his place when Luke Kennedy – a Volunteer and IRB member who knew Tom's importance – warned him that water should be stored up in case the British could cut off the supply and probably the electricity and gas as well. Tom brought Kennedy to the headquarters room where Pearse instructed Tom to get Kennedy to take lorries to Bachelor's Walk, seize dairy churns, fill them with water and finally deposit them in a GPO yard.[9] This reversal of roles with Pearse caused Tom no difficulty; indeed he knew it was essential for the greater good that he was seen to be following proper protocol, not undermining Pearse and Connolly's authority or confusing the chain of command. Ever vigilant, Clarke was also constantly on the alert for breaches of discipline. He was especially concerned about enforcing the leadership's ban on consuming alcohol and its order to destroy any stocks found in occupied buildings. When Catherine Byrne discovered a small bar containing beer and minerals, she asked a Volunteer for a bottle of lemonade, but Clarke suddenly appeared and emptied out a beer bottle. Typically he wasn't taking any chances – either with Byrne, the Volunteer or the rest of the garrison. She recalled that 'later on Tom Clarke came up and examined all the crates to make sure that all the stout was gone. He said he did not want the men to be tempted'.[10]

To Clarke's satisfaction, Easter Monday ended without interference from any of Dublin's nine functioning army barracks or a single shot fired at the GPO. The Military Council's plans in the capital had gone almost without a hitch and taken the British authorities completely by surprise, vindicating the tight security with which Tom had surrounded the work of the Military Council. British officers who regarded Dublin as an easy posting where they could frequent high-class brothels and enjoy weekend sojourns in the big houses of the Anglo-Irish ascendancy were about to find themselves in action once again.

However, everything hinged now on how the Irish people and British government reacted to the Rising. Tom must have hoped – even expected – that the country would respond enthusiastically to rebels occupying Dublin city centre. But ominously, J.J. Walsh, a Volunteer and trained wireless operator, had been able to contact Cork, Galway, Athlone and Wexford from the Post Office, and learned that these counties had not risen. Shaken, Pearse warned Walsh to keep the bad news to himself.[11] Furthermore, the British authorities had recovered quickly from their initial shock and summoned reinforcements from across the country; they had also started to gather intelligence on the rebels' strength and dispositions. In Dublin itself, troops rapidly secured the Magazine Fort, Kingsbridge and Broadstone railway stations and the Vice-Regal Lodge in Phoenix Park. Just after lunch on Monday, soldiers from the Royal, Portobello and Richmond Barracks began arriving at the Castle and by evening its garrison had risen to 300 men. By 5.20 p.m., an additional 1,600 troops from the Curragh had arrived at Kingsbridge station to protect the docks and secure Amiens Street railway station and the Custom House. Soon considerable reinforcements were preparing to converge on Dublin from Belfast and Athlone and 10,000 soldiers encamped at St Albans in England had left for Ireland.

Oblivious of these developments, the GPO garrison was in a relaxed mood on Tuesday morning and in the yard younger Volunteers even passed the time doing trick-riding on bicycles belonging to telegraph boys.[12] So at ease were the rebels that Connolly strode up to Winifred Carney 'almost speechless and his face crimson with rage. Some of the Citizen Army have asked him if they can go to their work that day. With difficulty I repress a desire to laugh for I would never be forgiven such levity'.[13] The cheerful atmosphere was due in part to a welter of rumours that boosted Volunteer morale in the Post Office.

Cork and Limerick had supposedly risen, 10,000 Germans had landed in
Kerry and were closing in on Dublin, Verdun had finally fallen to the
Germans and Germany's North Sea fleet was about to land an expeditionary
force in England while its U-boats were already in Dublin Bay. Such fantasies
thrived because of a dearth of accurate information that was due in part to
the severing of communications between Dublin and the outside world and
within the capital itself. The telegraph connection to England was broken
within twenty minutes on Easter Monday, and although the telephone system
continued operating during the week, civilians were only able to receive calls.
In Dublin only a Unionist newspaper, the *Irish Times*, was able to continue
publishing for three days, though copies of English titles were brought in and
sold at a shilling each. No mail was collected or delivered.

Nevertheless, the initiative was already passing inexorably to the British.
The Military Council's original plan to sandwich enemy forces between
rebel garrisons in the city centre with Volunteers moving on Dublin from
the countryside had failed. Despite Pearse's claim that 'the country is rising',
a nationwide revolt had not materialised. Now the British began probing
the GPO's defences and from O'Connell Bridge an armoured car periodically sprayed the deserted street with machine-gun fire. By now the crowds
thronging O'Connell Street on Easter Monday had evaporated, but many
civilians had merely shifted a short distance across the bridge to become
spectators at a rising that seemingly they regarded as a spectacle laid on for
their enjoyment. Then Clarke's sisters-in-law Laura and Nora Daly arrived
in the Post Office, having travelled with Eamon Dore from Limerick.[14] They
verified Walsh's report of a day earlier that the Volunteers in Limerick, Cork
and elsewhere had not stirred, a setback that made a British counter-attack
in Dublin inevitable. Hurriedly Connolly began fashioning a new strategy
to deal with British infantry attempting to storm the GPO. As a revolutionary socialist he could not imagine the capitalist class allowing an artillery
bombardment of O'Connell Street that would cause widespread destruction
of property; instead he envisaged close, even hand-to-hand, fighting in the
Post Office and started to garrison buildings nearby that commanded routes
along which he thought British soldiers would advance. These included the
block on the opposite side of O'Connell Street that contained the Imperial
Hotel and Clery's department store. There was as yet no immediate danger of
a British frontal assault on the GPO since the enemy was confining himself
to isolating the building from other rebel garrisons in the capital.

On Tuesday afternoon, Brigadier-General William Lowe and another
1,000 troops from the Curragh arrived at Kingsbridge station and, in Friend's

absence, Lowe assumed command of British forces in Dublin. During the day increasing British military resources forced Mallin to evacuate Stephen's Green and seek refuge in the nearby College of Surgeons. Lowe also began establishing a 'protected line' of posts from Kingsbridge station in the west of the city through Dublin Castle and Trinity College to the Custom House on the docks in the east. This line split rebel forces in two and enabled advancing troops to begin extending their operations north and south. And on Easter Tuesday the reinforcements from England disembarked at Kingstown.

At about midnight on Tuesday, Dore and the Daly sisters left the GPO for Kingsbridge station. Both women carried messages from MacDermott for the Volunteer leaders in Limerick and Cork; on the way out MacDermott had told them: 'For God's sake try and do something to help the fighting men in Dublin'.[15] Separately and more candidly, he informed Dore that 'you need not come back as you know it's all over'.[16] But at Kingsbridge station Dore recognised a detective who knew him, and sending the sisters ahead for the train he returned to the GPO. After parting from Laura at Limerick Junction, Nora travelled on to Cork where MacDermott's appeal failed to sway the Volunteer leaders Terence MacSwiney and Thomas McCurtain, who insisted that their men lacked the strength to take the military initiative and they would only respond to a British attack. Dore's reappearance in the GPO astounded Clarke and MacDermott who reproached him for coming back. Dore told them that the Daly sisters had got away safely, but he also revealed that the British were closing in fast: troops had reached the Rotunda and the bank at the corner of Parnell and O'Connell Streets and were also at Phibsboro and south of Mountjoy Gaol. Dore said the British soldiers were very nervous and suggested that he lead a commando raid to force them back: 'Tom Clarke replied "We have no authority. Connolly is in charge here and we will report what you have said". I heard no more about my suggestion, but I do know Clarke and MacDiarmada went to him'.[17]

Nevertheless Easter Tuesday in the GPO had been comparatively quiet and as darkness fell Clarke unwound by chatting in the kitchen to MacDermott's fiancée, Min Ryan. While acknowledging that the Irish people would initially condemn the Rising, he insisted the IRB leaders had to go through with it; they had brought the men to such a pitch of readiness that any last-minute retreat would have destroyed the Irish Volunteers. Asserting that shedding blood had always raised the Irish people's spirit, Tom also said the Military Council had declared a republic because 'you must have something striking in order to appeal to the imagination of the world'. Furthermore, despite the military tide turning against the rebels, Clarke was not downhearted: '"Of course", he added, "we shall all be wiped out". He said this almost with gaiety. He had got into the one thing he had wanted to do during his whole lifetime'. Light-heartedly Tom also ribbed a wretched-looking Seán McGarry that 'Miss Ryan will get you a cup of Bovril. She gave one to me; it is great stuff'.[18]

On Wednesday military activity increased to a relentless tempo throughout Dublin. British snipers attacked the Imperial Hotel and a naval vessel, the *Helga*, bombarded Liberty Hall rather ineffectively before heavy guns reduced the deserted building to ruins. Soon British machine guns on top of Trinity College were sweeping O'Connell Street and forcing Connolly to evacuate some Volunteer outposts. He transferred these men to the Metropole block which stretched from Middle Abbey Street to Prince's Street and by the evening Volunteers also dominated Sackville Place, the Lower Abbey Street approach and the whole of lower O'Connell Street. British soldiers attempting to storm GPO would suffer considerable casualties.

Across the capital other rebel garrisons had mixed fortunes. On Wednesday one of Ned Daly's most important outposts at the Mendicity Institution surrendered after an epic siege. Earlier in the day as a British cordon closed rapidly around the building, its young commandant Seán Heuston had appealed to Connolly for reinforcements. Connolly was euphoric that the Mendicity's small garrison was still holding out and summoned Clarke, MacDermott and Pearse to hear the news. But all he could send to Heuston and his men was a message of praise because another British military cordon was tightening around the GPO itself. Late on Wednesday night, the British fired shrapnel shells into O'Connell Street and some hit the Metropole Hotel. But Volunteer morale in the Post Office soared when dispatch carriers brought news of fierce fighting that had taken place earlier in the day at Mount Street Bridge where Volunteers from Eamon de Valera's Third Battalion had ambushed a column of British reinforcements that had landed at Kingstown and was marching into the city. Enemy losses amounted to four officers killed and fourteen wounded, while 216 men of other ranks were killed and wounded – over half the British casualties in the entire Rising.

A Volunteer in the GPO, Michael Staines, recalled that 'Wednesday night was immensely calm. Scarcely a sound was to be heard outside the garrison. It was indeed the calm before the storm'.[19] By now the garrison knew Ireland had not risen and that British reinforcements were pouring into both Dublin and Ireland itself. But the prospect of facing a massed British infantry assault only hardened their resolve to fight to the finish. A heroic last stand appealed very much to Clarke who now anticipated ending his life in the

GPO – either from a sniper's bullet or from being buried under a pile of rubble. Dr Jim Ryan recollected that:

> On Wednesday Tom Clarke came to the hospital and sitting down quietly beside me began to talk … I was now Red Cross and so he said I might possibly be spared by the enemy in the final bayonet charge which was evidently expected by him as well as by the rest of us. If therefore I should survive he hoped I now understood and would make known the motives of those who signed the Proclamation.[20]

Increasingly gripped by a vision of going down fighting, Clarke brought Desmond FitzGerald – who ran the commissary – to an outside yard and showed him a concrete shelter. Tom instructed Fitzgerald that just before the final British assault he should move all the women into it, though Fitzgerald himself would most likely perish or be executed soon afterwards.[21] Tom's more sombre mood deepened on Wednesday when he learned that British soldiers had advanced to the North Circular Road and threatened Kathleen's safety in Richmond Avenue. He sent Seán T. O'Kelly out with another letter for his wife, but troops detained O'Kelly on the North Circular Road, thus severing contact between Tom and Kathleen until after the Rising ended.[22]

On Easter Thursday 27 April, the GPO garrison awakened early to another glorious cloudless day, but everyone sensed that militarily this day would be different. By now the British had a firm grip on the capital, having identified the most important rebel garrisons, had built up vastly superior troop levels, and were starting to establish an inner cordon around the GPO that would isolate the nerve centre of the Rising. British soldiers were now strongly concentrated in College Street, Trinity College, the Custom House, Liberty Hall and Amiens Street, and in O'Connell Street from Parnell Street to Findlater Place. Shortly after dawn, British machine-gun fire and heavy sniping was concentrated on the Post Office though a shell had not yet hit the building. One British sniper wounded Connolly's left leg as he returned from outposts in Liffey Street and in the GPO a captured British army doctor treated him using chloroform as an anaesthetic. For the rest of Thursday, Connolly was out of action and thereafter survived on frequent injections of morphine. Carney chided Connolly for exposing himself to British marksmen, but he replied 'Do not blame me now, I must take risks like the others'.[23] Although The O'Rahilly now assumed military leadership in the Post Office, overall control passed to Clarke and MacDermott. With Pearse suffering from lack of sleep and Plunkett seriously ill after the operation on his glandular neck, Tom and Seán's increasingly open authority was accepted without question by the GPO garrison. Irish Volunteers in the IRB knew of the pair's importance, now publicly proclaimed by their membership of the Provisional Government and their frequent interaction in the Post Office with Pearse, Connolly and Plunkett. Clarke and MacDermott now began promoting officers, moving munitions and prisoners around the building and deciding whether or not to continue manning outposts.

Looking in control and undaunted by a deteriorating military situation, the reassuring presence of both men was vital in sustaining morale. Hitherto, Pearse had irritated Winifred Carney by never smiling or laughing once in the GPO. She recalled that:

> About Wednesday Pearse, standing with his usual sad demeanour annoyed J.C. Fearful of the effect he may have on the Volunteers J.C. remonstrates with him. Afterwards I ask Connolly how could he speak so to Pearse and wearily he replies 'it is so difficult to get these people to understand the sordidness of a revolution'.[24]

Long inured to stress and sleeplessness, Clarke was imperturbably calm at the centre of a storm. Seán McGarry 'never knew him to be cooler. His normal air of business seemed to have been accentuated and he gave his orders decisively and as calmly as if he were in his own shop'.[25] Patrick Rankin thought he 'looked about thirty years younger and seemed so happy you could imagine you were talking to him in his old shop in Parnell Street'.[26] As probably the oldest person in the GPO, Tom also looked and acted like a father figure, one especially protective of the garrison's younger men and women. After a teenage courier, Mary McLoughlin, found a revolver lying on the ground near Abbey Street on Easter Thursday, Tom saw her playfully pretending to hold up a Fianna boy scout in the Post Office. Still injured himself by McGarry carelessly handling a weapon, he warned Mary gently but firmly about the dangers. As a former schoolmaster, Tom also resorted to the frightener of sending a wayward pupil to the headmaster: 'He told me I would have to give the gun up to James Connolly himself. I did so when James Connolly, who was lying on a stretcher, held my hand, saying the gun could not have been in better hands'.[27]

Although not a religious man, Clarke knew its importance to many Volunteers in the GPO whose confessions earlier in the week had been heard by Father Michael Flanagan of Dublin's Pro-Cathedral. However the priest had departed without a replacement or a promise that he would return. At about 4 p.m. on Easter Thursday, Tom summoned Leslie Price, a Cumann na mBan dispatch carrier, and told her to fetch a priest from the cathedral presbytery. With the Post Office practically surrounded, Price was frightened: 'Tom Clarke looked at me. He had sort of steely eyes. He said, "You are to cross O'Connell Street". I could have cried but, when I looked at his courageous face, I said, "All right". I did not cry'.[28] After a scary journey she reached the presbytery safely and delivered Clarke's message to Father Flanagan. To Price's astonishment he exclaimed that 'no one here will go into the Post Office. Let these people be burned to death. They are murderers'.[29] Attributing his resentment to the left-wing Citizen Army's participation in the Rising, Price retorted that she would go back alone. But she managed to change his mind by saying that Volunteers prepared to die simply wanted to do so in the presence of a priest. At the Post Office Clarke quietly instructed Mick Staines not to allow Flanagan out of the building again, something that proved vital next day when Flanagan led a group of nurses out of the Post Office to safety.

By mid-afternoon on Easter Thursday, the rebel dispatch system had completely collapsed, strongly reinforcing the Post Office's isolation. Like every other Volunteer garrison, it was now on its own. At 3.45 p.m. British howitzers began bombardment lasting two and a half hours, dropping shrapnel shells over the roof of the GPO and forcing defenders down to lower floors. The assault inflicted hardly any damage on the building, though British snipers on top of the Gresham Hotel poured bullets through its windows. It was a different story during the evening on the opposite side of O'Connell Street. There Winifred Carney watched the British strategy unfold as incendiary shells ignited an inferno:

The firing from the enemy is incessant, a continuous shower of bullets from machine guns and the explosion of incendiary bombs. They apparently cannot get a clear range at the G.P.O. And so have been burning down the buildings that surround us from the Liffey side. The scene is fascinating as the fire consumes each building and octopus like grips the adjoining one as it stands untouched until it too is a blazing mass, and so on until the whole block is an inferno with the noise of burning and falling masonry.[30]

One Volunteer witnessed how:

A solid sheet of blinding death white flame rushes hundreds of feet into the air with a thunderous explosion which shakes the walls. It is followed by a heavy bombardment as hundreds of drums of oil explode.

The intense light compels one to close the eyes. Even here the heat is
so terrible that it strikes one like a solid thing as blast and scorching air
come in through the glassless windows. Millions of sparks are floating
in masses for hundreds of yards around O'Connell Street. The whole
thing seems too terrible to be real.[31]

Another Volunteer, Michael Staines, recalled that:

The heat from the burning block opposite the GPO was beyond
belief. Despite the great width of O'Connell Street the sacks, etc. in
the windows began to scorch and show signs of smouldering. Batches
of men had to be hastily formed to continually drench the window
fortifications with water. Dense volumes of acrid smoke, myriads of
sparks and splinters of falling debris were being blown to the GPO by
a strong north-east wind. Lurid flames leapt skywards and the spectacle
in the gathering darkness could only be likened to Dante's Inferno.
The intensity of the heat grew steadily worse and the water being
poured from buckets and hoses was converted into steam as it touched
the fortifications. There had to be a withdrawal from the front of the
building of all save those who were combating the risk of a conflagration in the Post Office itself. Our struggle with this new danger seemed
to go on for interminable hours. The men were soot-stained, steam-
scalded and fire-scorched, sweating, weary and parched.[32]

At last the terrific heat died down and the smoke lessened. Although the fires
smouldered for days, the immediate danger had passed. During the night the
big guns were silent and only occasionally did a British sniper open fire.

At daybreak on Easter Friday 28 April, Clarke could see with his own eyes
that British soldiers had inflicted on his capital the kind of destruction that
he had tried to visit on theirs over thirty years earlier. On the eastern side of
O'Connell Street only the façade of many buildings still stood, numerous fires
were still burning and swirling clouds of grey smoke shrouded O'Connell
Bridge. Sometimes a British soldier or rooftop sniper was glimpsed, but no
troops were massing for a frontal attack on the Post Office. This indicated that
the British now intended to avoid suffering heavy casualties by proceeding
to level the western side of O'Connell Street. By 2.30 a.m. when Major-
General Sir John Maxwell arrived in Dublin to replace Friend, he had
between 18,000 and 20,000 troops at his disposal with substantially more due
within forty-eight hours. After consulting with senior officers, he decided to

further isolate any 'infectious patches' and began by ordering Lowe to close in on O'Connell Street.

By now Clarke had come to terms with the grim situation that confronted the rebels, telling Volunteers that 'things are looking serious now, we are surrounded'.[33] His time in the GPO had truly been a baptism of fire for someone like Tom who had just turned 59, was probably the oldest Volunteer in the Post Office and had never experienced battle. Cooped up during Easter Week, he had endured sniper fire, incendiary shells, artillery bombardment, flames and the danger of ammunition exploding or the roof collapsing and burying him alive. For days Clarke's eyes and ears were assailed by memorable sights and sounds. He saw men terribly injured, dying and dead rebels, enemy soldiers and Dublin civilians, the rotting corpses of cavalry horses and O'Connell Street burning. He was also assailed by the sounds of exploding shells, cries for help and the screams of men who just could not take any more. Tom also faced extreme heat from the fires and the steam from water hoses used to fight the flames. Physically, emotionally and psychologically, the Easter Rising tested him – and many others – to the limit. Although in the scale of military operations, Dublin 1916 was nothing like the Western Front, the combat was intense. One British officer, Lieutenant Jameson, wrote that 'everybody who had been in France seemed to think the Dublin fighting was a far worse thing to be in!'[34] But Clarke passed the test. He possessed physical and moral courage and an unconquerable will. A lifetime acquiring absolute control over his emotions enabled Tom to convey calmness to other Volunteers in the GPO. Sleeplessness hardly troubled a person who had suffered sleep deprivation regularly during many years in prison. Nor was fire, great heat and steam a new experience for someone who had worked in the iron foundry at Chatham Prison. And it was not by chance that Clarke and other Provisional Government members were in the Post Office sharing the dangers with ordinary Volunteers. A common image from the First World War is that of military commanders directing armies from the safety of a their châteaux situated far behind the front lines where infantry are fighting and dying. But a cardinal principle of Clarke's life had been never to ask of his followers something that he was not prepared to do himself. He and his fellow leaders were determined in a sense to get down into the trenches, fight alongside rank-and-file Volunteers and demonstrate that they really were all in it together. This led to Connolly suffering two wounds from enemy sniper fire and despite the second incapacitating him, he insisted on remaining in the GPO to the end. In less dramatic ways, Clarke insisted on sharing others' suffering. Michael Staines, Quartermaster of the Irish Volunteers' Dublin

Brigade, recalled that on Easter Wednesday night he managed to get some sleep in the room set aside for the leaders:

> When I awakened on Thursday I saw Tom Clarke lying on another mattress. He appeared to be very cold; I remonstrated with him for not taking one of my blankets and he replied that as I was sleeping so soundly he did not wish to disturb me. I gave him some of my blankets and he went asleep.[35]

Like Clarke, many Volunteers in the GPO also sensed that the end was near. To Seán MacEntee it seemed that 'the air was heavy with premonition, and the brooding calm forebode a storm'. True enough, at daybreak the British launched a bombardment of incendiary shells and continuous bursts of machine-gun fire raked O'Connell Street. Having discovered a winning formula on the previous day, their tactics for Easter Friday were simply more of the same. Faced with the imminent possibility of the GPO garrison being obliterated or incinerated, the rebel leaders must have convened early on Friday to decide on a response. Almost certainly they were joined in their discussions by The O'Rahilly and possibly Willie Pearse. Having never retreated or surrendered, Clarke would have argued for a glorious last stand, but once again he was probably in a minority of one. Connolly in particular had always insisted on giving his men a fighting chance of surviving. Undoubtedly a decision was taken to evacuate the GPO, and its continued occupation on Friday was purely a holding exercise to buy time – time for the rebel leadership to find an alternative strategy and withdraw men from outposts into the building so that the entire garrison could depart the GPO together.

MacDermott now ordered Diarmuid Lynch to transfer munitions from the upper floor to a basement room and then bring back Volunteers from outposts in Henry Street and Middle Abbey Street. He also instructed the medical officer, Jim Ryan, to prepare sixteen wounded Volunteers for removal to Jervis Street Hospital. About noon British howitzers situated behind the Rotunda Hospital lobbed shells and incendiaries into the GPO, setting fire to a corner of the roof and precipitating the first phase of the evacuation. Thirty women were assembled in the main hall where Pearse told them they would have to leave. Angry and determined to stay with the Volunteers to the end, the women prevailed on MacDermott to intercede on their behalf, but Pearse stood firm. During a brief lull in the fighting, they were ushered into Henry Street. At about 3 p.m., Clarke, MacDermott, Diarmuid Lynch, Seán McGarry and Eamon Dore went up to the commissary for a surprisingly relaxed final meal. Tucking into mutton chops they joked about sinning on a meatless Friday, while Clarke considerately opened a tin of pears for the younger Dore.[36] Afterwards the group returned to the ground floor. Having at last got their range, the British intensified the bombardment and serious fires broke out around the GPO as flames on the roof burned through the top of the portico and into the interior of the building. Seán MacEntee

was fascinated by the long snakes of fire that went curling and writhing across the glass canopy of the central hall. I watched them with the rapture of a young boy at a great fireworks display. Death had been so close for the last few days that, now when it came still nearer, I almost laughed in its face. Over the glass roof, the water from the hoses, a bluish, translucent liquid, came pouring from above in a fiery stream. The end of the stream, impinging on the tough glass, would shape itself for a moment to a star before it burst and sent flying from its blazing rays a hundred fiery particles. Often a spurt of water from the hoses would sweep across the glass, carrying the fire before it, and then, when the mass of water was large, it would go billowing back and forward from end to end of the transparent ceiling, so that the flame, like fire-fairies in play, went glissading to and fro on the crystal above us.

Despite the fire-fighters' best efforts

the fire grew fiercer and spread until it seemed as though we stood underneath a lake of flame. The heat was intense; we could hear the glass plates crack above our heads and see the hungry flames leap through the broken spaces. We concentrated now in the main hall of the building, the fire following us with amazing rapidity.[37]

Soon afterwards the final British assault began. Inside the General Post Office, the first fires had been quickly brought under control, but about 3 p.m. a shell inflicted serious damage over the portico. Having at last got their range, the British intensified the bombardment and fires broke out around the building where every hose, fire extinguisher and bucket of water was employed against them. Soon the flames had eaten their way through the roof of the cupola and into the interior. Two streams of water were thrown against the lower part of the roof and lines of buckets were also organised. Just when it seemed the flames were being contained, incendiary bullets ignited another part of the roof. Despite frantic efforts, Dick Humphries recalled that:

After a few minutes, however, we see that all is useless. The fire is gaining ground in all directions. Huge masses of the roof commence to fall inwards with terrific noise. The floor on which the men are working threatens to give way with each blow. Clouds of smoke from the burning debris writhe around the corridors and passages. It gets into our eyes and noses and compels fits of coughing. The floors are covered to a depth of three inches with grimy water.[38]

MacDermott and Patrick Pearse were actively involved in trying to keep the fires at bay until the wounded had gone and a full evacuation could get under way. Despite every available hose, extinguisher and bucket of water being used to combat the fires, the situation was becoming untenable as intense heat melted the glass overhead. Volunteer Seamus Scully feared that 'the shaft descending to the crammed ammunition cellar would ignite at any moment. The wild suggestion of an escape by the filth choked sewer was impossible. Headquarters had lost contact with the main outlying positions and the enemy now had a clear field for military attack'.[39]

To avoid panic, the leaders had kept secret from the rank and file until the last moment their decision to evacuate the GPO. Now every man was ordered to assemble in the general sorting office at the rear. There, at about 6 p.m., the wounded and their Volunteer escort were readied for evacuation, except for Connolly who utterly refused to leave. Father Flanagan led them out accompanied by most of the remaining nurses who were carrying Volunteers' farewell messages. Clarke had told one, 'If you see my wife, tell her the men fought …' but then broke down and turned away.[40] Only three women remained now – Connolly's secretary, Winifred Carney, and two nurses, Elizabeth O'Farrell and Julia Grenan. By now sparks were coming down the elevator and air shafts, through the doorways and every other opening, and nothing could be done to stop the fire spreading. It was time to go. Pearse now required an advance guard to precede the main garrison and make ready a new headquarters at Williams & Woods jam factory in Parnell Street. These premises were full of foodstuffs and close enough, Pearse believed, to British lines to make shelling them a risky enterprise for the enemy. For this attempted breakthrough, he chose The O'Rahilly, who in turn selected twenty-five men. Leading them out from the side entrance on Henry Street, he arranged his men into fours, took his place at the front, drew his sword and ordered them to follow him. Initially they advanced without incident, but upon turning into Moore Street saw a British barricade about 250yds away. Suddenly rifle and machine-gun fire opened up on the Volunteers and when The O'Rahilly rallied his men and resumed the advance, he was cut down and mortally wounded. Inside the GPO an increasingly perplexed Pearse waited in vain for a dispatch from The O'Rahilly announcing that he had occupied Williams & Woods.

In the sorting office, over 300 men of the GPO garrison were lined up while barely 30yrds away a wall of flame extended to the roof, loose ammunition was exploding like machine-gun fire and bombs detonated. In the midst of this Wagnerian denouement, men with rifles slung or at the slope stood to attention. Pearse now made his final speech to the assembled garrison, praising their gallantry, and they responded spontaneously with 'The Soldier's Song'. Shortly afterwards at about eight o'clock, Volunteers began evacuating the GPO, filing past Pearse and leaving through the Henry Street side entrance. Outside the Post Office was almost as dangerous as inside. When the prisoners were released, most took their chances by running across Moore Lane, where one British soldier was cut down by a British sniper on the roof of the Rotunda dressed in a nurse's uniform. Volunteers ran straight into a gauntlet of exploding shells, machine-gun fire and bullets striking walls and pavements like hailstones. In the canteen of the GPO on Easter Friday, Volunteer Joseph O'Rourke was guarding British prisoners and he recalled that 'shells were screaming and exploding with periodic regularity, the ear was assailed with the roar of machine-guns in full action; the incessant pattering and zipping of bullets; the crash of falling beams and tumbling masonry and a circle of blazing fires menaced them'.[41]

Clarke had intended staying in the GPO to the end. Now as his dreams literally went up in flames, he stood amidst falling beams and masonry, brandishing an automatic pistol and shouting 'You can all go and leave me here. I'll go down with the building'.[42] However, just in time MacDermott cajoled him into joining the exodus. When everyone had gone, Pearse made a final sweep of the building for any stragglers before dashing into Henry Street to catch up with the other leaders. By now nobody was actually in charge; only confusion and latent panic reigned. Even MacDermott's self-control cracked. In front of Pearse and Connolly, he shouted despairingly: 'My God, we are not going to be caught like rats and killed without a chance to fight. We have no chance now: this is the end'.[43]

Volunteers managed to shield themselves from enemy fire by dragging a motorcar across the end of Moore Lane. It was only a brief respite, because crossing into Moore Street exposed them once again to British machine-gunners on the roof of the Rotunda Hospital. At great personal risk, Plunkett stood in the middle of the road, periodically dipping his sword as a signal for men to run over. Then a Volunteer in uniform was shot in the breast and fell over the handles of the stretcher carrying Connolly. Seeing the uniform, Connolly thought it was Plunkett and became very agitated. Trying to roll off his stretcher, Connolly shouted for Plunkett to be carried immediately into a building, but Plunkett strolled up and pacified him.[44] During the first lull in enemy fire, MacDermott ordered Connolly to be rushed across towards Moore Street and into Cogan's grocers' shop at the corner of Henry Place and Moore Street. Sheltering inside the shop was a policeman and when Connolly saw him, he let out a roar that the man should be thrown out to hell.[45] The devoted Carney protected Connolly until his stretcher bearers lifted him through the window of Cogan's shop. In Henry Place, British machine-gun fire had stampeded Clarke's group and after trying unsuccessfully to shoot off a door lock and get his men safely inside a building, Tom led them to the corner of Henry Place and Moore Lane. Hoping to die by an enemy bullet, he raised a hand and with the cry 'one more rally for Ireland', led a charge across the road.[46] Against all odds Tom and his men reached Cogan's shop. Inside, Clarke and MacDermott discovered Connolly on the ground, weeping and proclaiming bitterly, 'I would not like to have MacNeill's conscience'.[47] Everyone was tense, thirsty and exhausted. Winifred Carney recalled that 'death has no terrors in an overwhelming desire just to sleep'.[48] At least the famished leaders could ease their hunger because Mrs Cogan who lived on the premises provided boiled ham for a meal. MacDermott even lifted an egg and sucked out the raw contents through a hole.

Farther along Moore Street, Volunteers had forced entry into other houses whose frightened residents had locked their doors, and throughout the night they smashed holes in walls to create a line of communication. Since Connolly was now unable to exercise effective command, he and Pearse transferred their military authority to Seán McLoughlin, an 18-year-old Fianna scout whose bravery and intelligence had impressed them.[49] McLoughlin also knew the area well and he offered at least a chance of reaching the Four Courts before the British completed their encirclement. Enemy pressure was now becoming relentless. Artillery shells had already set alight four houses in Moore Street and a British officer had warned occupants that he would level as many buildings as were necessary to root out the rebels. McLoughlin believed that at noon the British would commence burning or shelling the rebels out and he began assembling a 'Death or Glory Squad' to storm the Moore Street barricade in an attempt to open an escape corridor to Capel Street and the Four Courts. During the early hours, Clarke, MacDermott, Pearse and Plunkett clambered after Volunteers who laboriously manoeuvred Connolly's stretcher from house to house until finally they all reached Nos. 15 and 16 Moore Street. There

MacDermott slept briefly on a mattress in the kitchen, while Pearse and his brother Willie covered themselves with their coats and lay on a table, underneath which snored a weary Volunteer clutching his rifle. Volunteer Charles Saurin recalled that in the darkened room he

> could dimly make out men sitting all around the walls and lying on the floor. In the corner quite near to me sat Tom Clarke with his hands clasped around his knees. A Volunteer beside him was irritably taxing him with taking his place. Even making allowances for the state of nerves everyone might have been in, I thought this was going too far and leaned across and told him who he was attacking, at the same time placing a hand upon his knee. He ceased complaining and clung to my hand as if it were a sheet anchor. Just then the door opened and Lieutenant Leo Henderson came into the room. He called out, 'Is Mr Clarke here?' Tom Clarke answered, and Leo Henderson said, 'Mr Clarke, I have a bed for you'. Tom Clarke got up and with some difficulty made his way over the men stretched out on the floor, the majority of whom were now asleep.[50]

Outside, shelling and machine-gun fire continued until 3 a.m. when the GPO munitions dump went up in a massive explosion that created a sparkling volcano and shook surrounding streets.

By daybreak McLoughlin's 'Death or Glory Squad' was all set to go when he was suddenly called to meet the leaders.[51] As Pearse sat on Connolly's bed, Clarke and MacDermott occupied chairs and Plunkett hunkered down in a corner, McLoughlin realised that doubts had arisen among them about the wisdom of fighting on. After suspending McLoughlin's breakout plan, they began debating whether or not to continue the Rising. Their hesitation arose in part from the suffering of civilians in the Moore Street area. Having been largely cocooned from non-combatants inside the GPO, Pearse was deeply affected by the sight of British soldiers firing on women attempting to flee Moore Street and killing a man with a white flag when he ran from his burning house. MacDermott had witnessed a Volunteer accidentally blow out the brains of a young girl standing in a doorway and Connolly told Winifred Carney that 'we must save the lives of the people for the military are burning down the city'.[52] And how many more sacrifices could they reasonably demand of Volunteers already at the limit of their endurance? It was a question posed by the intended assault on the British barricade in Moore Street. Its probable outcome had dawned on MacDermott earlier when he stood over The O'Rahilly's bullet-ridden body and two or three more dead Volunteers. Another frontal attack on a well-defended enemy position might well be a suicide mission resulting in death rather than glory. And to what end? Even if at great cost the leaders reached the Four Courts, only their location would have changed, not the unpalatable reality of a British counter-attack becoming unstoppable. Continued resistance would make even greater carnage inevitable. It was over.

Only Clarke resisted – and voted against – capitulation, almost as if he believed that even now sheer force of will could rouse the nation and turn the tide of battle. His colleagues, however, decided to seek terms from the British in order to prevent 'further slaughter of the civil population and to save the lives of as many as possible of our followers'. Having surmounted this psychological hurdle, Pearse, Connolly and MacDermott could finally relax, laugh and chat together. But Carney saw Tom in anguish

> standing near the wall against the window. Suddenly he turns his face to the wall and breaks down. I go over to calm him only to break into an uncontrollable fit of weeping myself. It is so sad to see him cry. This steadies him and he begs me to control myself.[53]

Carney too was greatly affected by the news of imminent surrender. As Dr Jim Ryan attended to Connolly's wounded leg and Julia Grenan combed his hair, a weeping Carney tidied his dust-covered Citizen Army uniform on to which dropped her tears.[54]

At about 12.45 p.m. Elizabeth O'Farrell left No. 15 carrying a stick with a white handkerchief and a verbal message from Pearse to the commander of the British forces requesting a discussion about surrender terms. A British officer took her to General Lowe, whose headquarters, by coincidence, was located in Clarke's Parnell Street shop. After listening courteously, Lowe drove O'Farrell back to the top of Moore Street and at about 2.25 p.m. gave her verbal and written demands for Pearse's unconditional surrender within half an hour. Instead O'Farrell returned with a note attempting to bargain. But Lowe simply repeated that unless Pearse appeared with O'Farrell within half an hour, followed by Connolly, he would recommence hostilities. Reluctantly the Provisional Government members accepted the British ultimatum.

After silently shaking the hands of every Volunteer, Pearse stepped into Moore Street and marched with O'Farrell to the British barricade. There he handed Lowe his sword, pistol and ammunition, signed a formal document of surrender, shook O'Farrell's hand and stepped into a military car. Soon afterwards a stretcher party brought Connolly to Clarke's shop from where fifty heavily armed soldiers escorted him to Dublin Castle. Back in Moore Street, Carney recalled that 'when Pearse and Connolly have gone we kneel down and say the Rosary in Irish, Seán MacDermott giving it out while we respond. It is tragedy in the extreme'.[55] But suddenly she noticed Clarke was missing: 'Seán becomes uneasy for Tom had always said he would never surrender to the enemy. They search for him and in about half an hour he comes into the room. He had been in the basement'. But it is inconceivable that Tom contemplated suicide, having never once in his life fled a battlefield of any kind or deserted his band of brothers. And maintaining the Provisional Government's unity to the end was vital for the Rising's historical credibility. Almost certainly Clarke had simply needed time and space to compose himself after breaking down in front of a woman for the first time in his life – something he would have thought unmanly. And Tom also needed to brace himself for the difficult personal, political and legal trials that undoubtedly lay ahead. Bound by collective responsibility, he now helped maintain a rock-like solidarity as news of the surrender spread among the dumbfounded rank and file. Seán McGarry recalled that 'after what seemed like an eternity MacDermott called me and with tears falling said "We are going to ask the lads to surrender. It would have been far better to go down in a good fight but it is too late now"'.[56] He remembered seeing a flag of truce being prepared and then they went anxiously from room to room, not talking but looking at each other in disbelief that it had come to this. Many Volunteers were demanding that the fight go on, but Clarke and Plunkett called on them to support their leaders. MacDermott finally regained control of the situation by warning that prolonged resistance would only result in many more civilians lying dead in the streets. Their duty now, he declared, was to survive and after a hopefully brief imprisonment renew the armed struggle.

First the wounded were carried out on blankets, placed on the street pavement and propped against the walls of a chip shop. Ambulances would collect them later. Willie Pearse and another officer now began searching lanes and alleyways, gathering up Volunteers until eventually over 320 men had assembled in Moore Street, lined up behind Plunkett, Clarke and MacDermott. Carney recorded a furious young Volunteer, Michael Collins, shouting, 'By Christ, I'll have my revenge for this'.[57] After being ordered to slope arms, the column marched down Moore Street. Volunteer Seamus Scully recalled that at the head was Willie Pearse 'victoriously waving his white flag as if rousingly leading his St Enda's boys in colourful pageant'.[58] It then turned left into Henry Place and then Henry Street, where a British NCO stood ostentatiously loading a revolver. In O'Connell Street MacDermott walked calmly on the pavement alongside Clarke who had his hands in his pockets and a cap on the back of his head.

Finally the Volunteers stopped outside the Gresham Hotel and laid down their
rifles, shotguns, revolvers, ammunition, bayonets, bandoliers and belts. But they
refused to act like a defeated army and some insouciantly smashed weapons at
their captors' feet or puffed on cigarettes and cigars. Carney recalled that:

> Julia Grenan and myself are in the front line. Tom Clarke is behind us.
> The officers indulge in sneers and laughter at our expense, turning over
> the rifles contemptuously with their feet. Two officers come to where
> Tom Clarke is standing and ask his name. Afterwards Tom whispers
> to me 'That's their way' or words to that effect.[59]

As darkness fell British soldiers marched the prisoners a short distance to
a grassy space in front of the Rotunda Hospital at the northern end of
O'Connell Street. There armed soldiers ordered the Volunteers to lie down
while machine guns on the roofs of the Rotunda and nearby buildings
covered the entire area. British officers moved angrily among the Volunteers,
one calling MacDermott a cripple while another kicked Plunkett on the
soles of his shiny boots. Captain Lea Wilson, the commanding British officer
at the Rotunda, was a 31-year-old Englishman who whipped his men to a
crescendo of anti-rebel fury. A Volunteer, Desmond Ryan, recalled Wilson as

> a dark browed florid, thick-lipped man, either drunk or mad with
> hysteria who behaves in a bullying half-crazed manner. He strides
> around, yelling that no one must stand up, that no one must lie down,
> and as for the needs of nature, anyone who chooses the Rotunda
> Gardens for a bedroom can use it as a lavatory as well, and – well lie
> in both. He threatens his own men. He will have them shot in the
> morning as looters. He threatens the Volunteers in similar terms.
> He strikes matches and hold them in the Volunteers' faces, yelling at
> his men, 'Anyone want to see the animals?' A Volunteer snaps out at
> him, 'You are a nice specimen of an English gentleman'. He walks on
> and ignores the taunt. When the relief guard comes, he begins a litany
> of 'Who are the worst, the Germans or the Sinn Féiners?' 'The Sinn
> Féiners' chant the Tommies. 'What shall we do with them?' 'Shoot 'em,
> stick a bayonet in 'em' chorus the Tommies, or some of them, and their
> tone is rather one of humouring a maniac than real conviction.[60]

Discovering Plunkett's will, Wilson returned it, saying Plunkett would need
it as he was going to be shot. Wilson then pounced on Clarke, shouting 'This

old bastard has been at it before. He has a shop across the street there. He's an old Fenian'.[61] Frog-marching Tom to the Rotunda steps, he began searching him thoroughly. Since Clarke's recent injury had only partly healed, he still could not fully flex his elbow and Eamon Dore claims he saw Wilson forcibly straightening the arm to remove Tom's coat.[62] Wilson's action reopened the wound and caused terrible pain. According to Dore, Wilson also stripped Tom to the skin in front of the prisoners with nurses watching from the Rotunda's windows. Carney recalled that 'I feel my blood boil. In no mild language I whispered to Seán, "what I wouldn't do if I just had my revolver" and he puts his arm around me, afraid I might attempt something foolish'.[63] For an hour detectives questioned Tom and read out information about his life in prison, America and Ireland. After re-joining the prisoners, he said his interrogators knew his life story: 'Everything, they have everything'. During the night Ned Daly and his men arrived at the Rotunda, but although Clarke might have seen his brother-in-law they certainly did not speak to each other. A British officer, Captain Cherry, immediately approached Ned, saying 'That's the leader', and ordered four soldiers to guard him closely.[64]

Prisoners at the Rotunda remembered a cold, miserable and hungry 'night of horror'.[65] Lacking sanitation and privacy, the men as well as Carney and Grenan had to relieve themselves on the grass in front of each other. In one small space, over 400 Volunteers huddled together for greater warmth with many of them suffering severe cramps. From inside the hospital the screams and cries for help that rang through the night may have been from women in labour or from other causes but to one of the prisoners they seemed more like those of people driven mad by the fighting and destruction. By early Sunday morning, said one prisoner, 'the sound of heavy guns, machine gun staccato and the crack of the rifles had gradually died down the previous day and Saturday night had been unnaturally quiet. It was obvious that the struggle for Dublin was finished'.[66] Finally at 9 a.m., armed soldiers led the column of prisoners towards the southern end of O'Connell Street and across O'Connell Bridge. Their destination was Richmond Barracks, 2 miles away at Inchicore on the western edge of the city, an exhausting journey for men who badly needed a wash, a shave and a change of clothing. There, William Whelan recorded that 'Tom Clarke was in the file in front of me when we halted in Richmond Barracks and he gave me a large sum of money. He said, "Bill, you take this, I will not need it anymore". Clarke knew he was finished then'.[67] Believing that he and MacDermott would be summarily executed, Tom scribbled his wife a last letter in which he expressed his pride and satisfaction at the Rising and a conviction that 'all will be well eventually – but this is my goodbye and now you are ever before me to cheer me.

God bless you and the boys. Let them be proud to follow [the] same path – Seán
[i.e MacDermott] is with me and McG [i.e McGarry] – They are all heroes'.[68]
After searchers seized any incriminating documents and photographs, British
military policemen and G-men diverted the Volunteers into a gymnasium.
Within two hours, they had identified about 200 prominent suspects including
Clarke, MacDermott, Ceannt, MacDonagh, Plunkett and Major John MacBride.
Eventually prisoners were issued with blankets and then packed into bare rooms
containing buckets for latrines. Their rations consisted of a daily tin of bully beef,
a few hard biscuits and a mug of tea. Despite everything, an old friend observed
Clarke withstanding the physical and emotional pressures well, 'sitting there just
as we had seen him twenty times in his shop in Parnell Street, with the same
clothes, the same look, quiet, silent, with the suspicion of a smile. Tom was very
satisfied with himself and the situation'.[69] Tom in fact coped better than the
younger MacDermott:

> After a while Seán fell asleep with his head on Tom's chest. I don't think
> Tom slept at all. Seán would start a little and we would hear a mutter
> from him saying 'The fire! The fire! Get the men out!' Then you would
> hear Tom's quiet voice saying gently: 'Quiet, Seán, we're in the Barracks
> now. We're prisoners now, Seán'.[70]

Clarke's fate was now in the hands of Major-General Sir John Maxwell,
a 56-year-old Scot who had spent his military career in Africa and the Middle
East defending the British Empire. Invested with full authority to restore
order, he would inevitably punish rebels who had imperilled both imperial
unity and the British Army. Furthermore, the Rising had occurred at a time
when the Allies were on the defensive on all fronts with the Gallipoli expedition stalled, the Germans deep in Russia and the French Army was being
destroyed at Verdun. Maxwell had also been appalled at the loss of life and
destruction in Dublin; he reported the city as 'still smouldering and the blood
of the victims of this mad rebellion is hardly dry'.[71] But as an intelligent,
broad-minded and civilised man, Maxwell never contemplated imposing
massive repression on Ireland, preferring instead a short sharp shock in the
form of 'the most severe sentences on the known organisers of this detestable
Rising'.[72] Maxwell believed the rebel leadership had criminally exploited the
naiveté and blind loyalty of ordinary Volunteers and that only by decapitating
it could he free the rank and file from political extremism. So Maxwell
quickly released many of the 3,500 men and 79 women in custody after
the Rising, while an appeals procedure soon freed almost 1,300 internees.

This left 186 men (including Clarke and the other Provisional Government members) and a single woman, Constance Markievicz. All of them would be tried by court martial.

Ironically just like Maxwell, Clarke and his fellow rebel leaders wanted the highest penalty inflicted on themselves while clemency was extended to ordinary Volunteers. When Sean Murphy encountered MacDermott in a washroom at Richmond Barracks:

> By way of conversation I said: well that's all, Seán. I wonder what's next. And in reply he said to me, Seán, the cause is lost if some of us are not shot. Surely to God you do not mean that, Sean. Aren't things bad enough? I replied. They are, he said, so bad that if what I say does not come true they will be very much worse.[73]

Unlike Patrick Pearse, Clarke and MacDermott's desire for a supreme sacrifice – a blood sacrifice – came not from any messianic desire to die but a coldly rational calculation that only through their executions could they snatch political victory from military defeat. Whereas Maxwell thought that shooting them would act as a terrible deterrent against another Rising, the rebel leaders envisaged their deaths inspiring survivors to resume the armed struggle and eventually win Ireland's freedom. Both sides then were playing for the highest stakes and the winner would shape Ireland's political future. Joseph Gleeson, Clarke's Supreme Council colleague and fellow prisoner, recalled that Tom quickly came to see the brighter side of defeat: 'Tom Clarke seemed pleased with the outcome of the Rising. I think he said, "We have a minimum loss which will result in a maximum gain"'.[74] Soon afterwards in the gymnasium, Piaras Béaslaí encountered Clarke who told him proudly that 'the Rising will do great good for the nation'. Tom also had personal reasons for wanting to face a firing squad. Far more than death he dreaded re-incarceration, the horrors of Chatham and Portland being etched in his memory. Moreover since Clarke's fragile health made it unlikely that he would survive long into another imprisonment, any sentence a court martial imposed would be in effect a death sentence. In that case Tom preferred to die soon on his feet like a soldier rather than have jailers discover him one day lying dead in a lonely cell.

At extremely short notice, Clarke learned that his court martial would be held on the afternoon of Tuesday 3 May in Richmond Barracks and that he faced a charge of rebelling 'for the purpose and with the intention of helping the enemy'. An accusation of being in effect a German agent impelled Tom to plead not guilty while informing his fellow prisoners that he did so only to set the historical record straight. His actions had been on behalf of Ireland, not Germany. Uniquely among the 187 persons court-martialled, Tom was on trial for his life a second time. However, unlike the majesty of the Old Bailey thirty-three years earlier, he appeared now in a small and sparsely populated room, and not before the three highest judges in England but a trio of legally unqualified military officers. His trial in 1883 had been held in open court, its benches packed with spectators, reporters and Clarke's friends; it was conducted with great formality and according to the rules of evidence the proceedings were extensively reported in newspapers that the general public read avidly. Lasting four days, the trial had been thorough and fair and with a real chance of walking free, Tom had fought hard for a not-guilty verdict, defending himself with zest, skilfully questioning witnesses and picking holes in the prosecution case. But this time around he believed a guilty verdict was pre-ordained and simply went through the motions just — as he assumed — like his accusers. In a secret trial lasting barely fifteen minutes, Tom displayed supreme indifference and though not of course charged with contempt of court, he displayed it in full measure. He made no statement from the dock, called no witnesses and only intervened briefly once to elicit agreement from the sole prosecution witness — a British Army lieutenant — that his rebel captors had treated him well in the GPO. The prosecutor, William Wylie, recalled Clarke being 'perfectly calm and brave throughout the proceedings. He struck me as a particularly kindly man who could not injure anyone'.[75]

Since military judges did not immediately announce a verdict, Tom remained technically ignorant of his fate when he left the courtroom. In Richmond's now empty gymnasium, he was reunited with Pearse and MacDonagh whose courts martial had also finished. Piaras Béaslaí, Ned Daly's second-in-command, remembered how:

> Pearse sat down on the floor apparently deep in thought. He did not once address any of us. Clarke seemed in a mood of quiet deep satisfaction that he had lived to see what he had seen. He said confidently as he had said on the Sunday in the same place, 'This insurrection will have a great effect on the country. It will be a different Ireland'. As for MacDonagh he chatted freely and seemed in the highest spirits.[76]

Soon after Tom was returned to his cell, a British officer brought him news that he had been sentenced to death and would be shot early next day in Kilmainham Gaol. The verdict still required Maxwell's final confirmation, and there were mitigating circumstances such as Clarke's age, a Volunteer

status humbler than that of Pearse, Plunkett and MacDonagh, and his relatively low-profile role during the actual Rising. Nor was he captured in
uniform or in possession of a rifle and Tom had almost certainly dumped
his revolver in O'Connell Street after the surrender. But his name occupied
pride of place on the Proclamation, visible proof that he had been at the
heart of the conspiracy; Maxwell described him as one of its 'most prominent
leaders'.[77] Clarke had also been seen giving orders in the GPO, the rebellion's
centrepiece and a scene of heavy fighting during Easter Week. Especially
offensive to Maxwell's Scottish Presbyterian morality were British intelligence reports on Tom's political influence and his lengthy revolutionary
career. These persuaded the general that Clarke had grievously abused his
authority by turning impressionable young men into 'infernal rebels' and
ruining their lives. Maxwell also believed Tom had cynically taken advantage
of his 1898 amnesty, spurning the opportunity to repent his crimes and
ultimately bringing about far greater destruction than was ever caused by
the Fenian bombing campaign. Maxwell would have regarded himself in
dereliction of duty if he had let such a person live when the British Army
was executing soldiers for walking away from enemy gunfire on the Western
Front. For Tom there would be no second chance.

In the late afternoon of Tuesday 2 May 1916, armed British soldiers
marched Clarke, Pearse and MacDonagh to Kilmainham Gaol. Closed to
civilians in 1911, it had been hurriedly reopened as a military prison after the
outbreak of war only for its inmates to be hurriedly replaced by an influx of
captured rebels. Kilmainham still bore the hallmark of abandonment. Dank
and smelly, its gloom was only partly relieved by light from candles in jam
jars or naked gas flames. Overwhelmed by so many prisoners, the authorities were unable to provide many basic facilities. Soon after their arrival the
three condemned men learned that Maxwell had speedily confirmed their
death sentences and as dusk gathered they were separately confined in rooms
containing Volunteer prisoners. In his room Clarke sat on an upturned bucket
surrounded by men keen to hear the details of his court martial. Tom said he
had no illusions about a last-minute reprieve; having decided Clarke would
never stop his subversion, the British were determined to eliminate him:
'The British have been watching for their chance down through the years,
and are not going to let it slip now'. Despite knowing that he would face
a firing squad within six hours, Clarke radiated confidence and optimism,
believing in his heart and soul that short-term defeat would be followed by
long-term victory. He assured the younger Volunteers that 'this is not the end
of our fight for Irish Freedom; it is only the beginning and I believe from this

last week's fighting that men will come forward to carry on from where we left off. Some of you will live to see Ireland respond to the call'.[78] Eventually the prisoners lay down close together on blankets spread out on the floor with Clarke lying in some discomfort on the arm of Gerald Doyle beside him. Doyle recalled that when they awoke after dozing off they heard soldiers talking outside the door. Then the door opened, they came in,

> flashed a light in our faces and then called out the name of Tom Clarke. We then immediately got to out feet and Tom shook hands with us in turn. I being next to the door was the last to shake hands with him and they took him away. We then said the Rosary for him.[79]

Prior to his execution, Tom spent his final hours in a cell where the British authorities allowed him to see his wife one last time. Kathleen had been held in Dublin Castle since her arrest a day earlier and a military car drove her to Kilmainham. A soldier admitted her to the cell but insisted on remaining in the open doorway throughout holding a candle. Tom was lying on the ground but jumped up when he saw Kathleen moving towards him. He confirmed what she had sensed but not known officially – that he would be shot in the morning. But Tom was serene: 'All through our interview, I was conscious of the exalted, very exalted state of mind he was in'.[80] She found him 'wild with the joy of being able to hold out the week and full of hope for the future and admiration of his comrades in arms. His years seemed to have fallen away from him in the pride of their achievement'.[81] But he also expressed sorrow that they too would die; he already knew that Pearse and MacDonagh would be shot along with him and assumed that MacDermott, Connolly, Plunkett, Ceannt and others would soon follow. Only briefly could they bear to discuss the children's future:

> He begged me not to let his death shadow their lives. 'They have been so far such happy children, but train them to follow in my footsteps'. I said I would do my best to carry out his wishes, but his death would shadow their lives no matter what I did and I thought it was a hard road he had picked for them, to follow in his footsteps; children did not always carry out their parents' wishes.[82]

For Kathleen this last meeting with Tom was almost unbearably sad and very different from their final encounter before the Rising when there was still a chance of their dreams coming true. Now with brutal suddenness she was about to lose the love of her life and as a young woman in her mid-thirties, faced the bleak prospect of decades of widowhood; no man could possibly replace Tom in her heart or provide the happiness that he had brought. Alone too she would have responsibility for raising their children. The realisation of her imminent loss and what lay ahead was almost impossible to bear and Kathleen cried out 'I don't know how I am going to live without you. I wish the British would put a bullet in me too'.[83]

Ever the forward planner, Tom ordered her to expose MacNeill's 'treachery' and drive him out of political life; he also told Kathleen to visit Devoy in New York and explain everything about the Rising. As he prepared to depart the battlefield, Clarke made Kathleen memorise his last message to the Irish people. It was a clarion call to resume the struggle and win through to final victory:

> My comrades and I believe we have struck the first successful blow for freedom, and so sure as we are going out this morning, so sure will freedom come as a direct result of our action. It will not come today or tomorrow, and between this and freedom Ireland will go through Hell, but she will never lie down again until she has attained full freedom. With this belief, we die happy. I am happy and satisfied at what we have accomplished.[84]

Before they parted Tom told Kathleen something that she did not know, that her beloved brother Ned had also been sentenced to death. But Kathleen did not tell Tom something that he did not know, that she had been pregnant for some weeks with their fourth child. Kathleen had kept the news secret because of the great political pressure that Tom was under just before the Rising, and she thought it would have been cruel to reveal now that he would never set eyes on their new baby. After a short time the guard said, 'Time up' and Kathleen had to leave. Decades later she recalled that 'the sound of that door closing has haunted me ever since'.[85]

Despite later assertions that either one or two priests attended Tom at the end, he actually died unreconciled to the Catholic Church – the one rebel leader executed without having received the sacraments. Only two priests had permission to be present at Kilmainham Gaol in the early hours of Wednesday morning, 3 May 1916, both of them Capuchins from the Franciscan friary in Church Street. One, Father Aloysius, was there at the request of Patrick Pearse and on arrival he learned that MacDonagh had also asked for his ministrations.[86] Aloysius spent some hours with the two men, heard their confessions and gave them Holy Communion, declaring later that he could not 'easily forget the devotion with which they received

the Most Blessed Sacrament'. Afterwards Pearse and MacDonagh prayed and
sometime between 2 a.m. and 3 a.m. Aloysius left them 'in a most edifying
disposition'. Aloysius recorded that he had been driven to Kilmainham in
a British military car 'accompanied by another Father' from the Franciscan
friary and Kathleen Clarke described meeting at Tom's cell door an agitated
priest wearing the Capuchin's brown habit. Named in some accounts as
Father Columbus, he had refused Tom absolution unless he expressed contri-
tion for participating in the Rising. Clarke told Kathleen he had thrown the
priest out: 'I was not sorry for what I had done, I gloried in it and the men
who had been with me. To say I was sorry would be a lie, and I was not going
to face my God with a lie on my tongue'.[87]

Shortly before 3 a.m. a party of British soldiers removed Tom from his cell
and escorted him along corridors and down steps towards a stone-breakers'
yard where he, Pearse and MacDonagh would be executed in quick succession. Upon reaching a long corridor that ran down to the yard, Tom was
blindfolded and had his hands tied behind his back, and a white piece of
cloth was pinned above his heart. Never having flinched from looking his
enemy in the eye, Clarke vainly offered to forego the blindfold. At the end
of the passageway soldiers guided him through a doorway and into the
stone-breakers' yard. Awaiting Tom was a firing squad of a dozen marksmen,
arranged in two rows, one kneeling and the other standing. The official
records stated that Clarke, Pearse and MacDonagh 'all met their fate
bravely'. The last sounds they heard are unknown. During the executions at
Kilmainham the officer in charge sometimes silently dropped his hand, while
in other cases he yelled 'Fire!' Samuel Henry Lomas, the British officer who
provided the firing squad recorded that MacDonagh – who had entered the
stone-breakers' yard happy and whistling – was executed first. Pearse was shot
next. Both men died instantaneously. But Clarke 'an old man was not quite so
fortunate, requiring a bullet from the officer to complete the ghastly business.'
The dead bodies did not receive absolution as the British authorities ignored
Aloysius's demand that he be allowed to accompany the condemned men
into the execution yard.[88]

Afterwards the corpses were carried to a nearby stone-breakers' shed. Just
before his own execution, Tom had been granted permission to exchange
farewells with Ned Daly, but complex administrative arrangements delayed
Daly's military escort leaving Richmond Barracks until Clarke's firing squad
was making its final preparations. Just as the escort hastened through the gates
of Kilmainham at 3.30 a.m., a volley of shots rang out. Two more followed
in the next twenty minutes, signifying that Clarke, Pearse and MacDonagh

had all been executed. Even so, Daly was still allowed to pay homage to Tom's body. As Clarke's commanding Volunteer officer, Daly gave him the soldier's farewell to which he was entitled. Standing at attention over the remains, Daly saluted, removed his cap and knelt for a while in prayer and quiet contemplation. After donning his cap and saluting again, Daly turned round and rejoined his escort.[89]

Later that day Madge and Laura Daly travelled from Limerick to Richmond Avenue. Madge recalled that:

> My sister Kathleen saw us at once and was awaiting us at the door. I hope never to see on any human face such absolute desolation. She looked as if life could do no more to her, as if some vital part of her was dead. Madge plied Kathleen with whiskey but it had no effect whatsoever on the rigid teetotaller.[90]

And life in fact could do more damage to Kathleen. Soon afterwards, British soldiers raided and searched the Clarkes' house, stealing many personal items and leaving Kathleen 'beyond feeling or heeding anything'.[91] Troops had also ransacked the Parnell Street shop, looted all the valuable stock of tobacco, cigarettes and cigars and left it open for civilians to finish the job. A few days later a neighbour boarded up the premises, but while Kathleen was recuperating in Limerick, the landlady took possession and installed new tenants. This deprived Kathleen of a good livelihood, but the landlady was deaf to her protests. Dangerously ill, Kathleen miscarried a few weeks after the Rising and temporarily lost the will to live.[92] The deaths of Tom and Ned had also devastated Uncle John whose health deteriorated steadily; he suffered acute headaches and the motor neurone's paralysis had spread inexorably. The doctor's drugs could only dull Uncle John's pain until he finally passed away on 30 June 1916.[93]

Kathleen lost not only Tom's baby but his body as well. On 3 May after a final meeting with their brother Ned, Kathleen and Madge formally asked the prison authorities to let them have Tom and Ned's bodies in coffins that they intended delivering to the prison. The two sisters planned to bury both men in family plots. Afterwards, on behalf of a sick Kathleen, Madge and Laura appealed for the return of Tom's corpse on the basis that he was an American citizen. They also wrote to the American consul but he did not reply. The British officer in charge of the executions, Major Kinsman, replied that he had been directed to turn down the request.[94] It was Maxwell himself who decided how the executed men's corpses were to be disposed of and he was adamant about not returning them to the families. Maxwell feared that 'Irish sentimentality will turn those graves into martyrs' shrines to which annual processions etc will be made'.[95] Instead, after Clarke, Pearse and MacDonagh were shot, a medical officer certified them dead and name labels were pinned to their breasts. The bodies were then wrapped in army blankets and laid on a horse-drawn ambulance which later that morning drove them the short distance to Arbour Hill. There they were buried in the exercise yard of the military prison located behind the Royal (now Collins) Barracks. Tom was placed in an unmarked grave alongside Pearse and MacDonagh, the bodies were covered in quicklime and the grave filled. Over the next nine days, another eleven were executed at Kilmainham and subsequently interred at Arbour Hill. They have lain there ever since.

★★★

For almost a century Tom Clarke's historical legacy has been overshadowed by that of Patrick Pearse and James Connolly and other members of the Provisional Government. An early, adulatory biography benefited his reputation little and there were few posthumous public honours, a neglect which for many years after his death caused Kathleen Clarke to grieve that her husband had been so eclipsed in the story of 1916. But in a way this was appropriate. Self-effacing and devoid of vanity, Clarke cared nothing for fame and high position. He had preferred to work in the shadows, biding his time, manipulating his way through people towards the goal he had set his heart on: Irish freedom. His fierce simplicity caused him to focus on one dream with a revolutionary fervour that never dimmed even in the most difficult times. It was a mission that cost him over fifteen years in prison and eight years of exile in a foreign land and finally, of course, it cost him his life. For all this Clarke would have had no regrets, only satisfaction that the rebellion to which he had dedicated his life had happened, even if not on the scale he had envisaged. He had pride, too, in the rebel performance and confidence that in time successors would complete what he had set out to achieve.

His had been a full life and one of extremes. Clarke experienced failure and despair as well as great personal happiness and success. That success was only made possible by his tenacity and a determination to overcome all adversity. It has been said that adversity is like a strong wind that tears away from us all but the things that cannot be torn, so that we see ourselves as we really are. And that was certainly true of Tom Clarke. Equally he personified the dictum that one should beware the fury of a patient man. Seán McGarry said of Clarke that 'to fight England was to him the most natural thing in the world'[96] and to that fight he brought soldierly qualities of courage, patriotism and loyalty: to him betraying a comrade or deserting the cause was something unforgivable. Tom was someone who literally preferred death to dishonour. In his mind, Ireland was a country on its knees and, like another revolutionary, he believed that it was better to die standing on your feet than to live upon your knees.

Tom Clarke was a self-made man who started life with few advantages and rose to the top of the republican movement through his natural talent and willpower. He revived the moribund Irish Republican Brotherhood, groomed a new generation of leaders, and supervised the military planning that eventually led him and his colleagues into the GPO on Easter Monday, 1916. Symbolically too he linked the past with the future in the Irish struggle. Having organised O'Donovan Rossa's funeral, it was coincidentally fitting that Tom was buried behind the Arbour Hill detention barracks where O'Donovan Rossa was imprisoned after the Fenian Rising of 1867. It was appropriate also that fighting alongside him in the Post Office was a young Volunteer, Michael Collins, who would lead the campaign that resulted in the creation of an Irish Free State – the stepping stone, as Collins said, to full political independence.

Clarke was not without flaws and limitations. Concentration on one great objective and a harsh unforgiving nature made him intolerant of dissent and ungenerous towards political opponents. Believing like Wolfe Tone that the connection with England was the source of Ireland's woes, he gave little thought to the political shape Ireland might take after it was broken. And his naïve belief that the Ulster Volunteer Force and the Irish Volunteers were really brothers under different skins showed his blindness to Unionist realities. Nevertheless, Clarke's significance in modern Irish history is indisputable. His contemporaries knew that well. John Devoy declared that 'but for him there would have been no IRB left in Ireland and no fight in 1916'.[97] P.S. O'Hegarty regarded Clarke as 'the embodiment of Fenianism, an impregnable rock' whose life and work inspired a younger generation and 'made him easily the first of us and the best of us'.[98] Increasingly, the passage of time has vindicated these judgements as a new generation rediscovers the importance of Tom Clarke – the true leader of the Easter Rising.

NOTES

1   Kathleen Clarke, *Revolutionary Woman*, p. 93.
2   Kathleen Clarke, 'A Character Sketch of Tom Clarke', Clarke Papers, NLI MS 49,355/12
3   Winifred Carney, in a memoir of Easter Week that was loaned to me by its owner who preferred to remain anonymous. Hereafter, Winifred Carney, 'GPO Memoir'.

4   Desmond Ryan, BMH WS 724.

5   Diarmuid Lynch, 'Recollections and Comments on the IRB', BMH WS 4.

6   Seán McGarry, Lecture on the Easter Rising, NLI MS 33,913 (8).

7   Charles MacAuley, BMH WS 735.

8   Seán T. O'Kelly, BMH WS 1765.

9   Luke Kennedy, BMH WS 165.

10   Catherine Byrne, BMH WS 848.

11   J.J. Walsh, 'Recollections of a Rebel', BMH Collected Documents, no. 296.

12   Michael Staines, BMH WS 284 and M.W. Reilly, 'The Defence of the GPO', *An tOglac* (23 January 1926).

13   Winifred Carney, 'GPO Memoir'.

14   Madge Daly, 'The Memoirs of Madge Daly'. Also, Eamon Dore, BMH WS 153.

15   'The Memoirs of Madge Daly'.

16   Eamon Dore, BMH WS 153.

17   Ibid.

18   Min Ryan (Mrs Richard Mulcahy), BMH WS 399.

19   Michael Staines, BMH WS 284.

20   Jim Ryan, 'General Post Office Area', *Capuchin Annual* (1966).

21   Desmond Fitzgerald, *The Memoirs of Desmond Fitzgerald 1913–1916*, p. 148.

22   Seán T. O'Kelly, BMH WS 1765.

23   Winifred Carney, 'GPO Memoir'.

24   Ibid.

25   Seán McGarry, Lecture on the Easter Rising, NLI MS 33,913 (8).

26   Patrick Rankin, BMH WS 163.

27   Mary McLoughin, BMH WS 934.

28   Leslie Price (Mrs Tom Barry), BMH WS 1754.

29   Ibid.

30   Winifred Carney, 'GPO Memoir'.

31   Dick Humphries, GPO Diary, NLI MS 18,829.

32   Michael Staines, BMH WS 284.

33   Aoife De Burca, BMH WS 359.

34   Lieutenant A.M. Jameson's letters have been presented to the Imperial War Museum, London. Private Papers/Documents 7072.

35   Michael Staines, BMH WS 284.

36   Dore, BMH WS 153.

37   Seán MacEntee, BMH WS 1052.

38   Dick Humphries, 'GPO Diary', NLI MS 18,829.

39   Seamus Scully, 'Moore Street 1916', NLI MS 27,834.

40   Joe Good, *Enchanted by Dreams* (Dingle: Brandon Books, 1996), p. 53.

41   Volunteer Joseph O'Rourke, BMH WS 1244.

42   Liam Tannam, BMH WS 242.

43   Seán McLoughlin, BMH 290.

44   Sean Price, BMH WS 769.

45   Ibid.

46   Kathleen Clarke, *Revolutionary Woman*, p. 95. At their last meeting Tom told Kathleen that he had hoped to go down under enemy gunfire.

47   Winifred Carney, 'GPO Memoir'.

48 Ibid.
49 Seán McLoughlin, BMH WS 290.
50 Charles Saurin, BMH WS 288.
51 Seán McLoughlin, BMH WS 290.
52 Winifred Carney, 'GPO Memoir'.
53 Ibid.
54 Seamus Scully, 'Moore Street 1916', NLI MS 27,834.
55 Winifred Carney, 'GPO Memoir'.
56 Seán McGarry, Lecture on the Easter Rising, MS 33,913 (8).
57 Winifred Carney, 'GPO Memoir'.
58 Seamus Scully, 'Moore Street 1916', NLI MS 27,834.
59 Winifred Carney, 'GPO Memoir'.
60 Desmond Ryan, BMH WS 724.
61 Volunteer Joseph Sweeney in Kenneth Griffith and Timothy O'Grady,
    Curious Journey (Cork: Mercier Press, 1998), p. 79.
62 Eamon Dore, BMH WS 153.
63 Winifred Carney, 'GPO Memoir'.
64 Joseph O'Rourke, BMH WS 1244.
65 Piaras Béaslaí, *Irish Independent*, 20 January 1953.
66 Eamon (Bob) Price, BMH WS 995.
67 William Whelan, BMH WS 369.
68 Piaras F. MacLochlainn, *Last Words: Letters and Statements of the Leaders Executed
    after the Rising at Easter 1916*, p. 45.
69 Piaras Béaslaí, *Irish Independent*, 20 January 1953.
70 Liam Ó Briain quoted in Ruth Dudley Edwards, *Patrick Pearse: The Triumph of
    Failure*, p. 312.
71 Sean Price, BMH WS 769.
72 Sir George Arthur, *General Sir John Maxwell*, p. 264.
73 Michael Foy and Brian Barton, *The Easter Rising*, p. 304.
74 John J. (Sean) Murphy, BMH WS 204.
75 Joseph Gleeson, BMH WS 367.
76 William Wylie, unpublished memoirs (in typescript), National Archives,
    London, PRO30/89/2.
77 Piaras Béaslaí, *Irish Independent*, 21 January 1953.
78 Maxwell memorandum, 11 May 1916, entitled, 'Brief history of rebels on whom it
    has been necessary to inflict the supreme penalty', Asquith Papers, MS 43.
79 Gerald Doyle, BMH WS 1511.
80 Ibid.
81 Kathleen Clarke, *Revolutionary Woman*, p. 95.
82 Kathleen Clarke, 'A Character Sketch of Tom Clarke', Clarke Papers, NLI MS.
    49,355/12
83 Kathleen Clarke, *Revolutionary Woman*, p. 94.
84 Ibid.
85 Ibid.
86 Father Aloysius, BMH WS 200, and 'Lecture on the Rising Easter Week 1916',
    BMH Collected Documents, no. 117.
87 Kathleen Clarke, *Revolutionary Woman*, p. 93.

88   In an article by Mick O'Farrell in *The Irish Times*, 2 August 2014 containing excerpts from Lomas's diary.
89   Michael Soughley, BMH WS 189.
90   'The Memoirs of Madge Daly'.
91   Ibid.
92   Kathleen Clarke, *Revolutionary Woman*, p. 127.
93   'The Memoirs of Madge Daly'.
94   Ibid.
95   Maxwell to Bonham Carter, 20 May 1916, University College Dublin Archives, P150/152.
96   Sean McGarry, BMH WS 360.
97   John Devoy, *Gaelic American* , 25 June 1925
98   P.S. O'Hegarty, in his foreword to Thomas J. Clarke, *Glimpses of an Irish Felon's Prison Life*, p. 7.

Bibliography

PRIMARY SOURCES

Witness Statements

Bureau of Military Archives, Dublin

Rev. Fr. OFM Cap. Aloysius
Rev. Fr. OFM Cap. Augustine
Piaras Béaslaí
Robert Brennan
Aoife de Burca
Catherine Byrne
Ignatius Callender
Sean Cody
Martin Conlon
Matthew Connolly
Richard Connolly
Right Rev. Monsignor M. Curran
Mrs Sidney Czira
Francis Daly
Madge Daly
Paddy Daly
Seamus Daly
Thomas Devine
Geraldine Dillon
Eamon Dore
C. Doyle
Gerald Doyle
James Doyle
Thomas Doyle
Louise Gavan Duffy
Patrick Egan
Frank Gaskin
Joseph Gleeson
Frank Henderson
Bulmer Hobson
Julia Hughes
Valentine Jackson
Seamus Kavanagh
John Keegan
Luke Kennedy
Sean Kennedy
Diarmuid Lynch
Fionan Lynch
Michael McAllister
Alec McCabe
Patrick McCormick
Denis McCullough
John McGallgolly
Seán McGarry
Mary McLoughlin
Seán McLoughlin
Eamon Martin
Phyllis Morken

Mrs Richard Mulcahy (Min Ryan)
Fintan Murphy
Gregory Murphy
Seamus Murphy
Sean Murphy
Harry Nicholls
Liam Ó Briain
Annie O'Brien
Lawrence O'Brien
William O'Brien
Joseph O'Byrne
Mortimer O'Connell
Joseph O'Connor
Tommy O'Connor
Kitty O'Doherty
Con O'Donovan
Seán O'Duffy

Eamon O'Dwyer
Michael O'Flanagan
P.S. O'Hegarty
Seán T. O'Kelly
Joseph O'Rourke
Seamus O'Sullivan
Eamon Price
Leslie Price (Mrs Tom Barry)
Sean Price
Molly Reynolds
J. Ridgeway
Desmond Ryan
Charles Saurin
Michael Soughley
Michael Staines
Liam Tannan
William Whelan

Collected Documents

Bureau of Military Archives, Dublin
Eoin MacNeill
Seamus O'Connor
J.J. Walsh
Chief Secretary's Official Registered Correspondence
National Archives, Dublin

Limerick University
Daly papers

National Library of Ireland

Piaras Béaslaí papers
Thomas Clarke papers
Roger Casement papers
Bulmer Hobson papers
Dick Humphries diary
Diarmuid Lynch papers

Denis McCullough papers
Eoin MacNeill papers
William O'Brien papers
Florence O'Donoghue papers
Seán T. O'Kelly papers
Seán O'Mahony papers

John Devoy, *Germany Kept Faith with Ireland*. MS 17609 (11)
Diarmuid Lynch, Notes and comments on the manuscript of Louis Le Roux's book, *Tom Clarke and the Irish Freedom Movement*. MS 11123
Patrick McCartan, Manuscript notes on Louis Le Roux's biography of Thomas Clarke. MS 44683
Louis Le Roux, Typescript of an unpublished biography of John Daly. MS 44690
Letters and contribution sent to Louis Le Roux for his biography of Thomas Clarke. MS 44684
Seamus Scully, Moore Street 1916. MS 27834

National Archives, London
Colonial Office papers
Home Office papers
War Office papers

Bodleian Library, Oxford
Asquith papers
Sir Edmund du Cane papers
Nathan papers

Princeton University
Sir John Maxwell papers

In Private Hands
Edith Carney memoir

SECONDARY SOURCES

Books

aan de Wiel, Jerome, *The Catholic Church in Ireland 1914–1918: War and Politics* (Dublin: Irish Academic Press, 2003).
aan de Wiel, Jerome, *The Irish Factor 1899–1919: Ireland's Strategic and Diplomatic Importance for Foreign Powers* (Dublin: Irish Academic Press, 2008).
Arthur, Sir George, *General Sir John Maxwell* (London: Murray, 1932).
Augusteijn, Joost, *Patrick Pearse: The Making of a Revolutionary* (Basingstoke: Palgrave Macmillan, 2010).
Barton, Brian, *The Secret Court Martial Records of the Easter Rising* (Stroud: The History Press, 2010).
Bateson, Ray, *They Died By Pearse's Side* (Dublin: Irish Graves Publications, 2010).
Bayor, Ronald H. and Meagher, Timothy, *The New York Irish* (Baltimore: John Hopkins University Press, 1997).
Clarke, Kathleen, *Revolutionary Woman: An Autobiography, 1878–1972* (Dublin: The O'Brien Press, 1991).
Clarke, Thomas J., *Glimpses of an Irish Felon's Prison Life* (Dublin: Maunsel & Roberts, 1922).
Connell Jnr, Joseph, *Dublin in Rebellion: A Directory, 1913–23* (Dublin: Lilliput Press, 2006).
Cooke, Pat, *A History of Kilmainham Gaol, 1796–1924* (Dublin: Stationery Office, 1995).
Davitt, Michael, *Leaves from a Prison Diary* (London: Chapman and Hall, 1885).
Devoy, John, *Recollections of an Irish Rebel* (Shannon: Irish University Press, 1929).
Dolan, Jay P., *The Irish Americans: A History* (New York: Bloomsbury Press, 2010).
Doyle, David Noel and Dudley Edwards, Owen, *America and Ireland 1776–1976: The American Identity and the Irish Connection* (Westport, CT: Greenwood Press, 1980).
Dunleavy, Janet Egleson and Dunleavy, Gareth W., *Douglas Hyde: A Maker of Modern Ireland* (Berkeley, CA: University of California Press, 1992).
Edwards, Ruth Dudley, *Patrick Pearse: The Triumph of Failure* (Dublin: Irish Academic Press, 2006).

Fitzgerald, Desmond, *The Memoirs of Desmond Fitzgerald 1913–1916* (London: Routledge and Kegan Paul, 1968).

Foy, Michael and Barton, Brian, *The Easter Rising* (Stroud: The History Press, 2011).

Gannt, Jonathan, *Irish Terrorism in the Atlantic Community, 1865–1922* (Basingstoke: Palgrave Macmillan, 2010).

Golway, Terry, *Irish Rebel: John Devoy and America's Fight for Irish Freedom* (New York: St Martin's Press, 1998).

Gonne, Maud, *A Servant of the Queen* (London: Gollancz, 1938).

Greaves, C. Desmond, *Liam Mellows and the Irish Revolution* (London: Lawrence and Wishart, 1971).

Griffiths, Arthur, *Fifty Years of Public Service* (London: Cassell, 1905).

Hay, Marnie, *Bulmer Hobson and the Nationalist Movement in Twentieth-Century Ireland* (Manchester: Manchester University Press, 2009).

Hegarty, Shane and O'Toole, Fintan, *The Irish Times Book of the Easter Rising* (Dublin: Gill & Macmillan, 2006).

Henry, William, *Supreme Sacrifice: The Story of Éamonn Ceannt 1881–1916* (Cork: Mercier Press, 2005).

Hobson, Bulmer, *Ireland: Yesterday and Tomorrow* (Tralee: Anvil Books, 1968).

Jeffery, Keith, *The GPO and the Easter Rising* (Dublin: Irish Academic Press, 2006).

Le Caron, Henri, *Twenty-Five Years in the Secret Service: The Recollections of a Spy* (London: W. Heinemann, 1893).

Le Roux, Louis, *Tom Clarke and the Irish Freedom Movement* (Dublin: Talbot Press, 1936).

Lynch, Diarmuid, *The I.R.B. and the 1916 Insurrection* (Cork: Mercier Press, 1957).

Kenna, Shane, *War in the Shadows: The Irish-American Fenians who Bombed Victorian Britain* (Dublin: Irish Academic Press, 2013).

MacAtasney, Gerard Seán MacDiarmada, *The Mind of the Revolution* (Manorhamilton: Drumlin Publications, 2004).

—, *Tom Clarke: Life, Liberty and Revolution* (Dublin: Irish Academic Press, 2013).

McGarry, Fearghal, *The Black Hand of Republicanism: Fenianism in Modern Ireland* (Dublin: Irish Academic Press, 2010).

—, *The Rising Ireland: Easter 1916* (Oxford: Oxford University Press, 2010).

McGee, Owen, *The IRB: The Irish Republican Brotherhood from the Land League to Sinn Féin* (Dublin: Four Courts Press, 2007).

MacLochlainn, Piaras F., *Last Words: Letters and Statements of the Leaders Executed after the Rising at Easter 1916* (Dublin: Stationery Office, 1990).

McConville, Seán, *Irish Political Prisoners, 1848–1922* (Abingdon: Routledge, 2005).

Martin, F.X., *The Irish Volunteers, 1913–1915* (Dublin: James Duffy, 1963).

—, *The Howth Gun-Running 1914* (Dublin: Brown & Nolan, 1964).

—, *The Easter Rising and University College, Dublin* (Dublin: Browne & Nolan, 1966).

—, *Leaders and Men of the Easter Rising* (London: Methuen, 1967).

Morrissey, Thomas J., *William O'Brien 1881–1968* (Dublin: Four Courts Press, 2007).

Nevin, Donal, *James Connolly* (Dublin: Gill & Macmillan, 2005).

— (ed), *Between Comrades: James Connolly, Letters and Correspondence 1889–1916* (Dublin: Gill & Macmillan, 2007).

Novick, Ben, *Conceiving Revolution: Irish Nationalist Propaganda During the First World War* (Dublin: Four Courts Press, 2001).

O'Brien, William and Ryan, Desmond, *Devoy's Postbag 1871–1918* (Dublin: Fallon, 1953).

Ó Broin, Leon, *Dublin Castle and the 1916 Rising: The Story of Sir Matthew Nathan* (Dublin: Helican, 1966).

—, *W E Wylie and the Irish Revolution, 1916–1921* (Dublin: Gill & Macmillan 1989).

Ó Dubhghaill, M., *Insurrection Fires at Eastertide* (Cork: Mercier Press, 1966).

O'Rahilly, Alfred, *The Secret History of the Irish Volunteers* (Dublin: Irish Publicity League, 1915).

—, *The Secret History of the Irish Volunteers* (Dublin: Irish Publicity League, 1915).

Oram, Gerard, *Death Sentences Passed by Military Courts of the British Army, 1914–24* (London: Francis Boutle, 1998).

Pennell, Catriona, *A Kingdom United: Popular Responses to the Outbreak of the First World War in Britain and Ireland* (Oxford: Oxford University Press, 2012).

Reid, B.L., *The Lives of Roger Casement* (New Haven: Yale University Press, 1978).

Robbins, Frank, *Under the Starry Plough: Recollections of the Irish Citizen Army* (Dublin: The Academy Press, 1977).

Ryan, Desmond, *The Rising: The Complete Story of Easter Week* (Dublin: Golden Eagle Books, 1949).

Short, K.R.M., *The Dynamite War: Irish American Bombers in Victorian Britain* (Dublin: Gill & Macmillan, 1979).

Thompson, William, *The Imagination of an Insurrection: Dublin, Easter 1916* (Oxford: Oxford University Press, 1967).

Tierney, Michael, *Eoin MacNeill: Scholar and Man of Action, 1867–1945* (Oxford: Clarendon Press, 1980).

Townshend, Charles, *Easter 1916; The Irish Rebellion* (London: Penguin Books, 2005).

Wheatley Michael, *Nationalism and the Irish Party* (Oxford: Oxford University Press, 2005).

Yeates, Padraig, *A City in Wartime: Dublin 1914–18* (Dublin: Gill & Macmillan, 2012).

Articles

Bisceglia, Louis, 'The Fenian Funeral of Terence Bellew MacManus', *Eire-Ireland*, vol. XIV, no. 3, 1979.

Bowman, Tim, 'The Irish Recruiting and anti-Recruiting Campaigns, 1914–1918', in Taithe, Bernard and Thornton, Tim, *Propaganda: Political Rhetoric and Identity, 1300–2000* (Stroud: Sutton, 1999).

McConnell, James, 'Recruiting Sergeants for John Bull? Irish Nationalist MPs and Enlistment in the Early Months of the Great War', *War and History*, 14(4), 2007.

Mulcrone, Mick, 'On the Razor's Edge: The Irish-American Press on the Eve of the First World War', a paper presented to the Annual Meeting of the Association for Education in Journalism and Mass Communication (Washington, 10–13 August 1989).

Nina Ranalli, 'The Dust of Some: Glasnevin Cemetery and the Politics of Burial', Independent Study Project (ISP) Collection Paper 589 (2008).

Index

Also from The History Press

Irish Women

Also from The History Press

Irish Revolutionaries

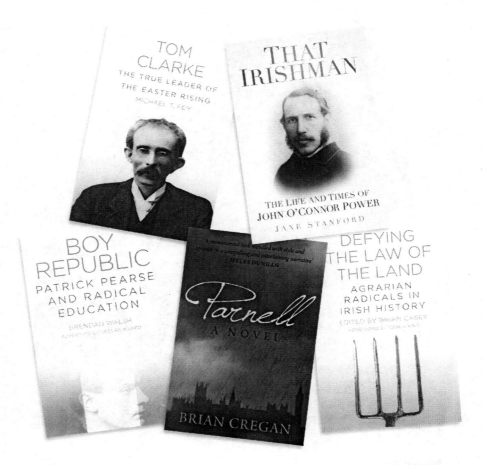

Lightning Source UK Ltd.
Milton Keynes UK
UKOW04f0604071014

239734UK00005B/55/P